Camping Wyoming and the Black Hills

Help Us Keep This Guide Up to Date

Every effort has been made by the author and editors to make this guide as accurate and useful as possible. However, many things can change after a guide is published—trails are rerouted, regulations change, techniques evolve, facilities come under new management, etc.

We would love to hear from you concerning your experiences with this guide and how you feel it could be improved and kept up to date. While we may not be able to respond to all comments and suggestions, we'll take them to heart and we'll also make certain to share them with the author. Please send your comments and suggestions to the following address:

The Globe Pequot Press
Reader Response/Editorial Department
P.O. Box 480
Guilford, CT 06437

Or you may e-mail us at:

editorial@globe-pequot.com

Thanks for your input, and happy travels!

Camping Wyoming and the Black Hills

Kenneth L. Graham

FALCON®

Guilford, Connecticut
An imprint of The Globe Pequot Press

A FALCON GUIDE®

Library of Congress Cataloging-in-Publication Data

Graham, Kenneth Lee.
Camping Wyoming and the Black Hills / Kenneth Graham.
p. cm.—(A FalconGuide)
Includes index.
ISBN 1-56044-894-6
1. Camping—Wyoming—Guidebooks. 2. Black Hills (S.D. and Wyo.)—Guidebooks. I. Title. II. Falcon guide.

GV191.42.W8 G73 2001
647.787'09'025—dc21

2001033559

Manufactured in the United States of America
First Edition/First Printing

Contents

About This Book

In the early days of Wyoming territory, scouts such as Jim Bridger and Jedediah Smith provided a valuable service for travelers, whether they were fortune seekers, homesteaders, or cavalry. These scouts blazed trails and directed travelers toward their goals along routes with food and water for man and beast within this unknown territory. Travel time was slow because the animals pulling the wagons required frequent stops for grazing, and travelers were able to explore areas near the paths their animals followed.

In many places little has changed, and for the most part travel today targets the unique features discovered by these previous visitors. But the sense of exploration does not end with days gone by. Today travelers use automobiles, synthetic tents, and "tin tepees." Campsites are no longer required to provide water and grass for livestock. Campfires are mostly used to roast marshmallows and to take off the evening chill at sundown, not for cooking dinner. And the nearby wildlife is an added attraction—not the evening meal.

Some of today's modern "wagons" are absolutely not equipped to make the trip into some spots. A 30-foot pull trailer behind a full-sized pickup does not easily fit on a mountain road hairpin turn. Neither do small tunnels and large RVs mix. Though the hazards are well marked and signed, it is usually very inconvenient to run across them in places involving a lot of backtracking. I have attempted to provide information on access requirements along with what you

A camper in the Black Hills enjoys a delectable ending to a perfect day: popcorn roasted over an open fire.

will find upon arrival. Out of almost 300 campgrounds, there are plenty that all vehicles can reach. This book allows you to plan your routes with your specific type of "wagon" in mind. This should eliminate hours of driving only to find that the last few miles are only accessible by short-wheelbase, all-terrain vehicles. There are too many wonderful things in Wyoming to spend precious time backtracking out of unannounced difficult country.

The appeal of camping for me is the relaxation offered in the fresh mountain air with an occasional wisp of campfire smoke and the smells of cowboy coffee and marshmallows roasted to a golden brown. For anglers there are plenty of trout in both lakes and streams offering both challenge and exploration. In Wyoming there are undesignated wilderness areas that have fewer visitors than designated ones. These hideaways are not openly advertised—adding to the thrill of discovery. This also implies an obligation to let others find these wild areas on their own, while we share the secret with only those that have been there before us.

Please keep in mind that Wyoming remains primitive by definition of modern camping practices. Hookups, with extremely few exceptions, do not exist. Drinking water is mostly produced through hard labor from ancient hand pumps and has an unmistakable iron flavoring. Self-contained units offer alternatives; however, finding sources for filling holding tanks will take some research. There are a lot of miles between towns with no services available. In many places, the only residents will be the wildlife common to the area. So

Marshmallows roasted to a golden brown are a traditional part of the camping experience.

plan your route in advance, check out the features of available resources in this book, and get ready for an adventure.

Wyoming Wildlife

Bears and campgrounds just seem to match like frosting on brownies. Not all camping areas identified in this book have bears, but most do. The Yellowstone area offers a healthy number of grizzly bears. A variety of measures minimize human-bear encounters, including campground closure. Sleeping Giant Campground west of Cody has been closed for just that reason. Other areas no longer allow tents, and bear boxes provide safe storage in camping areas where tents are still allowed. Information on bear sightings and human-bear encounters gets posted on signs at key places in individual campgrounds. Usually this will be at the fee sign near the entrance.

Large game animals such as moose, deer, elk, pronghorn (antelope), and bison (buffalo) live in Wyoming. All are potentially dangerous, and interaction with humans can lead to fatal results. Buffalo are commonly seen in Yellowstone National Park and Custer State Park in and around campgrounds. Moose run a close second on the hazard list. These huge animals blatantly blunder past tents and trailers alike when they please, seeming to dare people to "knock the chip off." Do not get in their way.

Fun to watch but dangerous to approach, buffalo have the right of way in Custer State Park in the Black Hills.

Rattlesnakes are more talked about than seen as a rule. However, they are present and no less dangerous than larger wildlife. Late August or early September finds numerous snakes warming on the warm asphalt late in the evening. These dead-looking snakes are very much alive, and can become contentious about their turf. At this time of year, a rattlesnake is preserving all the energy it can and will not necessarily warn you of its intentions by rattling its tail, so be wary of the not-so-dead snake on the road.

Even though larger animals and snakes represent potential dangers and/or death, the most annoying to me is the pesky mosquito. There are also ticks and horse and deer flies, although they don't buzz in your ear all night causing sleeplessness. Adequate bug repellent is of great value. There are a lot of miles between stores in Wyoming, so stock up before you leave home.

Wyoming Weather

Wyoming's high elevations result in a relatively cool climate. A hot sunny day will often require a coat by day's end. This is especially true of the high, mountain country where most campgrounds in this book are found. Wyoming's lowest elevation is located near the northeastern corner and is 3,125 feet. The highest elevation tops off at over 13,000 feet with plenty of heights in between.

Wind in Wyoming leaves permanent impressions on any visitor. A story once circulated through a mining camp in central Wyoming about a local wind indicator. Supposedly, a half-inch log chain was left dangling just off the ground on a pole near a public gathering place. If the chain held steady at 45 degrees from the vertical, it was an ordinary day. A truly windy day was when this chain stretched out at 90 degrees like a bicycle streamer on a downhill ride. There are days when it is easy to believe this story, and the wind can create very dangerous driving conditions in bad weather.

Storms can be fast and furious in any part of Wyoming, though they seem to be much more severe in the wide-open desert. There is plenty of desert between campgrounds. If your travels take you into some backcountry, it might pay to sit out the storm.

Campsite Fee Ranges	
$	less than $10
$$	$10–$20
$$$	more than $20

Map Legend

Interstate Highway	90
U.S. Highway	25 191
State or County Road	22 120
Lake	
National Park, Monument, Recreation Area	*Yellowstone National Park*
National, State Forest	SIX RIVERS NATIONAL FOREST
Public Campgrounds	▲89
Cities	• Sheridan
Compass	

Overview Map

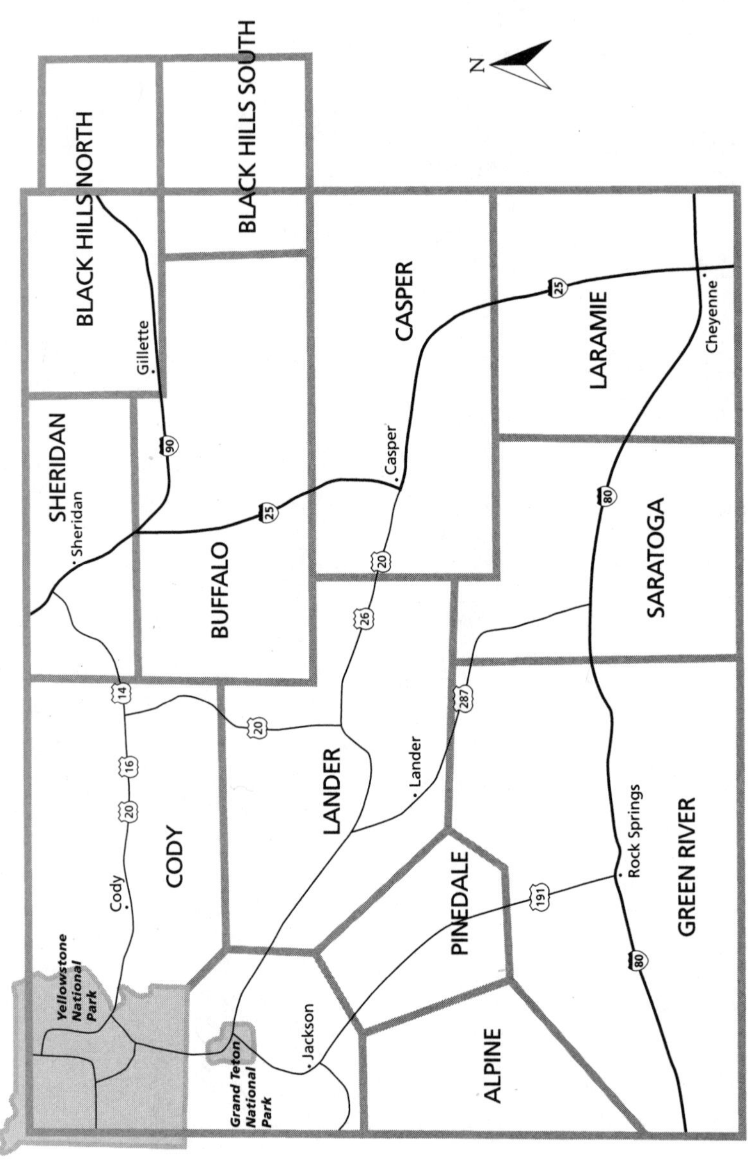

Yellowstone National Park

Without a doubt, Yellowstone National Park is the number one destination of travelers in Wyoming. The unique geologic phenomenon and plentiful wildlife has a reputation that continues to motivate increasing numbers of visitors worldwide. Wyoming, Montana, and Idaho all share a part of this great park, though Wyoming holds the lion's share with more than 90 percent, and of the five entrances, three are in Wyoming. Measures are aggressively enforced to maintain a natural environment, a most difficult task with the increased influx of visitors in larger vehicles.

Camping in Yellowstone National Park can become a test of nerves for the unprepared. Each year the number of visitors increases, putting an even greater strain on the available camping. The increasing size of RV units also creates a very frustrating problem for campers and rangers alike. The campgrounds were originally constructed with pickup campers and tents in mind. No one at that time ever dreamed that the huge trailers and busses of today would seek a parking area for camping. Larger units and more visitors also result in more frequent road repair, among other services. With a need to provide greater protection of the environment and wildlife, no small thought is being given to vehicle restriction.

Fishing Bridge RV Park is not a campground as the definition of campground is taken to mean that fire rings and picnic tables are present. This RV park was developed specifically for the larger RVs with the hopes that some of the tremendous pressure on the other campgrounds would be relieved.

Keep in mind that the days of touring the park during the day and then finding a camping spot just before dark are long gone. The more popular areas find visitors waiting for campers to leave in the morning. Reservations can be made in 5 out of the 12 campgrounds, but some already have been reserved as early as 18 months in advance. If you have your heart set on camping in the park, make your plans well in advance. If you are the sort that prefers to be in quiet, isolated places, it would be best to look to the often overlooked campgrounds in the adjacent national forest. Your entrance permit to both Yellowstone and Teton National Park allows you to exit and reenter for seven days. This opens opportunities to explore adjacent forests and enjoy some truly serene solitude at day's end.

YELLOWSTONE NATIONAL PARK

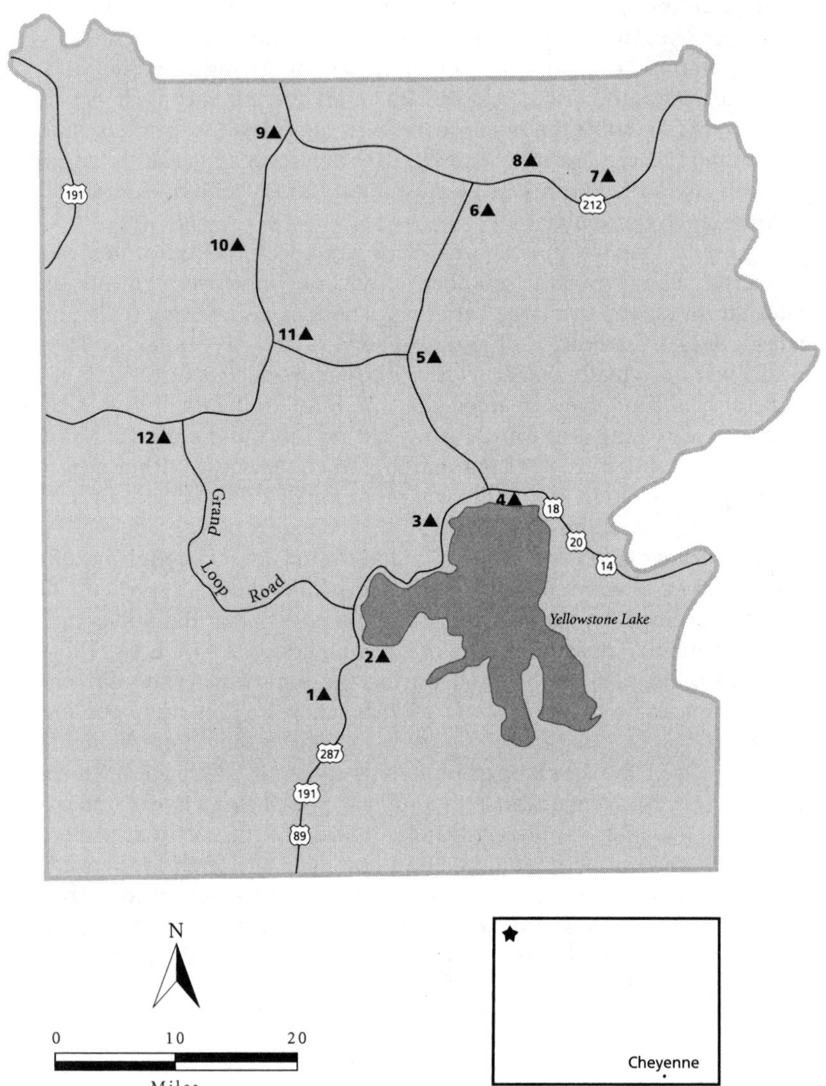

	Group sites	Tents	RV sites	Total sites	Hookups	Toilets	Showers	Drinking water	Dump station	Phone	Disabled access	Fee ($)	Season	Can reserve	Length of stay	Recreation
1 Lewis Lake		16	69	85		V		X				$	6/11-11/7		14	FHBW
2 Grant Village		110	315	425		C		X	X			$$	6/21-10/3	X	14	FHBW
3 Bridge Bay	10	90	330	430		C		X	X		X	$$	5/21-9/26	X	14	FHBW
4 Fishing Bridge RV Park			340	340	A		X	X	X		X	$$$	5/14-9/12	X		W
5 Canyon Village			272	272		C	X	X	X			$$	6/21-10/3	X	14	HW
6 Tower Fall			32	32		V		X				$	5/21-9/27		14	HW
7 Pebble Creek			32	32		V		X				$	6/4-9/27		14	FHW
8 Slough Creek		8	21	29		V		X				$	5/28-10/31			FHW
9 Mammoth			85	85		C		X				$$	All Year		14	WH
10 Indian Creek			68	68		V		X				$$	6/11-9/20		14	FHW
11 Norris		22	94	116		C		X		X		$$	5/21-9/27		14	FHW
12 Madison		40	240	280		C		X	X	X	X	$$	5/1-11/7	X	14	FHW

A=all, C=comfort stations, V=vault toilet, F=fishing, H=hiking, B=boating, W=wildlife viewing

1 Lewis Lake

Location: 10 miles north of the South Entrance.
Facilities: Vault toilets, fire rings, tables, drinking water, picnic area, boat ramp.
Sites: 16 for tents and 69 for RVs up to 30 feet long.
Fee: $ per day, 14-day maximum stay.
Reservations: First-come, first-served.
Agency: Yellowstone National Park, 1-307-344-7381.
Activities: Fishing, hiking, boating, wildlife viewing.
Finding the campground: The South Entrance to Yellowstone National Park is 57 miles north of Jackson. Take the South Entrance Road north from the fee booth for 10 miles. Turn left at the sign for Lewis Lake and travel a short distance. Turn left at the campground access.

About the campground: Pine and spruce trees shelter the RV sites in three confusing loops. Loop A bears left at the entrance with table designation open to interpretation, and 24 units haphazardly fit together like a jigsaw puzzle; the table could almost be divided in half the long way. The rolling knolls make it difficult for parking, as well. Loop B takes up the center on a rollercoaster–like setting with similar conditions for 16 sites. Loop C bears dead ahead with a tents-only section bearing to the right at the entrance. Longer RVs have managed to squeeze into a few of the 29 sites that snake along in this loop. It gets very tight. The lake nestles into place a pretty fair distance away. An active picnic area complete with boat ramp slides off to the right side just after leaving the highway.

2 Grant Village

Location: 80 miles north of Jackson.
Facilities: Comfort stations, fire rings, tables, drinking water, RV dump.
Sites: 110 for tents and 315 for RVs up to 20 feet long.
Fee: $$ per day, 14-day maximum stay.
Reservations: 1-307-344-7311.
Agency: Yellowstone National Park, 1-307-344-7381.
Activities: Fishing, hiking, boating, wildlife viewing.
Finding the campground: The South Entrance to Yellowstone National Park is 57 miles north of Jackson. Take the South Entrance Road north from the fee booth for 22 miles. Turn right at the Grant Village sign and travel 1 mile. Turn left at the well-marked campground entrance.

About the campground: These compact sites are neatly settled between pine trees. As with other campgrounds in the park, tents and pickup campers work best here, but larger units do fit with forethought and extra effort. Three of the eleven loops are set aside for tents only. Most of the parking units are short pullouts on both sides of the access roads.

3 Bridge Bay

Location: 83 miles west of Cody.
Facilities: Comfort stations, fire rings, tables, drinking water, RV dump.
Sites: 10 group for tents, 90 for tents, and 330 for RVs up to 40 feet long.
Fee: $$ per day, 14-day maximum stay.
Reservations: 1-307-344-7311.
Agency: Yellowstone National Park, 1-307-344-7381.
Activities: Fishing, hiking, boating, wildlife viewing.
Finding the campground: The East Entrance is 53 miles west of Cody. Take the East Entrance Road west from the fee booth for 27 miles. Turn left at the junction (toward West Thumb) and travel 3 miles. The campground is on the right side of the road.

About the campground: The more desirable units nestle into a thick pine forest, and some of these sites are reserved several months in advance. At one point in the history of this campground, pine trees became a threat to campers. Because of the small root base and other complications, trees would topple over within the camping area. The huge open area resulted from clearing that threat. Recently, new trees have been planted for forest renewal. Few units accommodate the longer RVs. Five of the ten loops are set aside for tents. Back-in parking dominates the tent areas. Remaining loops have more pullouts, though they are short.

4 Fishing Bridge RV Park

Location: 79 miles west of Cody.
Facilities: Full hookups. No fire rings, tables, or cable TV.
Sites: 340 for hard-sided RVs only.

Fee: $$$ per day.
Reservations: 1-307-344-7311.
Agency: Yellowstone National Park, 1-307-344-7381.
Activities: Wildlife viewing.
Finding the campground: The East Entrance is 53 miles west of Cody. Take the East Entrance Road west from the fee booth for 26 miles.

About the campground: Campfires and picnic tables do not exist in this RV park. The parking is tight, but this really is the place for long RVs, as it is the one park campground truly designed for this kind of camping and has most amenities associated with RV camping (no cable TV—but who needs it with the park outside?). Campers who have discovered these conveniences make reservations up to 18 months in advance. Don't plan on pulling in here at the last minute.

5 Canyon Village

Location: 96 miles west of Cody.
Facilities: Comfort stations, fire rings, tables, drinking water, RV dump.
Sites: 272 for tents or RVs up to 30 feet long. Limited spaces are available for longer units.
Fee: $$ per day, 14-day maximum stay.
Reservations: 1-307-344-7311.
Agency: Yellowstone National Park, 1-307-344-7381.
Activities: Hiking, wildlife viewing.
Finding the campground: The East Entrance is 53 miles west of Cody. Take the East Entrance Road west from the fee booth for 27 miles. Turn right at the junction and travel 16 miles. Turn right at the sign and follow directions to the registration office on the left.

About the campground: Eleven separate loops wind through the pine forest here. Most of the units are back-in spots of various lengths. Tents seem to be the most common, though a few larger motor homes do manage. Canyon Village offers gift shops, a cafeteria, and other amenities nearby. In the campground a laundry and showers are available. Reservations are a must if you have definite plans to stay here.

6 Tower Fall

Location: 115 miles west and north of Cody.
Facilities: Vault toilet, fire rings, tables, drinking water.
Sites: 32 for tents or RVs up to 30 feet long.
Fee: $ per day, 14-day maximum stay.
Reservations: First-come, first-served.
Agency: Yellowstone National Park, 1-307-344-7381.
Activities: Hiking, wildlife viewing.
Finding the campground: The East Entrance is 53 miles west of Cody. Take the East Entrance Road west from the fee booth for 27 miles. Turn right at the junction and travel 35 miles.

About the campground: This small campground fills fast. Nearby Tower Creek drops 132 feet on its way to the Yellowstone River below. Grizzly bears are not too far away, along with other wildlife.

7 Pebble Creek

Location: 77 miles southwest of Red Lodge, Montana.
Facilities: Vault toilets, fire rings, tables, drinking water.
Sites: 32 for tents or RVs up to 30 feet long.
Fee: $ per day, 14-day maximum stay.
Reservations: First-come, first-served.
Agency: Yellowstone National Park, 1-307-344-7381.
Activities: Fishing, hiking, wildlife viewing.
Finding the campground: The Northeast Entrance is 69 miles southwest of Red Lodge, Montana. Take the Northeast Entrance Road for 8 miles west of the fee booth. The campground is on the right side of the road.

About the campground: Pebble Creek rumbles by this campground, just far enough off the road to avoid hearing most traffic sounds. Smaller pine trees are scattered throughout the area, giving some campsites more shade than others. Tents, tent trailers, or pickup campers fit here best. Longer RVs will not have room if they have to unhook either a trailer or a towed car. Distance between units does not offer the best in privacy, but most all campers have the same goal—get out and see the park. A host occupies one of the units. Bring firewood with you from another source, as deadfall is not readily available. Get here before noon if you want to camp. On our visit—a Tuesday—every unit was occupied as of 11 A.M.

8 Slough Creek

Location: 86 miles southwest of Red Lodge, Montana.
Facilities: Vault toilets, fire rings, tables, drinking water.
Sites: 8 for tents and 21 for RVs up to 30 feet long.
Fee: $ per day.
Reservations: First-come, first-served.
Agency: Yellowstone National Park, 1-307-344-7381.
Activities: Fishing, hiking, wildlife viewing.
Finding the campground: The Northeast Entrance is 69 miles southwest of Red Lodge, Montana. Take the Northeast Entrance Road for 24 miles west of the fee booth. Turn right at the sign and travel 3 miles.

About the campground: Campers can easily hear Slough Creek pound corners off the boulders in its way, as most of the parking areas are only a few feet from the creek bank. Old spruce trees shade tables and fire rings alike with an open meadow above. As with Pebble Creek Campground, tents, tent trailers, and pickup campers fit best here. Longer RVs could fit in very few spaces with some tricky maneuvering. A host occupies one of the available spots. Firewood is best bought before arrival. The rough gravel road leading back here does not keep the campground from filling up long before noon.

9 Mammoth

Location: 61 miles south of Livingston, Montana.
Facilities: Comfort station, fire rings, tables, drinking water.
Sites: 85 for tents or RVs up to 50 feet long.
Fee: $$ per day, 14-day maximum stay.
Reservations: First-come, first-served.
Agency: Yellowstone National Park, 307-344-7381.
Activities: Hiking, wildlife viewing, thermal features.
Finding the campground: The North Entrance is 56 miles south of Livingston via U.S. Highway 89. The official entrance is at Gardiner. From there, take the North Entrance Road south for 5 miles. The campground is on the right side of the road.

About the campground: Cottonwood trees don't offer much shade on this side hill. The level pull-thrus make parking easy for larger RVs, but please be considerate of tent campers, who may not appreciate generator noise. Sagebrush and rocky ground make up the distance between trees and parking units. This campground generally fills before noon. When we visited the campground several units appeared empty, but the vacant spots turned out to be previously claimed by campers touring the park.

10 Indian Creek

Location: 73 miles south of Livingston, Montana.
Facilities: Vault toilets, fire rings, tables, drinking water.
Sites: 68 for RVs up to 30 feet long.
Fee: $$ per day, 14-day maximum stay.
Reservations: First-come, first-served.
Agency: Yellowstone National Park, 1-307-344-7381.
Activities: Fishing, hiking, wildlife viewing.
Finding the campground: The North Entrance is 56 miles south of Livingston via U.S. Highway 89 at Gardiner. Take the North Entrance Road for 5 miles to Mammoth. In Mammoth, follow signed directions south toward Norris and travel about 12 miles. Turn right at the campground sign.

About the campground: Bear activity has changed this tenting campground into a hard-sided only area, and its former purpose is apparent in the placement of the parking aprons. Trailers up to 25 feet can fit, but little room is left over for parking your towing vehicle. The park service does not allow parking off of the pavement, further complicating matters. Pickup campers, pop-up vans, and smaller RVs work well here. The sites are not all that close, though if everyone gets up at the same time generator noise could escalate. Indian Creek is a short hike away, offering fishing and wildlife viewing. Pine trees (living and dead) help isolate camping spots. This campground tends to be the last to fill up, possibly because tents are not allowed.

11 Norris

Location: 29 miles east of West Yellowstone.
Facilities: Comfort stations, fire rings, tables, drinking water, pay phone.
Sites: 22 for tents and 94 for RVs up to 25 feet long.
Fee: $$ per day, 14-day maximum stay.
Reservations: First-come, first-served.
Agency: Yellowstone National Park, 1-307-344-7381.
Activities: Fishing, hiking, wildlife viewing.
Finding the campground: Take the West Entrance Road east of West Yellowstone for 14 miles. Turn left at Madison Junction and travel 14 miles. Turn left toward Mammoth and travel 1 mile. Turn right at the sign for the Museum of the National Park Ranger to access the campground.

About the campground: Three loops snake around pine-forested knolls above the river. Loop A provides walk-in sites for tents only. Short, not-too level parking spots dominate the rest of the campground. Larger RVs manage to find spaces but not without risk and effort. Tents find room without getting too close. Otherwise things get real crowded. Firewood must either be bought or brought since previous campers have long since picked up all available deadfall.

12 Madison

Location: 14 miles east of West Yellowstone.
Facilities: Comfort stations, fire rings, tables, drinking water, RV dump, vending machines, pay phone.
Sites: 40 for tents and 240 for RVs up to 30 feet long.
Fee: $$ per day, 14-day maximum stay.
Reservations: 1-307-344-7311.
Agency: Yellowstone National Park, 1-307-344-7381.
Activities: Fishing, hiking, wildlife viewing.
Finding the campground: Take the West Entrance Road east of West Yellowstone for 14 miles. Turn right just before Madison Junction to access the campground.

About the campground: Pine trees shade the asphalt access and parking area. Two of the ten loops are set aside for tents only, with the others turning into a sort of zoo. Larger RVs manage to find spaces, but it does crowd things. The Madison River rushes by just south of the campground, inviting anglers and wildlife watchers. This campground fills during the peak season as early as 7:00 A.M.

Cody Area

History, high mountains, and two of the three Yellowstone National Park entrances from Wyoming are the highlights of this area. The Buffalo Bill Historic Center in Cody presents an overwhelming collection of historical artifacts for interpretation. Be prepared for the disappointment of inadequate time.

The main highlight, of course, is Yellowstone National Park. And that means the campgrounds along the main route fill very quickly. Preplanning and a little extra time will allow campers to explore the out-of-the-way places listed in this book. Backtracking a portion of Chief Joseph's trail to the Northeast Entrance presents travelers with less traffic and scenic views missed by the majority of national park visitors.

Grizzly bears and other wildlife are frequently seen in this area, requiring proper safety measures. Keep in mind the wild in wildlife comes first, and this is their home. We as travelers are not always, if ever, welcome guests.

1 Wood River

Location: 25 miles southwest of Meeteetse.
Facilities: Vault toilets, fire rings, tables, drinking water.
Sites: 5 for tents or RVs up to 32 feet long.
Fee: Donation, 14-day maximum stay.
Reservations: First-come, first-served.
Agency: Shoshone National Forest, Greybull Ranger District, 1-307-868-2379.
Activities: Fishing, hiking, wildlife viewing, rockhounding.
Finding the campground: Meeteetse is 31 miles southeast of Cody on Wyoming Highway 120. At Meeteetse turn onto Wyoming Highway 290 and travel 6 miles. Turn left onto the still-paved Wood River Road and travel 19 miles. The pavement will change to gravel in about 4 miles. The campground is on the left side.

About the campground: Washakie Wilderness access keeps this campground very active. Evergreen trees shade the units, though just outside the campground sagebrush takes over. Larger units do make the trip, but most are very familiar with the terrain. The Kirwin ghost town draws plenty of curious types. Some of the cars hosting the curious really do not belong on this backcountry road. So on your way into this place be cautious.

2 Brown Mountain

Location: 28 miles southwest of Meeteetse.
Facilities: Vault toilets, fire rings, tables, drinking water.
Sites: 6 for tents or RVs up to 30 feet long.
Fee: Donation, 14-day maximum stay.
Reservations: First-come, first-served.
Agency: Shoshone National Forest, Greybull Ranger District, 1-307-868-2379.

Cody Area

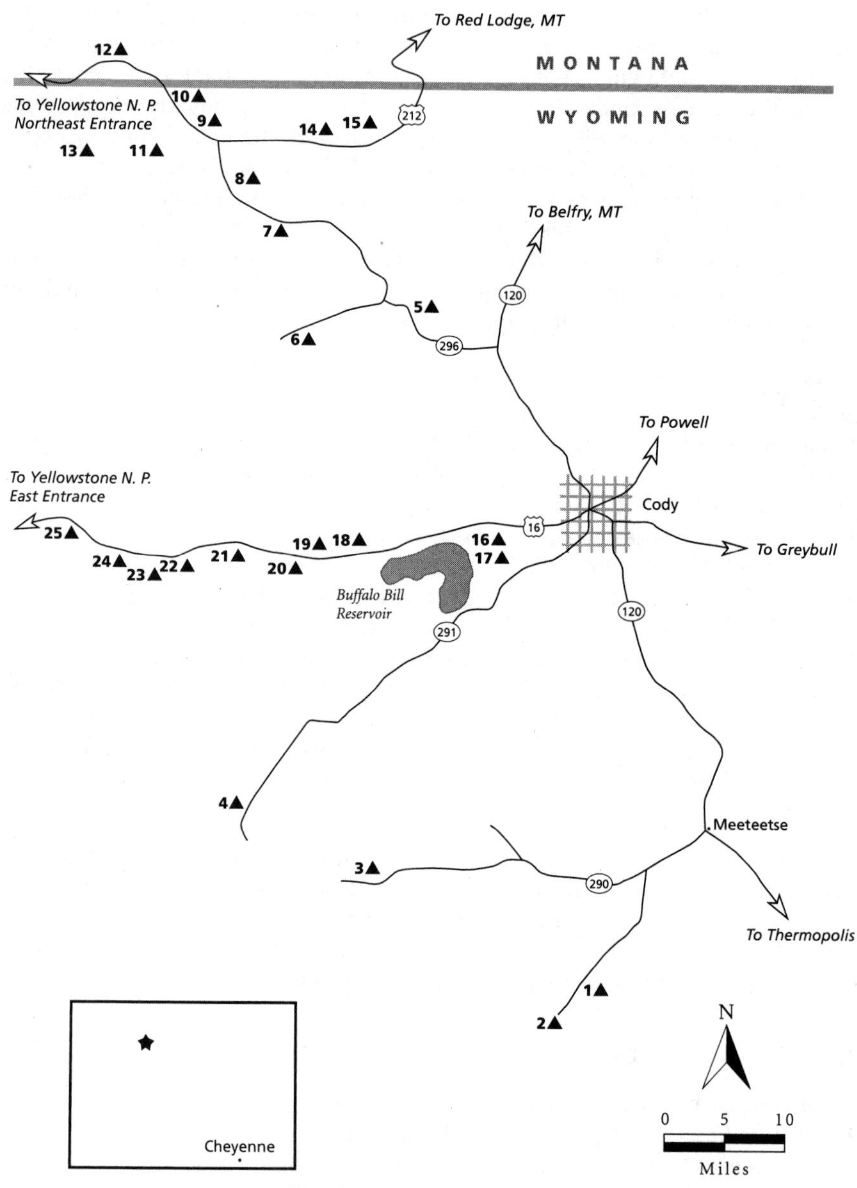

To Red Lodge, MT
MONTANA
WYOMING
To Yellowstone N. P.
Northeast Entrance
To Belfry, MT
To Powell
Cody
To Yellowstone N. P.
East Entrance
To Greybull
Buffalo Bill
Reservoir
Meeteetse
To Thermopolis
Cheyenne
N
0 5 10
Miles

	Group sites	Tents	RV sites	Total sites	Picnic area	Toilets	Showers	Drinking water	Dump station	Phone	Disabled access	Fee ($)	Season	Can reserve	Length of stay	Recreation
1 Wood River			5	5		V		X				D	6/1-11/1		14	FHWR
2 Brown Mountain			6	6		V		X				D	6/1-11/1		14	FHWR
3 Jack Creek			7	7		V						D	6/1-11/3		14	FHW
4 Deer Creek			7	7		V						D	All Year		14	FHR
5 Dead Indian			12	12		V						$	6/15-9/1		16	FHW
6 Little Sunlight			4	4		P						D	5/1-11/30		16	FHWR
7 Hunter Peak			20	20		V		X				$	6/15-9/1		16	FHW
8 Lake Creek			6	6		V		X				$	6/15-9/5		16	FH
9 Crazy Creek			16	16		V		X				$	6/15-9/1		16	FH
10 Fox Creek			27	27		V		X				$	6/15-9/1		16	FH
11 Chief Joseph (MT)			6	6		V		X				$	6/1-9/30		16	H
12 Colter (MT)			23	23		V		X				$	6/1-9/30		16	H
13 Soda Butte (MT)			20	20		V		X				$	6/1-9/30		16	H
14 Beartooth Lake			21	21	X	V		X				$	7/1-9/15		14	FHBS
15 Island Lake			20	20		V		X				$	7/1-9/15		16	FHBSP
Buffalo Bill State Park														G		
16 North Shore Bay	1	5	27	32		V		X	X		X	$	5/1-10/1		14	FBS
17 North Fork		6	50	56	X	V		X	X	X	X	$	5/1-10/1		14	F
18 Big Game			16	16		V		X				$	6/1-9/30		14	FHR
19 Wapiti			41	41		V		X				$	5/15-10/30		14	FHR
20 Elk Fork			13	13		V						$	6/1-9/30		14	FHR
21 Clearwater		10	5	15		V		X				$	6/1-9/30		14	FHR
22 Rex Hale			8	8		V		X				$	6/15-9/30		14	FHR
23 Newton Creek			31	31		V		X				$	6/1-9/30		14	FHR
24 Eagle Creek			20	20		V		X				$	6/1-9/30		14	FHWR
25 Threemile			33	33		V		X				$	6/15-9/3		14	FHWR

V=vault toilets, P=pit toilets, D=donation, F=fishing, H=hiking, B=boating, S=swimming, W=wildlife viewing, R=rockhounding, P=photography

Activities: Fishing, hiking, wildlife viewing, rockhounding.
Finding the campground: Meeteetse is 31 miles southeast of Cody on Wyoming Highway 120. At Meeteetse turn onto Wyoming Highway 290 and travel 6 miles. Turn left onto the still-paved Wood River Road and travel 22 miles. The pavement will change to gravel in about 4 miles. The campground is on the left side.

About the campground: The forest stretches far enough to shade these units, which are really an extension of the Wood River Campground. Wood River rages by with plenty of things to say. Horses and riders get real plentiful. Dust clouds hang around pretty steadily during weekends while visitors attempt to reach nearby Kirwin. Snowcapped mountains squeeze this ghost town so tight that the road into it seems to change yearly. At one point we found ourselves forced to drive a quarter mile up the creek bed, as only one half of the road remained on the hill. This gem of a place is 9 miles past the campground.

3 Jack Creek

Location: 28 miles west of Meeteetse.
Facilities: Vault toilets, fire rings, tables.
Sites: 7 for tents or RVs up to 20 feet long.
Fee: Donation, 14-day maximum stay.
Reservations: First-come, first-served.
Agency: Shoshone National Forest, Greybull Ranger District, 1-307-868-2379.
Activities: Fishing, hiking, wildlife viewing.
Finding the campground: Meeteetse is 31 miles southeast of Cody on Wyoming Highway 120. Turn onto the paved Wyoming Highway 290 and travel west out of Meeteetse for 11 miles. Bear right onto the paved County Road 41X for 1 mile. Follow the directional signs to the Jack Creek Trailhead, traveling 17 miles. The last 10 miles become a single-lane roller coaster.

About the campground: Aspen and willow trees shade almost all of the tables. One unit sets on a high bank of the Greybull River. The others sneak into the trees. Tall willow brush line the riverbanks. Sagebrush, rocks, and a little grass make up the steep hillsides all around. Firewood could take some traveling to find. Bear warning signs are posted for good reason. During our visit a black bear wandered through the brush along the river. This remote camping area offers plenty for those wanting to escape civilization. Snowcapped mountains in the background are better seen on the way in. Be sure to have plenty of supplies and warm clothes. If the weather turns bad, it could be some time before you get out. Keep in mind that when the sun goes down in this high mountain country, the heat goes with it. It might be desert, but it is a high-altitude desert. Days are hot and nights are cold.

4 Deer Creek

Location: 47 miles southwest of Cody.
Facilities: Vault toilet, fire rings, tables.
Sites: 7 for tents or RVs up to 32 feet long.
Fee: Donation, 14-day maximum stay.
Reservations: First-come, first-served.
Agency: Shoshone National Forest, Wapiti Ranger District, 1-307-527-6921.
Activities: Fishing, hiking, rockhounding.

Black bears and anglers alike fish the Greybull River near Jack Creek Campground.

Finding the campground: On the western end of Cody, take Wyoming Highway 291 southwest for 47 miles. The road turns to gravel for about the last 7 miles.

About the campground: The road splits this little camping place in two. A small stream gurgles happily by on the left side, which includes the toilet. Pull-thrus on the opposite side appeared a bit more roomy. Watch out for passing traffic. The South Fork Shoshone River holds both trout and petrified wood. Late August would be the best time for finding the wood, as the water level drops. Pine trees and willow brush help shelter campers from dust raised by passing traffic.

5 Dead Indian

Location: 40 miles northwest of Cody.
Facilities: Vault toilet, fire rings, tables.
Sites: 12 for tents or RVs up to 40 feet long.
Fee: $ per day, 16-day maximum stay.
Reservations: First-come, first-served.
Agency: Shoshone National Forest, Clarks Fork Ranger District, 1-307-754-7207.
Activities: Fishing, hiking, wildlife viewing.
Finding the campground: Take Wyoming Highway 120 north out of Cody for 17 miles. Turn left onto Wyoming Highway 296 and travel 23 miles.

About the campground: Dead Indian Creek divides the campground in two, and there are separate access roads. Chief Joseph of the Nez Perce led his people this way during their historic flight from the U.S. Army in 1877. A mixture of trees including spruce, cottonwood, and willow stand alone in this highway loop near the raging waters of the creek. Most of the units are fairly level, though not all are the same length. A few accommodate larger RVs. A host occupies one of the sites in the campground. As you wind down the hairpin turns, keep an eye out for the bottom—the campground area can be spotted long before you get there. Keep your camera loaded and handy for the scenic views offered from any one of the pullouts. Traffic can be noisy, as every year seems to have road construction nearby. Fill up your water jugs before you come. There is no drinking water here.

6 Little Sunlight

Location: 55 miles northwest of Cody.
Facilities: Pit toilet, fire rings, tables, corrals.
Sites: 4 for tents or RVs up to 40 feet long.
Fee: Donation, 16-day maximum stay.
Reservations: First-come, first-served.
Agency: Shoshone National Forest, Clarks Fork Ranger District, 1-307-754-7207.

Activities: Fishing, hiking, wildlife viewing, rockhounding.
Finding the campground: Take Wyoming Highway 120 north out of Cody for 17 miles. Turn left onto Wyoming Highway 296 and travel 25 miles. Turn left onto the gravel Forest Road 101 and travel 13 miles.

About the campground: The corrals and nearby trailhead keep this area busy. Firewood isn't too far away, but that is about all one can consider available. Fishing or hunting for agates could provide entertainment for those without horses or the desire to backpack into the wilderness. It is a long way to the campground to gamble on one of the four units to be vacant. The gravel bars yield agates and some petrified wood.

7 Hunter Peak

Location: 59 miles northwest of Cody.
Facilities: Vault toilet, fire rings, tables, drinking water, corral, trailhead.
Sites: 20 for tents or RVs up to 40 feet long.
Fee: $ per day, 16-day maximum stay.
Reservations: First-come, first-served.
Agency: Shoshone National Forest, Clarks Fork Ranger District, 1-307-754-7207.
Activities: Fishing, hiking, wildlife viewing.
Finding the campground: Take Wyoming Highway 120 north out of Cody for 17 miles. Turn left onto Wyoming Highway 296 and travel 42 miles. The campground is on the left side of the road.

About the campground: The parking spots that do not accommodate long RVs make up for it in width. Trailers up to 32 feet long can be unhooked with room to put the towing vehicle alongside. Granite outcrops pop up at random with a creek cruising past nearby. Spruce and pine dominate this cubbyhole along the Clarks Fork Yellowstone River. A few aspen sneak in here and there with some grass between.

8 Lake Creek

Location: 63 miles northwest of Cody.
Facilities: Vault toilet, fire rings, tables, drinking water.
Sites: 6 for tents or RVs up to 20 feet long.
Fee: $ per day, 16-day maximum stay.
Reservations: First-come, first-served.
Agency: Shoshone National Forest, Clarks Fork Ranger District, 1-307-754-7207.
Activities: Fishing, hiking.
Finding the campground: Take Wyoming Highway 120 north out of Cody for 17 miles. Turn left onto Wyoming Highway 296 and travel 46 miles. The campground is on the right side of the road.

About the campground: The forest hides all but the first parking spot, which is also the closest to the hand pump for water. A small loop toward the back nestles in under pine and spruce trees. Plenty of space between the sites provides a sense of privacy. There is no host here, but firewood appears to be easy to gather. The Clarks Fork Yellowstone River requires a bit of a hike across the road.

9 Crazy Creek

Location: 69 miles northwest of Cody.
Facilities: Vault toilets, fire rings, tables, drinking water.
Sites: 16 for tents or RVs up to 30 feet long.
Fee: $ per day, 16-day maximum stay.
Reservations: First-come, first-served.
Agency: Shoshone National Forest, Clarks Fork Ranger District, 1-307-754-7207.
Activities: Fishing, hiking.
Finding the campground: Take Wyoming Highway 120 north out of Cody for 17 miles. Turn left onto Wyoming Highway 296 and travel 47 miles. Turn left onto U.S. Highway 212 and travel 5 miles.

About the campground: Wilderness and a waterfall are accessible from this campground. The semilevel parking spots seem out of place in the granite outcrops. The pine forest shades tables and parking alike, with a few spruce mingled within. Sagebrush takes over where the trees stop, just above the creek. A host is present. Numerous signs advise visitors that tour buses are not allowed. Pull-thrus dominate the available parking with fairly convenient drinking water access. If you plan on a picnic here, be advised that there is a fee.

10 Fox Creek

Location: 74 miles northwest of Cody.
Facilities: Vault toilets, fire rings, tables, drinking water.
Sites: 27 for tents or RVs up to 30 foot long.
Fee: $ per day, 16-day maximum stay.
Reservations: First-come, first-served.
Agency: Shoshone National Forest, Clarks Fork Ranger District, 1-307-754-7207.
Activities: Fishing, hiking.
Finding the campground: Take Wyoming Highway 120 north out of Cody for 17 miles. Turn left onto Wyoming Highway 296 and travel 47 miles. Turn left onto U.S. Highway 212 and travel 10 miles. The campground is on the right side of the road.

About the campground: Spruce and pine trees of varying heights grow between parking areas, offering privacy. Loop A holds 10 units of fairly level parking. Loop B bears left from the entrance, passing along a small meadow. A few spots accommodate RVs up to 40 feet long, but most push the limit at 30 feet. Firewood gathering should not be too difficult in this thick forest. The Clarks Fork Yellowstone River rages past within sight of some of the back spots. A host is present.

1 Chief Joseph (Montana)

Location: 78 miles northwest of Cody.
Facilities: Vault toilet, fire rings, tables, drinking water.
Sites: 6 for tents or RVs up to 16 feet long.
Fee: $ per day, 16-day maximum stay.
Reservations: First-come, first-served.
Agency: Gallatin National Forest, Gardiner Ranger District, 1-406-848-7375.
Activities: Hiking.
Finding the campground: Take Wyoming Highway 120 north out of Cody for 17 miles. Turn left onto Wyoming Highway 296 and travel 47 miles. Turn left onto U.S. Highway 212 and travel 14 miles. The campground is on the left side of the road.

About the campground: Spruce and lodgepole pine of all sizes hide this campground from passing traffic. Drinking water comes from a hand pump close to the entrance. Tents will find level spots more readily than RVs.

2 Colter (Montana)

Location: 79 miles northwest of Cody.
Facilities: Vault toilets, fire rings, tables, drinking water.
Sites: 23 for tents or RVs up to 30 feet long.
Fee: $ per day, 16-day maximum stay.
Reservations: First-come, first-served.
Agency: Gallatin National Forest, Gardiner Ranger District, 1-406-848-7375.
Activities: Hiking.
Finding the campground: Take Wyoming Highway 120 north out of Cody for 17 miles. Turn left onto Wyoming Highway 296 and travel 47 miles. Turn left onto U.S. Highway 212 and travel 15 miles. The campground is on the right side of the road.

About the campground: Fire touched this campground in the recent past. Open, stump-filled areas replace the forest along the road. The two loops circle about in an unusual manner. An inner, unmarked loop holds 13 sites. An outer loop really is more of a long pull-thru with an exit about 0.5 mile farther up the highway. Spruce trees inhabit the sites toward the back, offering a sample of what this campground was before the fire. Units have a lot of room in the outer loop, with a small draw hiding most from the upper sites. Plentiful deadfall is available for firewood. You will need a good saw, as the smaller pieces have been picked up. Numerous spigots provide tasty drinking water.

13 Soda Butte (Montana)

Location: 80 miles northwest of Cody.
Facilities: Vault toilets, fire rings, tables, drinking water.
Sites: 20 for tents or RVs up to 30 feet long.
Fee: $ per day, 16-day maximum stay.
Reservations: First-come, first-served.
Agency: Gallatin National Forest, Gardiner Ranger District, 1-406-848-7375.
Activities: Hiking.
Finding the campground: Take Wyoming Highway 120 north out of Cody for 17 miles. Turn left onto Wyoming Highway 296 and travel 47 miles. Turn left onto U.S. Highway 212 and travel 16 miles. The campground is on the left side of the road.

About the campground: Permanent campers reside in the old Cooke City Cemetery next to the access road. These campers were here long before any road wound its way to this remote spot. Tall pine and spruce trees share the meadows with camping units. Most of the parking areas are not level. Numerous water spigots are easily accessible, unlike firewood. Rugged mountains overlook the campground peeking through open spots. A turnaround allows trailers and longer RVs to scope out any available sites. The distance between units varies some, with most somewhat isolated.

14 Beartooth Lake

Location: 77 miles northwest of Cody.
Facilities: Vault toilets, fire rings, tables, drinking water, picnic area, boat ramp.
Sites: 21 for tents or RVs up to 40 feet long.
Fee: $ per day, 14-day maximum stay.
Reservations: First-come, first-served.
Agency: Shoshone National Forest, Clarks Fork Ranger District, 1-307-754-7207.
Activities: Fishing, hiking, boating, swimming.
Finding the campground: Take Wyoming Highway 120 north out of Cody for 17 miles. Turn left onto Wyoming Highway 296 and travel for 47 miles. Turn right onto U.S. Highway 212 and travel 13 miles. The campground is on the left side of the road.

About the campground: This is bear country. A warning sign posted at the fee depository at the time of our visit stated a grizzly bear and human encounter had recently occurred. Make sure you understand and follow the rules. Moose have been seen in the willow swamp along the south side of the campground. Beartooth Lake sits peacefully under the dramatic colors of Beartooth Butte. Hikers can exercise a little to get a closer view of the waterfall revealed along the road. For a wider view a short drive will place you in the Clay Butte Lookout Tower. Spruce and pine trees grow thick enough to keep grass from growing between. Loop A holds 6 units. Loop B offers some pull-thrus in the 9 spaces available. Loop C holds 4 shorter, sloping parking areas. Loop C accommodates tents best, though getting to a toilet from Loop C requires some footwork. The smaller pieces of firewood were picked up long ago. Deadfall can be found in places farther away—in areas you might consider driving to. A host is available.

15 Island Lake

Location: 80 miles northwest of Cody.
Facilities: Vault toilets, fire rings, tables, drinking water.
Sites: 20 for tents or RVs up to 30 feet long.
Fee: $ per day, 16-day maximum stay.
Reservations: First-come, first-served.
Agency: Shoshone National Forest, Clarks Fork Ranger District, 1-307-754-7207.
Activities: Fishing, hiking, boating, swimming, photography.
Finding the campground: Take Wyoming Highway 120 north out of Cody for 17 miles. Turn left onto Wyoming Highway 296 and travel for 47 miles. Turn right onto U.S. Highway 212 and travel 16 miles. The campground is on the left side of the road.

About the campground: Alpine meadows and the snowcapped Beartooth Mountains surround the granite outcrops this campground is perched on. White pine and spruce defiantly cling to the rock in all three loops. Loop A settles into southern exposure just out of sight of Island Lake. Loop B offers some of the more creative hideouts. One of the units perches tightly on top of a granite outcrop. Loop C grants some beautiful scenery with ice-cold Island Lake in front of the majestic mountains.

Buffalo Bill State Park

16 Buffalo Bill State Park: North Shore Bay

Location: 10 miles west of Cody.
Facilities: Vault toilets, fire rings, tables, drinking water, RV dump.
Sites: 5 for tents and 27 for tents or RVs up to 40 feet long.
Fee: $ per day (including entrance fee), 14-day maximum stay.
Reservations: First-come, first-served.
Agency: Buffalo Bill State Park, 1-307-587-9227.
Activities: Fishing, boating, swimming.
Finding the campground: Take U.S. Highway 14/16/20 west out of Cody for 10 miles. Turn left at the sign and travel past the fee station.

About the campground: Drinking water is within the RV dump drive-through. It would be wise to fill up before setting up in a permanent spot. A host is present in the second loop along with the 5 tent-only spots. Loop 1 holds 7 pull-thrus while Loop 3 holds 16 pull-thrus. The willow trees have a

North Shore Bay Campground offers access to Buffalo Bill Reservoir in Buffalo Bill State Park.

long way to go before much shade will be produced. The lake offers a refreshing way to cool off, which proves to be the activity of choice. Most anglers at the time of our visit were in boats.

17 Buffalo Bill State Park: North Fork

Location: 15 miles west of Cody.
Facilities: Vault toilets, fire rings, tables, drinking water, picnic area, RV dump, pay phone.
Sites: 6 for tents and 50 for RVs up to 50 feet long.
Fee: $ per day (including entrance fee), 14-day maximum stay.
Reservations: First-come, first-served.
Agency: Buffalo Bill State Park, 1-307-587-9227.
Activities: Fishing.
Finding the campground: Take U.S. Highway 14/16/20 west out of Cody for 15 miles. The campground is accessed from the county road on the left side of the highway.

About the campground: A loop with 14 pull-thrus sits closer to the North Fork Shoshone River just below the main campground. The trees here lean permanently in the direction of the wind. The grounds are well kept and even irrigated. A host is present at the campground. The larger portion is more of a continuous loop with other access roads cutting across. The wind seems to hit the main area with more gusto, but that keeps the mosquitoes down.

18 Big Game

Location: 28 miles west of Cody.
Facilities: Vault toilets, fire rings, tables, drinking water.
Sites: 16 for tents or RVs up to 40 feet long.
Fee: $ per day, 14-day maximum stay.
Reservations: First-come, first-served.
Agency: Shoshone National Forest, Wapiti Ranger District, 1-307-527-6921.
Activities: Fishing, hiking, rockhounding.
Finding the campground: Take U.S. Highway 14/16/20 west out of Cody for 28 miles. The campground is on the right side of the road.

About the campground: Willow brush engulfs the space between cottonwood trees in this campground. The level parking units have plenty of space and brush for individual privacy. The trees and brush make a wall of green that could be referred to as a country alley. Well-defined trails stay open through continued use. A host is available at one of the sites. Deadfall is plainly visible within the tangled brush, but it probably will stay visible due to the difficulty of extracting it.

9 Wapiti

Location: 29 miles west of Cody.
Facilities: Vault toilets, fire rings, tables, drinking water.
Sites: 41 for tents or RVs up to 40 feet long.
Fee: $ per day, 14-day maximum stay.
Reservations: First-come, first-served.
Agency: Shoshone National Forest, Wapiti Ranger District, 1-307-527-6921.
Activities: Fishing, hiking, rockhounding.
Finding the campground: Take U.S. Highway 14/16/20 for 29 miles west out of Cody. The campground is on the right side of the road.

About the campground: Cottonwood and cedar trees provide just the right amount of shade. Parking units stretch out along the south side of the North Fork Shoshone River with a lot of room between. A host is present at the campground. The sites closest to the river generally fill first. The traffic tends to die down after dark, though during daylight noise levels get high.

20 Elk Fork

Location: 30 miles west of Cody.
Facilities: Vault toilet, fire rings, tables, corrals, trailhead.
Sites: 13 for tents or RVs up to 40 feet long.
Fee: $ per day, 14-day maximum stay.
Reservations: First-come, first-served.
Agency: Shoshone National Forest, Wapiti Ranger District, 1-307-527-6921.
Activities: Fishing, hiking, rockhounding.
Finding the campground: Take U.S. Highway 14/16/20 for 30 miles west out of Cody. The campground is on the left side of the road.

About the campground: Cedar and cottonwood trees add shade to this narrow end of the draw. Not all of the paved parking spots accommodate long RVs. The corrals and adjacent trailhead keep this place active. A host is present, but firewood will take some effort to find.

21 Clearwater

Location: 32 miles west of Cody.
Facilities: Vault toilets, fire rings, tables, drinking water.
Sites: 10 for tents and 5 for RVs up to 30 feet long.
Fee: $ per day, 14-day maximum stay.
Reservations: First-come, first-served.
Agency: Shoshone National Forest, Wapiti Ranger District, 1-307-527-6921.
Activities: Fishing, hiking, rockhounding.
Finding the campground: Take U.S. Highway 14/16/20 west out of Cody for 32 miles. The campground is on the left side of the road.

About the campground: Cedar, cottonwood, and willow trees provide a little shade in this desertlike setting. Larger RVs park along the road some distance away from the tables. Numbered tables match unit sites to avoid confusion. A host is present at the campground. Tents work best in this confusing layout. Firewood gathering requires some searching. Trout live in the river passing by. Well-rounded petrified wood surfaces in the gravel bars.

22 Rex Hale

Location: 36 miles west of Cody.
Facilities: Vault toilets, fire rings, tables, drinking water.
Sites: 8 for tents or RVs up to 25 feet long.
Fee: $ per day, 14-day maximum stay.
Reservations: First-come, first-served.
Agency: Shoshone National Forest, Wapiti Ranger District, 1-307-527-6921.
Activities: Fishing, hiking, rockhounding.
Finding the campground: Take U.S. Highway 14/16/20 west out of Cody for 36 miles. The campground is on the left side of the road.

About the campground: The road and river tightly squeeze compact parking spots. Pine trees and thick underbrush fill the gaps. The highway is scheduled for reconstruction in the future.

23 Newton Creek

Location: 38 miles west of Cody.
Facilities: Vault toilets, fire rings, tables, drinking water.
Sites: 31 for tents or RVs up to 30 feet long.
Fee: $ per day, 14-day maximum stay.
Reservations: First-come, first-served.

Agency: Shoshone National Forest, Wapiti Ranger District, 1-307-527-6921.
Activities: Fishing, hiking, rockhounding.
Finding the campground: Take U.S. Highway 14/16/20 west out of Cody for 38 miles. The campground is on the left side of the road.

About the campground: Fir trees grant plenty of shade in this hollow. The parking spots follow along a high bank of the North Fork Shoshone River. Be especially careful of young children getting too close. The highway tends to squeeze the left loop tighter to the river. Precious few spots will accommodate RVs 40 feet long.

24 Eagle Creek

Location: 45 miles west of Cody.
Facilities: Vault toilets, fire rings, tables, drinking water.
Sites: 20 for tents or RVs up to 35 feet long.
Fee: $ per day, 14-day maximum stay.
Reservations: First-come, first-served.
Agency: Shoshone National Forest, Wapiti Ranger District, 1-307-527-6921.
Activities: Fishing, hiking, wildlife viewing, rockhounding.
Finding the campground: Take U.S. Highway 14/16/20 west out of Cody for 45 miles. The campground is on the left side of the road.

About the campground: Bears visit more regularly now, and hard-sided RVs are required for camping. Just upstream, the former Sleeping Giant Campground went to day use only for the same reason. Pine and fir trees shade the tables and most of the parking spots. Two loops offer fairly private places with 7 on the right and 13 on the left upon entering. All of the units are within a very short distance of the river. If fishing is not very good, you can search the rock piles for pieces of petrified wood, which are actually more like agates than wood. Every year new specimens roll out with the spring high water.

25 Threemile

Location: 49 miles west of Cody.
Facilities: Vault toilet, fire rings, tables, drinking water.
Sites: 33 for tents or RVs up to 30 feet long.
Fee: $ per day, 14-day maximum stay.
Reservations: First-come, first-served.
Agency: Shoshone National Forest, Wapiti Ranger District, 1-307-527-6921.
Activities: Fishing, hiking, wildlife viewing, rockhounding.
Finding the campground: Take U.S. Highway 14/16/20 west out of Cody for 49 miles. The campground is on the left side of the road.

About the campground: Fir and pine trees live between the highway and the North Fork Shoshone River with the campground squeezed between. During the research for this book, the campground was not open due to road construction. Call ahead for information about closures.

Jackson Area

Mountain men frequented this scenic region even after the beaver were trapped out, and capable individuals can still revisit their steps in the backcountry—with the proper permission and equipment. The visitor center at Moose offers an excellent place to research your options.

Mountains jut out of the ground in stark beauty on both sides. Some less-visited campgrounds on the west must be accessed from Idaho, though they are in Wyoming. Grand Teton National Park is the major attraction here, though there are some wonderful and moderately secret hideaways nearby, like the Curtis Canyon Campground near the National Elk Refuge. Most travelers do not spend a lot of time exploring them, instead hurrying on their way to nearby Yellowstone National Park.

1 Cave Falls

Location: 26 miles east of Marysville, Idaho.
Facilities: Vault toilets, fire grates, grills, tables, drinking water, picnic area.
Sites: 23 pull-thrus for tents or RVs up to 50 feet long.
Fee: $ per day, 14-day maximum stay.
Reservations: First-come, first-served.
Agency: Targhee National Forest, 1-208-624-3151.
Activities: Fishing, hiking, wildlife viewing.
Finding the campground: Take Idaho Highway 47 east of Marysville for about 7 miles. Turn right at the sign onto the paved Grassy Lake Road and travel 19 miles. Thirteen miles of gravel divide two paved stretches across the national forest.

About the campground: This scenic little part of Wyoming is seldom visited, perhaps because it must be accessed from Idaho. The Grassy Lake Road does go through to Flag Ranch, in Grand Teton National Park, though four-wheel drives are advised. Cars were making the trip on our visit; however, a good rainstorm would stop their advance in one of the meadows. Water flows continuously from a pipe at the end of the campground, but not as fast as the Bechler River beside it. The first units are above the river out of sight of the noisy rapids. The farthest units are the closest to the river. Pine trees allow a few spruce into the long distances between camping spots. Regardless of whether you want to be close to the river or farther up, the rapids provide plenty of background music. The Cave Falls are a short distance past the campground. These wide and noisy falls are well worth the extra distance to get photographs. At the time of our visit, it appeared that the drinking water had been shut off in the picnic area and that garbage service had been discontinued.

Jackson Area

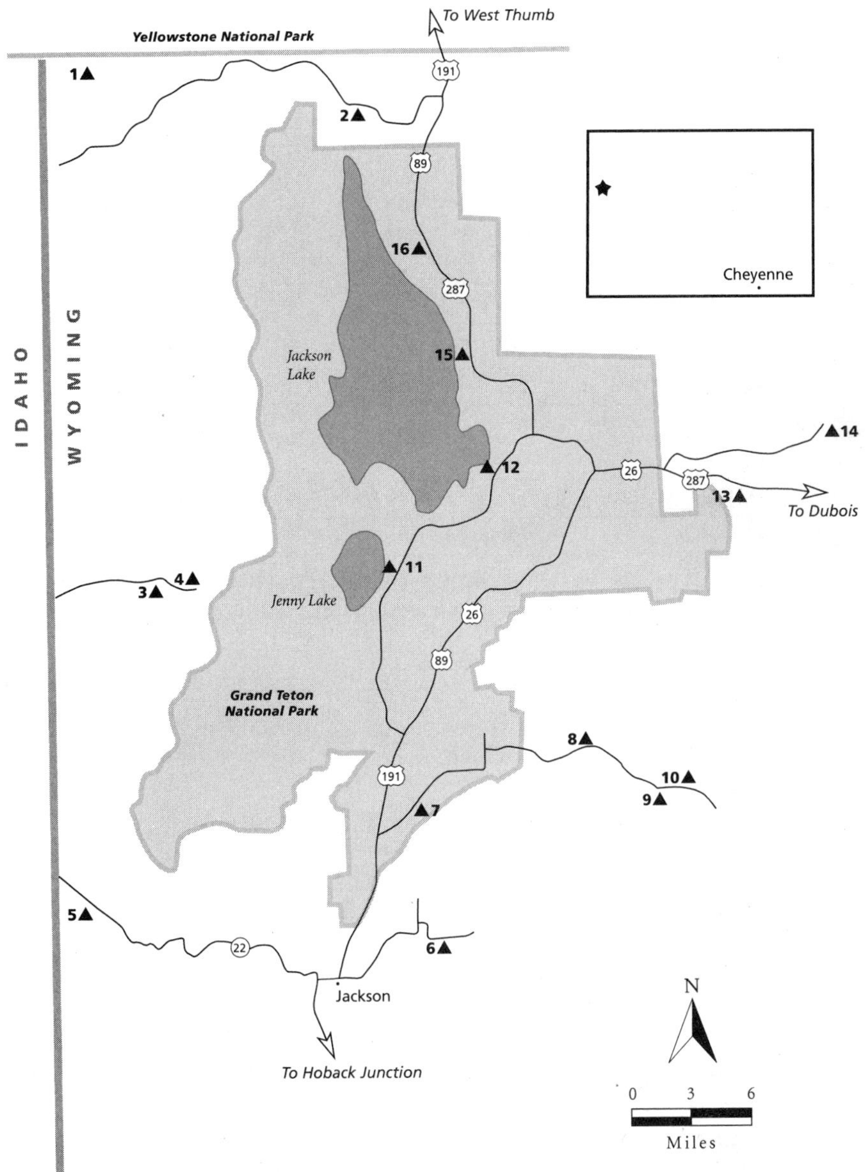

	Group sites	Tents	RV sites	Total sites	Picnic area	Toilets	Showers	Drinking water	Dump station	Phone	Disabled access	Fee ($)	Season	Can reserve	Length of stay	Recreation
1 Cave Falls			23	23	X	V		X				$	Summer		14	FHW
2 Snake River				D		V						N	Summer		14	FH
3 Reunion Flat	1			D		V		X				$	Summer	G		FH
4 Teton Canyon			19	19		V		X				$	Summer	X	16	FH
5 Trail Creek			11	11		V		X				$	Summer		14	FH
6 Curtis Canyon			12	12		V		X				$	6/5-9/10		14	HW
7 Gros Ventre			360	360		C		X	X	X	X	$$	5/1-10/15		14	FHW
8 Atherton Creek			20	20	X	V		?				$	6/5-10/30		10	FHBS
9 Red Hills			5	5		V		X				$	6/5-10/30		14	FH
10 Crystal Creek			6	6		V		X				$	6/5-10/30		14	FH
11 Jenny Lake		49		49		C		X				$$	5/15-9/20		7	FHW
12 Signal Mountain			86	86	X	C		X	X		X	$	5/15-10/4		14	FHBSW
13 Hatchet			9	9		V		X				$	6/1-9/30		10	HW
14 Turpin Meadow			18	18	X	V		X				$	6/1-9/30		6	FHW
15 Colter Bay			350	350	X	C		X	X	X	X	$$	5/22-9/20		14	FHBS
16 Lizard Creek		20	40	60	X	C		X				$$	6/12-9/6		14	FH

D=dispersed, N=none, G=group, V=vault toilets, C=comfort stations, F=fishing, H=hiking, B=boating, S=swimming, W=wildlife viewing

2 Snake River

Location: 5 miles west of Flag Ranch.
Facilities: Vault toilets, tables.
Sites: 8 dispersed sites for tents or RVs up to 30 feet long.
Fee: None, 14-day maximum stay.
Reservations: First-come, first-served.
Agency: Teton National Forest, Jackson Ranger District, 1-307-739-5500.
Activities: Fishing, hiking.
Finding the campground: Turn onto the paved access road for Flag Ranch. The Grassy Lake Road is the first right-hand turn after leaving the highway. This paved road turns to gravel as it heads toward the different units.

About the campground: Some of these isolated camping areas have more than one unit. Up to a mile or better separates these little-advertised riverbank hideaways. Site 1 advertises 4 units, though exactly how it is divided seems open to interpretation. Larger RVs could feasibly utilize the unit complete with newer toilets; however, it would be a real disappointment to drag, push, and pull over the ruts and rocks only to find occupants already there. Camping out of designated spots is not allowed. The Snake River winds past in willow brush thickets, with the camping units overlooking from the pine forest

Cave Falls, on the Bechler River, is a short distance upriver from the campground of the same name.

on the bank above. This could be a very welcome change of pace after swimming in the flood of visitors common to Yellowstone National Park.

3 Reunion Flat

Location: 10 miles east of Driggs, Idaho.
Facilities: Vault toilets, fire rings, tables, drinking water.
Sites: Group area for tents or RVs up to 40 feet long.
Fee: $ to $$$ depending upon group size.
Reservations: 1-877-444-6777.
Agency: Targhee National Forest, 1-208-624-3151.
Activities: Fishing, hiking.
Finding the campground: In Driggs turn at the Targhee National Forest Recreation sign and travel 7 miles. Turn right onto the gravel Forest Road 009 and travel 3 miles.

About the campground: This campsite is generally reserved for larger groups, though individuals are allowed to camp here if no group is present. The large, grassy area accommodates up to 150 people, though it could seem crowded. The wilderness access is a mile farther up the road. If you plan to hike in the backcountry, the Teton Canyon Campground would be a better choice. This spot would be more for when the other units are full.

Teton Canyon

Location: 11 miles east of Driggs, Idaho.
Facilities: Vault toilets, fire rings, grills, tables, drinking water.
Sites: 19 for tents or RVs up to 40 feet long.
Fee: $ per day, 16-day maximum stay.
Reservations: 1-877-444-6777.
Agency: Targhee National Forest, 1-208-624-3151.
Activities: Fishing, hiking.
Finding the campground: In Driggs turn at the Targhee National Forest Recreation sign and travel 7 miles. Turn right onto the gravel Forest Road 009 and travel 4 miles.

About the campground: Spruce trees shade the more popular units along a noisy creek. Other units fill the open area between the forest and trailhead parking. A few aspen trees pop out at various locations in this deep canyon. Photos of the western side of the Teton Mountains can be taken along the access road. After arriving at the campground, the steep, forested mountainsides hide the peaks, requiring a hike to view them.

Trail Creek

Location: 18 miles west of Jackson.
Facilities: Vault toilets, fire rings, grills, tables, drinking water.
Sites: 11 for tents or RVs up to 40 feet long.
Fee: $ per day, 14-day maximum stay.
Reservations: First-come, first-served.
Agency: Targhee National Forest, 1-208-624-3151.
Activities: Fishing, hiking.
Finding the campground: Take Wyoming Highway 22 west out of Jackson for 18 miles. NOTE: Teton Pass has 10 percent grades and sharp corners.

About the campground: Aspen trees greet campers at the entrance, while spruce trees take over the back portion. The semilevel parking spots are spread out between the highway and the raging Trail Creek. It will take a while for the sun to reach campers in this deep canyon. Traffic could be noisy during the day, though it is likely to get quiet after dark. A host is available at the campground. Firewood will take some footwork if not purchased.

6 Curtis Canyon

Location: 8 miles east of Jackson.
Facilities: Vault toilets, fire rings, tables, drinking water.
Sites: 12 for tents or RVs up to 20 feet long.
Fee: $ per day, 14-day maximum stay.
Reservations: First-come, first-served.
Agency: Teton National Forest, Jackson Ranger District, 1-307-739-5500.

Activities: Hiking, wildlife viewing.
Finding the campground: From Jackson proceed through the National Elk Refuge on the northeast side. Take the gravel road past the Twin Creek Ranch to the national forest access sign. Turn right onto this very rough gravel road and travel up the switchbacks for 3 miles.

About the campground: This secret hideaway is neatly tucked into the evergreen forest out of site from Jackson. A very short hike brings the Jackson Hole back into sight. Be sure to bring your camera and binoculars. The Elk Refuge lies below with a lot of area to study. A host is present at the campground. The rough road could prove very disheartening if the units are full. The reward for your perseverance would be isolated places to meditate on the panoramic mountains.

7 Grand Teton National Park: Gros Ventre

Location: 12 miles northeast of Jackson.
Facilities: Flush toilets, fire rings, tables, drinking water, RV dump, pay phone.
Sites: 360 for tents or RVs up to 50 feet long.
Fee: $$ per day, 14-day maximum stay.
Reservations: First-come, first-served.
Agency: National Park Service, 1-307-739-3600.
Activities: Fishing, hiking, wildlife viewing.

RVs find ample parking at the Gros Ventre Campground, within view of the Tetons.

Finding the campground: Take U.S. Highway 26/89/191 north out of Jackson for 8 miles. Turn right onto Gros Ventre Road and travel 4 miles. The campground is on the right side of the road.

About the campground: The Tetons provide a spectacular backdrop for this campground. Mature cottonwood trees grant a lot of shade but little firewood. Drinking water is located at the comfort stations. RVs should fill drinking water tanks from the provided spigot at the dump station. The Gros Ventre River meanders past to the east, inviting anglers. Tents do make use of the camping area, though generators and hot water heaters tend to produce complaints from time to time.

8 Atherton Creek

Location: 20 miles northeast of Jackson.
Facilities: Vault toilets, fire rings, tables, drinking water, picnic area, boat ramp.
Sites: 20 for tents or RVs up to 25 feet long.
Fee: $ per day, 10-day maximum stay.
Reservations: First-come, first-served.
Agency: Teton National Forest, Jackson Ranger District, 1-307-739-5500.
Activities: Fishing, hiking, boating, swimming.
Finding the campground: Take U.S. Highway 26/89/191 north out of Jackson for 8 miles. Turn right at Gros Ventre Junction and travel 6 miles, passing through Kelly. Turn right onto the paved Gros Ventre Road and travel 6 miles.

About the campground: The aspen and spruce trees share this sloping side hill along the banks of Lower Slide Lake. A landslide created this lake in 1923. The dam broke two years later, resulting in six deaths and a smaller lake. Three loops offer back-in sites with shorter aspen and spruce trees granting some shade. As of our visit a water pump was chained. The host was not in at the time, so drinking water could be a past service. Firewood should either be brought or bought at the campground.

9 Red Hills

Location: 25 miles northeast of Jackson.
Facilities: Vault toilets, fire rings, tables, drinking water.
Sites: 5 for tents or RVs up to 15 feet long.
Fee: $ per day, 14-day maximum stay.
Reservations: First-come, first-served.
Agency: Teton National Forest, Jackson Ranger District, 1-307-739-5500.
Activities: Fishing, hiking.
Finding the campground: Take U.S. Highway 26/89/191 north out of Jackson for 8 miles. Turn right at Gros Ventre Junction and travel 6 miles, passing through Kelly. Turn right onto the paved Gros Ventre Road and travel 11 miles.

Atherton Creek Campground nestles along the shore of Lower Slide Lake, which was created by a landslide in 1923.

About the campground: The road was closed upon our visit to the area. It would appear from the Atherton Creek Campground that the mountain backdrop changes. An evergreen forest carpets the mountainsides as they crowd the Gros Ventre River farther upstream. Trailers are not advised in this campground.

10 Crystal Creek

Location: 26 miles northeast of Jackson.
Facilities: Vault toilets, fire rings, tables, drinking water.
Sites: 6 for tents or RVs up to 20 feet long.
Fee: $ per day, 14-day maximum stay.
Reservations: First-come, first-served.
Agency: Teton National Forest, Jackson Ranger District, 1-307-739-5500.
Activities: Fishing, hiking.
Finding the campground: Take U.S. Highway 26/89/191 north out of Jackson for 8 miles. Turn right at Gros Ventre Junction and travel 6 miles, passing through Kelly. Turn right onto the paved Gros Ventre Road and travel 12 miles.

About the campground: As with the previous campground, the closed road kept us from visiting the area. An informational bulletin posted on the Internet advised that the campground is accessible to trailers, though the exact size of the trailer is not listed. Both this campground and the Red Hills Campground fill quickly during the summer and tend to stay that way.

Grand Teton National Park: Jenny Lake

Location: 21 miles north of Jackson.
Facilities: Comfort stations, fire rings, tables, drinking water.
Sites: 49 for tents.
Fee: $$ per day, 7-day maximum stay.
Reservations: First-come, first-served.
Agency: National Park Service, 1-307-739-3600.
Activities: Fishing, hiking, wildlife viewing.
Finding the campground: Take U.S. Highway 26/89/191 north out of Jackson for 13 miles. Turn left at Moose Junction onto the paved Teton Park Road and travel 8 miles. Turn left at the South Jenny Lake access road and travel 0.25 mile.

About the campground: Paved access winds through large boulders and tall spruce, pine, and fir trees. Sagebrush is scattered about with tall grass in places. The Tetons loom over the treetops, offering plenty of photographic views. This campground fills quickly every day. It has been reported that as one pulls out, two are waiting. It is a most beautiful spot, though somewhat maddening to obtain a unit.

Grand Teton National Park: Signal Mountain

Location: 33 miles north of Jackson.
Facilities: Comfort stations, fire rings, tables, drinking water, RV dump, picnic area, boat ramp.
Sites: 86 for tents or RVs up to 30 feet long.
Fee: $ per day, 14-day maximum stay.
Reservations: First-come, first-served.
Agency: National Park Service, 1-307-739-3600.
Activities: Fishing, hiking, boating, swimming, wildlife viewing.
Finding the campground: Take U.S. Highway 26/89/191 north out of Jackson for 13 miles. Turn left at Moose Junction onto the paved Teton Park Road and travel 20 miles.

About the campground: Stubby pine trees and tall sagebrush flow over the steep hillside overlooking Jackson Lake. Some of the units provide better mountain views than other spots. The units are well positioned, providing a sort of privacy. The Signal Mountain Trail, taking off from the camping area, is an excellent photographic tour. Moose, deer, and other wildlife are often spotted in the area as well.

13 Hatchet

Location: 9 miles east of Moran Junction.
Facilities: Vault toilets, fire rings, tables, drinking water.
Sites: 9 for tents or RVs up to 30 feet long.
Fee: $ per day, 10-day maximum stay.
Reservations: First-come, first-served.
Agency: Teton National Forest, Jackson Ranger District, 1-307-739-5500.
Activities: Hiking, wildlife viewing.
Finding the campground: Take U.S. Highway 26/287 east of Moran Junction for 9 miles. The campground is on the right side of the road just before the Blackrock Ranger Station.

About the campground: The campground sits almost within a forest of lodgepole pine. The parking units appear to have been placed so as to avoid cutting trees. Two pull-thrus and one long back-in could accommodate RVs up to 50 feet long without too much leveling work. The six remaining sites would be crowded for anything over 30 feet long. As of our visit the water dribbled slowly out of the spigots. If you have a large empty holding tank for drinking water, fill it up before arriving. Both Yellowstone and Grand Teton National Parks campgrounds fill toward late afternoon. If your travels run late, this campground could very well be the last place to camp. Deadfall lies a long ways away from this well-used campground, so firewood will not come easily. This is bear country. Be aware of the procedures.

14 Turpin Meadow

Location: 44 miles north of Jackson.
Facilities: Vault toilets, fire rings, tables, drinking water, picnic area.
Sites: 18 for tents or RVs up to 40 feet long.
Fee: $ per day, 6-day maximum stay.
Reservations: First-come, first-served.
Agency: Teton National Forest, Jackson Ranger District, 1-307-739-5500.
Activities: Fishing, hiking, picnicking, wildlife viewing.
Finding the campground: Take U.S. Highway 26/89/191 north out of Jackson for 30 miles. At Moran Junction continue on U.S. Highway 26/287 for 4 miles. Turn left onto the paved Buffalo Fork Road and travel 10 miles. Turn left onto the gravel access road just before crossing the Buffalo Fork River.

About the campground: Pine trees tower above grassy open spaces between units, where horses are allowed. The adjacent trailhead appeared more active than the campground upon our visit. This camping area is geared more toward horse riders, as evidenced by the extra-long parking units. Bear boxes located in the campground are not there for looks. Be aware of the proper procedures. Gathering firewood will require some hiking, so you may want to acquire some beforehand.

15 Grand Teton National Park: Colter Bay

Location: 40 miles north of Jackson.
Facilities: Comfort stations, fire rings, tables, drinking water, picnic area, RV dump, pay phone.
Sites: 350 for tents or RVs up to 50 feet long.
Fee: $$ per day, 14-day maximum stay.
Reservations: First-come, first-served.
Agency: National Park Service, 1-307-739-3600.
Activities: Fishing, hiking, boating, swimming.
Finding the campground: Take U.S. Highway 26/89/191 north out of Jackson for 30 miles. At Moran Junction turn left onto U.S. Highway 89/191/287 and travel 10 miles. Turn left at the Colter Bay Village sign just past the convenience store and gas station. The campground entrance is a short distance from the highway on the right side.

About the campground: The Tetons peek through mature evergreen trees and in roadway clearings. Paved access is provided to the 15 separate loops, with plenty of space between campers. Firewood tends to be rather scarce. Jackson Lake requires a short hike from the camping units, though some are a little closer than others. On an average summer day, this campground fills by noon. Some loops are set aside for tents only.

16 Grand Teton National Park: Lizard Creek

Location: 45 miles north of Jackson.
Facilities: Comfort stations, fire rings, tables, drinking water, picnic area.
Sites: 20 for tents and 40 for tents or RVs up to 30 feet long.
Fee: $$ per day, 14-day maximum stay.
Reservations: First-come, first-served.
Agency: National Park Service, 1-307-739-3600.
Activities: Fishing, hiking.
Finding the campground: Take U.S. Highway 26/89/191 north out of Jackson for 30 miles. At Moran Junction turn left onto U.S. Highway 89/191/287 and travel 15 miles. The campground is on the left side of the road.

About the campground: Spruce and pine trees of various heights shelter these units. A few of the back units are near the shoreline of Jackson Lake. The tent sites require some footwork from the parking spots. Tents are not allowed on the grass.

Lander Area

Mountains meet desert in random locations without offering an explanation. Some of the resulting formations include the historical sites known as Devil's Gate and Independence Rock. The unique geology also contains an abundance of agates and the famous Wyoming jade.

The Oregon Trail traversed this region, leaving a massive amount of outstanding evidence. Wagon ruts are still obvious to this day in select areas. The historical markers along the route are well worth the time to examine.

In a majority of places, you can turn completely around and not see any fences, power lines, or houses. Cattle have replaced the buffalo, and here and there two parallel ruts indicate current travel routes. Otherwise the scene remains much the same as when the mountain men and western emigrants passed through.

1 Cottonwood

Location: 73 miles southeast of Lander.
Facilities: Vault toilets, fire rings, tables, drinking water.
Sites: 18 for tents or RVs up to 20 feet long.
Fee: $ per day, 14-day maximum stay.
Reservations: First-come, first-served.
Agency: Bureau of Land Management, Rawlins District, 1-307-328-4200.
Activities: Fishing, hiking, rockhounding.
Finding the campground: Take U.S. Highway 287 southeast out of Lander for 62 miles (passing through Jeffrey City). Turn right onto the gravel Green Mountain Road/BLM 2411 and travel 11 miles.

About the campground: Lodgepole pine and a few aspen grow in the forest sheltering this campground. A somewhat narrow little draw directs a small stream past the parking units happily on its way to the Sweetwater River. This green oasis clings to the north side of the heavily forested Green Mountain. The mountain is easily seen from the vast sagebrush desert engulfing it. To the north, rock formations were once used in training World War II pilots. The granite outcrops were used for target practice, as rough equivalents to the battleships of the time. Ammunition cases and clips can still be found scattered among the rocks. This campground would be a good base for rockhounding. Jade and agates are found in the nearby desert. After a hot dusty day, the cool shade and refreshing mountain air of this campground would be a pleasant ending.

Lander Area

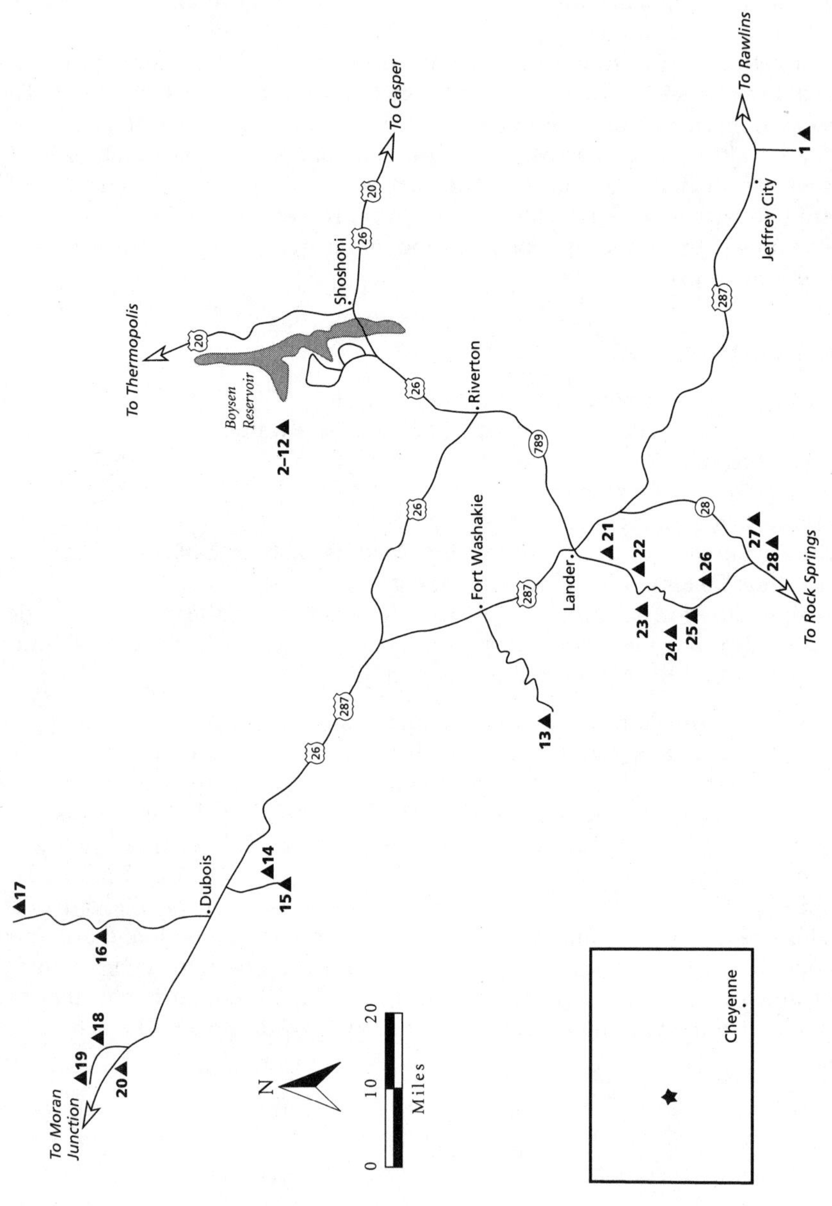

To Thermopolis
To Casper
To Rawlins
Shoshoni
Boysen Reservoir
2–12
Riverton
Jeffrey City
1
Fort Washakie
Lander
21
22
23
24
25
26
27
28
To Rock Springs
13
Dubois
14
15
16
17
18
19
20
To Moran Junction
20
26
287
789
28
N
0
10
20
Miles
Cheyenne

	Group sites	Tents	RV sites	Total sites	Picnic area	Toilets	Showers	Drinking water	Dump station	Phone	Disabled access	Fee ($)	Season	Can reserve	Length of stay	Recreation
1 Cottonwood			18	18		V		X				$	Summer		14	FHR
Boysen State Park								X	X							
2 Fremont Bay	1		3	3		V						$	All Year	G	14	FBS
3 South Muddy			1	1		V						$	All Year	G	14	FBS
4 North Muddy				D		V						$	All Year	G	14	FBS
5 Sand Mesa				D		V						$	All Year	G	14	FBSR
6 Cottonwood Bay	1			D		V						$	All Year	G	14	FBS
7 Poison Creek				D		V						$	All Year	G	14	FBS
8 Tough Creek			50	50		V		X				$	All Year	G	14	FBS
9 Brannon				D	X	V		X		X		$	All Year	G	14	FBS
10 Tamarask			25	25		V		X				$	All Year	G	14	FBS
11 Upper Wind River	1		50	50		V		X				$	All Year	G	14	F
12 Lower Wind River	1		40	40		V		X				$	All Year	G	14	F
13 Dickinson Creek			15	15		V						N	7/1-9/15		14	FHW
14 Ring Lake				D		V						N	All Year		14	FW
15 Trail Lake				D		V						N	All Year		14	FW
16 Horse Creek			9	9		V		X				$	6/1-10/30		16	FHW
17 Double Cabin			15	15		V		X				$	6/1-9/30		16	FHWR
18 Pinnacles			21	21		V		X				$	6/20-9/30		16	FHS
19 Brooks Lake			14	14		V		X				$	6/20-9/30		16	FHBSW
20 Falls			46	46		V		X				$	6/20-9/30		16	FHW
21 Sinks Canyon SP			30	30		V		X				$	All Year		14	FH
22 Sinks Canyon			9	9		V						$	6/1-10/31		10	FH
23 Worthen Meadow			28	28	X	V		X				$	7/1-9/15		10	FHBS
24 Fiddlers Lake		4	16	20	X	V		X			X	$	7/1-9/15		10	FHBS
25 Popo Agie			4	4		P						N	7/1-9/15		14	FH
26 Louis Lake			28	28		V						$	7/1-9/15		14	FHBS
27 Big Atlantic Gulch			8	8		V		X				$	All Year		14	H
28 Atlantic City			18	18		V		X				$	All Year		14	H

D=dispersed, V=vault toilets, P=pit toilets, N=none, G=group, F=fishing, H=hiking, B=boating, S=swimming, W=wildlife viewing, R=rockhounding

Boysen State Park

2 Boysen State Park: Fremont Bay

Location: 26 miles northeast of Riverton.
Facilities: Vault toilets, fire rings, tables, group area, playground, boat ramp. RV dump and drinking water are available at Park Headquarters across the highway a short distance before the Brannon and Tamarask Campgrounds access.
Sites: 3 for tents or RVs up to 30 feet long.
Fee: $ per day, 14-day maximum stay.
Reservations: Group only, 1-307-876-2796.
Agency: Boysen State Park, 1-307-876-2796.
Activities: Boating, fishing, swimming, volleyball, playground equipment.
Finding the campground: Take U.S. Highway 26 east out of Riverton for 22 miles. Turn left at the Boysen West Shore Road sign and travel about 1 mile. Turn right onto the West Shore Loop 1 road and travel 3 miles.

About the campground: Water recreation attracts campers to this desert reservoir. For the most part evenings are spent resting up for the next day's water sports. The group area here can be reserved and offers the best shelter from an intense sun—if it's not spoken for, individuals can use it. Other than the group area, there are only three fire rings with tables. A volleyball court settles into the sandy soil along with other playground equipment. Both drinking water and shade are not present. Be sure to bring the amount you need along with firewood, though driftwood does make a good fire when it can be found.

3 Boysen State Park: South Muddy

Location: 28 miles northeast of Riverton.
Facilities: Vault toilet, fire ring, table.
Sites: 1 for tents or RVs up to 40 feet long.
Fee: $ per day, 14-day maximum stay.
Reservations: Group only, 1-307-876-2796.
Agency: Boysen State Park, 1-307-876-2796.
Activities: Boating, fishing, swimming.
Finding the campground: Take U.S. Highway 26 east out of Riverton for 22 miles. Turn left at the Boysen West Shore Road sign and travel about 1 mile. Turn right onto the West Shore Loop 1 road and travel 5 miles.

About the campground: A few small trees struggle to provide a little shade along the shoreline. The only other shade comes from the shelter over the table. Water recreation attracts campers to this desert reservoir. Driftwood makes a good fire when it can be found. For the most part evenings are spent resting up for the next day's water sports.

4 Boysen State Park: North Muddy

Location: 32 miles northeast of Riverton.
Facilities: Vault toilet.
Sites: Dispersed for tents or RVs up to 20 feet long.
Fee: $ per day, 14-day maximum stay.
Reservations: Group only, 1-307-876-2796.
Agency: Boysen State Park, 1-307-876-2796.
Activities: Boating, fishing, swimming.
Finding the campground: Take U.S. Highway 26 east out of Riverton for 22 miles. Turn left at the Boysen West Shore Road sign and travel 6 miles. Turn right onto the paved West Shore Loop 2 road and travel 4 miles. The road turns to gravel just past Lake Cameahwait.

About the campground: Access roads drop off ridges to sandy shoreline. Some of the little draws snuggle up to sandstone formations that tend to keep the wind down. Water recreation attracts campers to this desert reservoir.

5 Boysen State Park: Sand Mesa

Location: 34 miles northeast of Riverton.
Facilities: Vault toilet, fire rings, tables.
Sites: Dispersed for tents or RVs up to 30 feet long.

North Muddy Campground lies just across Boysen Reservoir, the centerpiece of Boysen State Park.

Fee: $ per day, 14-day maximum stay.
Reservations: Group only, 1-307-876-2796.
Agency: Boysen State Park, 1-307-876-2796.
Activities: Fishing, boating, swimming, rockhounding.
Finding the campground: Take U.S. Highway 26 east out of Riverton for 22 miles. Turn left at the Boysen West Shore Road sign and travel 6 miles. Turn right onto the paved West Shore Loop 2 road and travel 6 miles. The road turns to gravel just past Lake Cameahwait.

About the campground: Water recreation is the main attraction at this desert reservoir, though not the only one for rockhounds. Shade is not available, in the typical desert fashion. All the same, hot sun and cool water make for plenty of visitors on holidays and weekends.

6 Boysen State Park: Cottonwood Bay

Location: 38 miles northeast of Riverton.
Facilities: Vault toilets, fire rings, tables, group area, boat ramp.
Sites: Dispersed for tents or RVs up to 40 feet long.
Fee: $ per day, 14-day maximum stay.
Reservations: Group only, 1-307-876-2796.
Agency: Boysen State Park, 1-307-876-2796.
Activities: Fishing, boating, swimming.
Finding the campground: Take U.S. Highway 26 east out of Riverton for 22 miles. Turn left at the Boysen West Shore Road sign and travel 6 miles. Turn right onto the paved West Shore Loop 2 road and travel 10 miles. The road turns to gravel just past Lake Cameahwait.

About the campground: Regulations state that campfires must be contained in designated rings, and this sandy beach offers only two such fire rings. Precious little shade comes from the few trees along the shore. About 15 large RVs filled the shoreline on our visit. More could park farther away from the water, though in the heat of summer, the closer the better.

7 Boysen State Park: Poison Creek

Location: 25.5 miles northeast of Riverton.
Facilities: Vault toilet, boat ramp.
Sites: Dispersed for tents or RVs up to 30 feet long.
Fee: $ per day, 14-day maximum stay.
Reservations: Group only, 1-307-876-2796.
Agency: Boysen State Park, 1-307-876-2796.
Activities: Boating, fishing, swimming.
Finding the campground: Take U.S. Highway 26 east out of Riverton for 24 miles. Turn left at the Poison Creek Recreation Area sign onto the gravel road and travel 1.5 miles.

About the campground: This seemingly remote spot drops down off the ridge into a somewhat sheltered area. There are no tables, fire rings, or drinking water in plain sight. We chose not to explore all of the parallel ruts leading in every direction. No one occupied the beach upon our visit, but plenty of telltale items spoke of numerous visitors.

8 Boysen State Park: Tough Creek

Location: 32 miles northeast of Riverton.
Facilities: Vault toilets, fire rings, tables, drinking water, boat ramp.
Sites: 50 for tents or RVs up to 50 feet long.
Fee: $ per day, 14-day maximum stay.
Reservations: Group only, 1-307-876-2796.
Agency: Boysen State Park, 1-307-876-2796.
Activities: Boating, fishing, swimming.
Finding the campground: Take U.S. Highway 26 east out of Riverton for 25 miles. At Shoshoni turn left onto U.S. Highway 20 and travel 6 miles. Turn left at the Tough Creek Campground sign onto the paved road and travel 1 mile. There is a very active railroad crossing just before reaching the campground. Be alert!

About the campground: Given a choice this would be the campground to stay in while visiting the state park. Most of the units find shade under one or more cottonwood trees. Fire rings, grills, and tables almost outnumber the trees. Firewood could be a problem so be sure to bring what you need, though driftwood makes a good fire when it's available. Drinking water spigots poke up near the restrooms. The parking areas could be considered dispersed after a fashion. Some forethought allows multiple vehicles and trailers to park together. A long peninsula hosts these units, granting easy access to the lake for all. Keep in mind that this is a reservoir with water sports and fishing foremost. It can smell kind of fishy.

9 Boysen State Park: Brannon

Location: 38 miles northeast of Riverton.
Facilities: Vault toilets, fire rings, tables, drinking water, picnic area, playground, boat ramp, telephone.
Sites: Dispersed for tents or RVs up to 50 feet long.
Fee: $ per day, 14-day maximum stay.
Reservations: Group only, 1-307-876-2796.
Agency: Boysen State Park, 1-307-876-2796.
Activities: Boating, fishing, swimming.
Finding the campground: Take U.S. Highway 26 east out of Riverton for 25 miles. At Shoshoni turn left onto U.S. Highway 20 and travel 13 miles. Turn left at the sign.

About the campground: It was difficult to tell where the picnic area started and the camping stopped. Watered and mowed grass marked what appeared to be the picnic area. Other roads took off toward the lake to the right of this area. Trailers were parked within sight of a sign giving directions to a swimming area.

0 Boysen State Park: Tamarask

Location: 38 miles northeast of Riverton.
Facilities: Vault toilets, fire rings, grills, tables, drinking water, playground.
Sites: 25 for tents or RVs up to 50 feet long.
Fee: $ per day, 14-day maximum stay.
Reservations: Group only, 1-307-876-2796.
Agency: Boysen State Park, 1-307-876-2796.
Activities: Boating, fishing, swimming.
Finding the campground: Take U.S. Highway 26 east out of Riverton for 25 miles. At Shoshoni turn left onto U.S. Highway 20 and travel 13 miles. Turn left at the sign.

About the campground: Tables and shade trees, of sorts, line separate peninsulas on a dead-end road. Drinking water appears to be relatively easy to obtain from one of the spigots. Driftwood makes a good fire when it can be found.

1 Boysen State Park: Upper Wind River

Location: 39 miles northeast of Riverton.
Facilities: Vault toilets, fire rings, grills, drinking water, group shelter, playground.
Sites: 50 for tents or RVs up to 50 feet long.
Fee: $ per day, 14-day maximum stay.
Reservations: Group only, 1-307-876-2796.
Agency: Boysen State Park, 1-307-876-2796.
Activities: Fishing, picnicking.
Finding the campground: Take U.S. Highway 26 east out of Riverton for 25 miles. At Shoshoni turn left onto U.S. Highway 20 and travel 14 miles. Turn left at the sign.

About the campground: Large cottonwood trees shade both sides of the paved access and parking units, but the sun can still get pretty intense by around noon. During our visit a host occupied a site toward the back of the campground. Firewood will need to be acquired before reaching this place. The green-colored Wind River rushes by on the west. Traffic noise gets a little heavy with the main highway directly beside and above the camping area.

12 Boysen State Park: Lower Wind River

Location: 40 miles northeast of Riverton.
Facilities: Vault toilets, fire rings, grills, tables, drinking water, group shelter, playground.
Sites: 40 for tents or RVs up to 50 feet long.
Fee: $ per day, 14-day maximum stay.
Reservations: Group only, 1-307-876-2796.
Agency: Boysen State Park, 1-307-876-2796.
Activities: Fishing, picnicking.
Finding the campground: Take U.S. Highway 26 east out of Riverton for 25

miles. At Shoshoni turn left onto U.S. Highway 20 and travel 15 miles. Turn left at the sign.

About the campground: The entrance divides this campground into two loops. Large cottonwood trees provide more shade on the northern loop. A special unit for the disabled begins this section of 15 units. The southern portion hosts a group area and playground along with the parking spots. Parking spots are gravel with a paved access road. As with the previous campground, traffic noise can get intense. When things quiet down, the Wind River can be heard working its way through the canyon. Three nearby tunnels add an orchestra of echoing car horns from time to time. Keep in mind that fishing downstream from Boysen State Park will put you onto the Wind River Indian Reservation. A special permit is required.

13 Dickinson Creek

Location: 34 miles northwest of Lander.
Facilities: Vault toilet, fire rings, tables.
Sites: 15 for tents or RVs up to 20 feet long.
Fee: None, 14-day maximum stay.
Reservations: First-come, first-served.
Agency: Shoshone National Forest, Washakie Ranger District, 1-307-332-5460.
Activities: Fishing, hiking, wildlife viewing.
Finding the campground: Take U.S. Highway 26/287 north out of Lander for 15 miles. At Fort Washakie turn left onto the paved Trout Creek Road (directly across from the Fort Wasakie Historic Marker sign). Trout Creek Road turns to rough gravel in 5 miles at a cattleguard. Continue on this very rough road for 19 miles. The steep switchbacks seem to go on indefinitely. It took one hour and fifteen minutes to travel the last 15 miles.

About the campground: High alpine meadows surround this forested campground. Dickinson Creek meanders by in the long continuous meadow with plenty of trout waiting for lunch. Bountiful elk, deer, and other wildlife award the observant with photographic options. Pack warm clothing. The summer wind carries a chill that goes to just plain cold when the sun goes down. Deadfall produces plenty of firewood from the forested areas. Trailers will have to be unhooked to make use of the parking aprons.

14 Ring Lake

Location: 7 miles southeast of Dubois.
Facilities: Vault toilet, boat ramp.
Sites: Dispersed for tents or RVs up to 40 feet long.
Fee: None, 14-day maximum stay.
Reservations: First-come, first-served.
Agency: Wyoming Game and Fish, Region 6, 1-307-332-2688.
Activities: Fishing, wildlife viewing.
Finding the campground: Take U.S. Highway 26/287 east out of Dubois for 3 miles. Turn right at the Whiskey Basin Recreation Area sign onto the gravel road and travel 4 miles bearing left. The camping area is on the left.

About the campground: Anglers frequent these super-clear waters with camping gear in tow. Sagebrush dominates the mountainsides, which have a sprinkling of pine trees. Camping here is more allowed than promoted. This camping area offers an abundance of level parking. Fire rings consist of circled rocks placed by previous visitors. No drinking water or firewood is available. Bring enough to take care of your length of stay. Bighorn sheep, moose, elk, and deer offer photographic opportunities from time to time.

5 Trail Lake

Location: 9 miles southeast of Dubois.
Facilities: Vault toilet, table.
Sites: Dispersed for tents or RVs up to 40 feet long.
Fee: None, 14-day maximum stay.
Reservations: First-come, first-served.
Agency: Wyoming Game and Fish, Region 6, 1-307-332-2688.
Activities: Fishing, wildlife viewing.
Finding the campground: Take U.S. Highway 26/287 east out of Dubois for 3 miles. Turn right at the Whiskey Basin Recreation Area sign onto the gravel road and travel 6 miles bearing left. The camping area is on the left.

About the campground: This area is a little smaller than the Ring Lake camping area. The lakes here flow almost directly from one to the other with the same crystal-clear water. The lakeshore is a bit steeper here with a few more pine trees. A boat ramp is located along the main access road just before the camping area. As of our visit more campers were parked at Ring Lake. Perhaps the fishing was better there at the time.

6 Horse Creek

Location: 11 miles north of Dubois.
Facilities: Vault toilets, fire rings, tables, drinking water.
Sites: 9 for tents or RVs up to 40 feet long.
Fee: $ per day, 16-day maximum stay.
Reservations: First-come, first-served.
Agency: Shoshone National Forest, Wind River Ranger District, 1-307-455-2466.
Activities: Fishing, hiking, wildlife viewing.
Finding the campground: Take the Wiggins Fork Road/Forest Road 285 north out of Dubois for 11 miles. The first 3 miles are paved.

About the campground: The level parking areas sit along the banks of Horse Creek. Some shade comes from the spruce and pine trees scattered about. Willow brush and grass spread out between trees and parking spots. The road gets rough in spots, making a longer stay more desirable. The units to the right tend to get a bit of dust from passing traffic. A host occupies one of the sites. Firewood will take some effort, though deadfall appeared at various places.

17 Double Cabin

Location: 27 miles north of Dubois.
Facilities: Vault toilets, fire rings, tables, drinking water.
Sites: 15 for tents or RVs up to 40 feet long.
Fee: $ per day, 16-day maximum stay.
Reservations: First-come, first-served.
Agency: Shoshone National Forest, Wind River Ranger District, 1-307-455-2466.
Activities: Fishing, hiking, wildlife viewing, rockhounding.
Finding the campground: Take the Wiggins Fork Road/Forest Road 285 north out of Dubois for 27 miles. The first 3 miles are paved. There are numerous roads shooting off of this one, but a directional sign was present at each intersection as of our visit.

About the campground: The pine forest closes in on these camping units. Some sites offer pull-thrus while the rest are back-in. Just outside the camping area, a sagebrush meadow slopes away into the Wiggins Fork. Huge mountains loom far into the sky on all sides. A nearby trailhead grants access to wilderness. For rockhounds the riverbed offers fresh specimens of agate and petrified wood every year, as high waters from spring thaw flushes new rocks to the surface. Keep in mind that this is grizzly bear country. Firewood will take some effort, though a short stop along the way in could make it easier. There were vacant spots with more than enough campers just outside the area to fill them at the time of our visit. A host is available at the campground.

18 Pinnacles

Location: 28 miles northwest of Dubois.
Facilities: Vault toilets, fire rings, tables, drinking water.
Sites: 21 for tents or RVs up to 40 feet long.
Fee: $ per day, 16-day maximum stay.
Reservations: First-come, first-served.
Agency: Shoshone National Forest, Wind River Ranger District, 1-307-455-2466.
Activities: Fishing, hiking, wildlife viewing.
Finding the campground: Take U.S. Highway 26/287 west out of Dubois for 23 miles. Turn right onto the gravel Forest Road 515 and travel 5 miles. Follow the directions as posted for the last mile.

About the campground: A lot of rolling knolls spotted with spruce and pine trees lie between the parking units here. Individual sites offer privacy and mountain scenery. Some pull-thrus are available. Brooks Lake settles into the shadows just west of the campground with some spots within view. Deadfall appeared plentiful at the time of our visit, but at some point in the future campers will need to go beyond the camping area for their firewood. The washboard access road tests nerves and endurance, but it's an acceptable sacrifice for such a beautiful haven. A host is available at the campground.

9 Brooks Lake

Location: 28 miles northwest of Dubois.
Facilities: Vault toilets, fire rings, tables, drinking water, boat ramp.
Sites: 14 for tents or RVs up to 40 feet long.
Fee: $ per day, 16-day maximum stay.
Reservations: First-come, first-served.
Agency: Shoshone National Forest, Wind River Ranger District, 1-307-455-2466.
Activities: Fishing, hiking, boating, swimming, wildlife viewing.
Finding the campground: Take U.S. Highway 26/287 west out of Dubois for 23 miles. Turn right onto the gravel Forest Road 515 and travel 5 miles.

About the campground: Brooks Lake snuggles up to a few of the parking units here. More isolated and private spots climb into the forest. Spruce trees inhabit the campground almost to the shoreline. Larger units will have to search some to find useable sites, but they do exist. Brooks Lake would be a good place for a canoe. Huge mountains overlook both the lake and campground, presenting plenty of postcard quality pictures. If you want scenic views including a mountain lake, this is the campground.

20 Falls

Location: 24 miles northwest of Dubois.
Facilities: Vault toilets, fire rings, tables, drinking water.
Sites: 46 for tents or RVs up to 40 feet long.
Fee: $ per day, 16-day maximum stay.
Reservations: First-come, first-served.
Agency: Shoshone National Forest, Wind River Ranger District, 1-307-455-2466.
Activities: Fishing, hiking, wildlife viewing.
Finding the campground: Take U.S. Highway 26/287 west out of Dubois for 24 miles. The campground is on the left side of the road.

About the campground: Engleman spruce and lodgepole pine shade both loops in equal percentages, with an open grassy meadow between. Brooks Lake Creek provides a smashing encore for an already serene setting. A waterfall crashes over a cliff edge so abruptly, one would not expect it. Obviously this pleasant addition resulted in the campground's name. Many travelers pass by never realizing the beauty they're missing. A parking area near the falls allows vehicles access with little effort. Firewood gathering doesn't require a lot of work yet, as this quiet spot seems to be passed by more frequently than other campgrounds. This would be an excellent place to relax either before or after a whirlwind tour of Yellowstone National Park. A host is available in the campground.

Pinnacles Butte is visible from the access road to Falls Campground.

21 Sinks Canyon State Park

Location: 6 miles southwest of Lander.
Facilities: Vault toilets, fire rings, tables, drinking water.
Sites: 30 for tents or RVs up to 40 feet long.
Fee: $ per day, 14-day maximum stay.
Reservations: First-come, first-served.
Agency: Sinks Canyon State Park, 1-307-332-6333.
Activities: Fishing, hiking.
Finding the campground: On Main Street in Lander, turn onto Fifth Street and travel to the end of the road. Turn right onto the paved Sinks Canyon Road and travel 6 miles following the signs.

About the campground: Two campgrounds occupy this park at either end. Sawmill Campground sits just below the Rise, with 4 compact sites. Popo Agie Campground perches on the banks of the Middle Fork of the Popo Agie River at the opposite end. A visitor center is between the two, where the river "disappears" into the limestone cliffs. Early French explorers studied this wonder in the early nineteenth century. The raging whitecaps are seemingly tamed by the mountain, as evidenced by the calm waters when the river emerges down canyon. Cedar, aspen, and willow brush saturate the boulder outcrops with coarse sand carpeting at both places. Very large trout pose for observant visitors at the "rise." Anglers won't get a tight line on these big ones. Fishing is allowed along other stretches, however.

22 Sinks Canyon

Location: 7 miles southwest of Lander.
Facilities: Vault toilet, fire rings, tables.
Sites: 9 for tents or RVs up to 20 feet long.
Fee: $ per day, 10-day maximum stay.
Reservations: First-come, first-served.
Agency: Shoshone National Forest, Washakie Ranger District, 1-307-332-5460.
Activities: Fishing, hiking.
Finding the campground: On Main Street in Lander, turn onto Fifth Street and travel to the end of the road. Turn right onto the paved Sinks Canyon Road and travel 7 miles. The campground is on the left side of the road.

About the campground: Sagebrush crowds the scattered cedar trees, making for more open area here than at the adjacent Popo Agie Campground. The cost is higher here than at the Sinks Canyon State Park. As a result this campground tends to be a last-resort stop. But on busy weekends and holidays, there is still a chance you will not find a space. The other campgrounds are farther up the rough gravel switchbacks on top. You might consider returning back through Lander to the other end of the loop road for access to the other campgrounds.

23 Worthen Meadow

Location: 18 miles southwest of Lander.
Facilities: Vault toilets, fire rings, tables, drinking water, boat ramp, picnic area.
Sites: 28 for tents or RVs up to 50 feet long.
Fee: $ per day, 10-day maximum stay.
Reservations: First-come, first-served.
Agency: Shoshone National Forest, Washakie Ranger District, 307-332-5460.
Activities: Fishing, hiking, boating, swimming.
Finding the campground: On Main Street in Lander, turn onto Fifth Street and travel to the end of the road. Turn right onto the paved Sinks Canyon Road and travel 18 miles. The paved road will end in about 9 miles. Steep gravel switchbacks begin just after the pavement ends.

About the campground: The boat ramp and picnic area divide the Hilltop and Lakeside camping areas. The eight units located in the Hilltop are on a knoll with a little more of a hike to the lakeshore. Tents or RVs up to 20 feet long find Hilltop suitable. Longer RVs and trailers will fit much easier in the Lakeside area. Lodgepole pine are thicker in the Lakeside sites, with plenty of deadfall for firewood. The forest does not quite classify as dog-hair, but it is close. Trout and grayling jump for lunch, leaving plenty of surface rings on the water for proof.

24 Fiddlers Lake

Location: 24 miles southwest of Lander.
Facilities: Vault toilets (disabled accessible), fire rings, grills, tables, drinking water, boat ramp, picnic area.
Sites: 4 for tents and 16 for tents or RVs up to 50 feet long.
Fee: $ per day, 10-day maximum stay.
Reservations: First-come, first-served.
Agency: Shoshone National Forest, Washakie Ranger District, 1-307-332-5460.
Activities: Fishing, hiking, boating, swimming.
Finding the campground: On Main Street in Lander, turn onto Fifth Street and travel to the end of the road. Turn right onto the paved Sinks Canyon Road and travel 24 miles. The paved road will turn to gravel in about 9 miles.

About the campground: Snowcapped mountains of the Wind River Range overshadow the pine forest surrounding this mountain lake. A separate parking area for tent campers sits quietly off to the right near the entrance. The remaining units have a good deal of distance between them for greater privacy than we found in most other campgrounds. The level parking areas included wide pullouts along the lakeshore with spacious back-in sites toward the back end. A solar-powered well provides water at numerous spigots, including disabled accessible drinking fountains. Firewood appeared to be easy to gather. Dust from passing traffic doesn't reach the camping area, and despite the rough and somewhat narrow road getting here, this campground provides plenty of beauty to make up for it. A host is present at the campground.

25 Popo Agie

Location: 27 miles southwest of Lander.
Facilities: Pit toilet, tables.
Sites: 4 for tents or RVs up to 16 feet long.
Fee: None, 14-day maximum stay.
Reservations: First-come, first-served.
Agency: Shoshone National Forest, Washakie Ranger District, 1-307-332-5460.
Activities: Fishing, hiking.
Finding the campground: On Main Street in Lander, turn onto Fifth Street and travel to the end of the road. Turn right onto the paved Sinks Canyon Road and travel 27 miles. The paved road will turn to gravel in about 9 miles.

About the campground: Tall pine and spruce march along the banks of the Little Popo Agie River with this little campground. A longer RV could park here, but it would crowd an already tight area. Stream fishing is the greatest attraction. Deep, calm pools meander past huge granite boulders both in and along the stream. Weekend traffic tends to make things a bit dusty, though it's a possibility at any time.

26 Louis Lake

Location: 28 miles southwest of Lander.
Facilities: Vault toilets, fire rings, tables.
Sites: 28 for tents or RVs up to 40 feet long.
Fee: $ per day, 14-day maximum stay.
Reservations: First-come, first-served.
Agency: Shoshone National Forest, Washakie Ranger District, 1-307-332-5460.
Activities: Fishing, hiking, boating, swimming.
Finding the campground: On Main Street in Lander, turn onto Fifth Street and travel to the end of the road. Turn right onto the paved Sinks Canyon Road and travel 28 miles. The paved road will turn to gravel in about 9 miles.

About the campground: This campground is a little tight for longer units, but trailers up to 25 feet long were present on our visit. The rock outcrops surrounding Louis Lake look like some huge giant tried stacking them like a house of cards.

27 Big Atlantic Gulch

Location: 28 miles south of Lander.
Facilities: Vault toilets, fire rings, tables, drinking water.
Sites: 8 for tents or RVs up to 40 feet long.
Fee: $ per day, 14-day maximum stay.
Reservations: First-come, first-served.
Agency: Bureau of Land Management, Lander Resource Area Office, 1-307-332-8400.
Activities: Hiking.
Finding the campground: Take Wyoming Highway 28 south out of Lander for 26 miles. Turn left at the South Pass Historic Area sign and travel 1.5 miles. Turn left onto the gravel access road and travel 0.5 mile. The campground is on the left side of the highway.

About the campground: Sagebrush carpets the ridges surrounding this gulch. A mature aspen grove defiantly defends campers from the encroaching desert brush with a touch of refreshing shade. The high elevation doesn't allow too much heat, but the sun's rays can still be brutal.

28 Atlantic City

Location: 28 miles southwest of Lander.
Facilities: Vault toilets, fire rings, tables, drinking water.
Sites: 18 for tents or RVs up to 60 feet long.
Fee: $ per day, 14-day maximum stay.
Reservations: First-come, first-served.
Agency: Bureau of Land Management, Lander Resource Area Office, 1-307-332-8400.
Activities: Hiking.

Finding the campground: Take Wyoming Highway 28 south out of Lander for 26 miles. Turn left at the South Pass Historic Area sign and travel 2 miles. The campground is on the right side of the road.

About the campground: The presence of bears here—they had visited the area recently when we made our trip—helps remind us of the wild. This area has probably remained very much as it was when miners first dipped gold pans into the mountain streams. The aspen trees seem taller here than at the Big Atlantic Gulch Campground. The sloping hillside gives a different identity to each unit. A host is present at the campground.

Pinedale Area

Jim Bridger of mountain man fame camped in this area many times. The Museum of the Mountain Man located in Pinedale is a must-see attraction, with its excellent displays of artifacts from the fur trade. Ice-cold mountain lakes snuggle into the canyons and other hideaways along the Bridger Wilderness boundary.

Most of the camping areas snuggle up against the Bridger Wilderness. Mountains climb upwards to more than 12,000 feet above sea level. Clear, cold natural lakes frequently reflect snowcapped splendor with occasional disturbances of rising trout.

The surrounding desert offers plenty of specimens for the diligent rockhound. The petrified wood of the Farson area is well worth investigating.

1 New Fork River

Location: 28 miles south of Pinedale.
Facilities: Pit toilet, fire rings, tables, boat ramp.
Sites: 5 for tents or RVs up to 50-plus feet long.
Fee: None, 14-day maximum stay.
Reservations: First-come, first-served.
Agency: Bureau of Land Management, Pinedale Resource Area Office, 1-307-367-4358.
Activities: Fishing, rafting.
Finding the campground: Take U.S. Highway 191 south out of Pinedale for 23 miles. Turn right onto Wyoming Highway 351 and travel 5 miles. The campground is across the bridge on the right side of the road.

About the campground: Water failed the test for drinking here. New Fork River flows past with plenty, though it is unlikely that you will want to make your coffee with it. Anglers probably find this spot more appealing. A contractor takes care of the upkeep, though the weeds may get a bit high from time to time, and there is no host or firewood. If you are running late in the day, this might be a great stopover for an early morning departure.

2 Big Sandy Reservoir

Location: 15 miles north of Farson.
Facilities: Vault toilets, fire rings, tables, drinking water.
Sites: Dispersed for tents or RVs up to 60-plus feet long.
Fee: None, 14-day maximum stay.
Reservations: First-come, first-served.
Agency: Bureau of Reclamation, 1-801-379-1000.
Activities: Fishing, hiking, boating, swimming, rockhounding.
Finding the campground: Take U.S. Highway 191 north out of Farson for 14 miles. Turn right at the Big Sandy Recreation Area sign onto the improved dirt road and travel 1 mile.

PINEDALE AREA

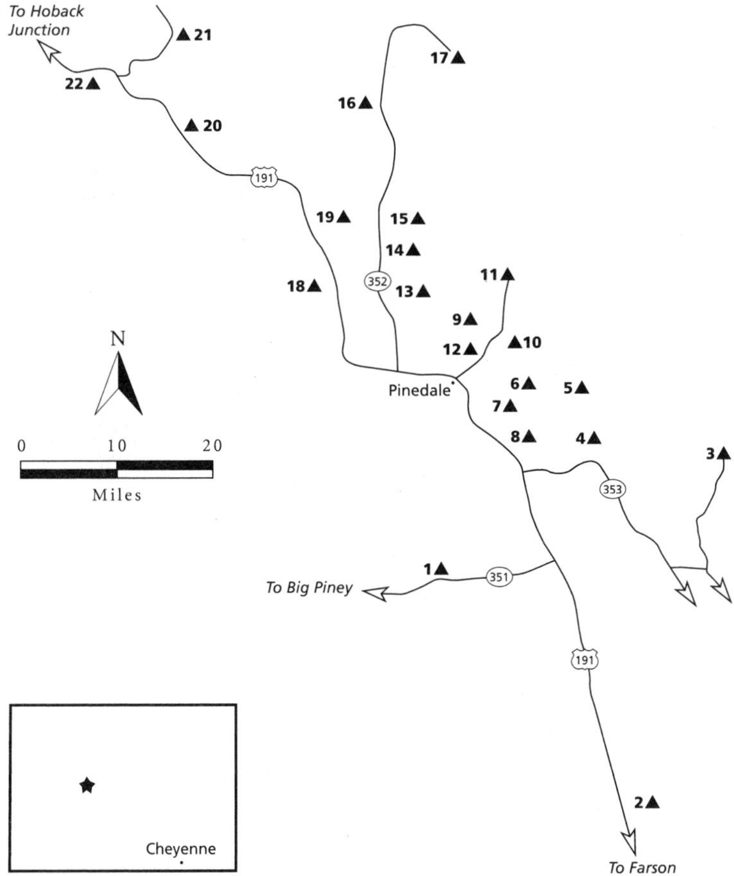

About the campground: There is really no developed campground here, but level parking outnumbers the tables. The more developed area is on the west shore of Big Sandy Reservoir. Don't count on any shade or firewood. Toilets are a long way off, across the lake.

3 Big Sandy Wilderness

Location: 60 miles southeast of Pinedale.
Facilities: Pit toilet, fire rings, tables.
Sites: 12 for tents or RVs up to 20 feet long.
Fee: None, 14-day maximum stay.
Reservations: First-come, first-served.

	Group sites	Tents	RV sites	Total sites	Picnic area	Toilets	Showers	Drinking water	Dump station	Phone	Disabled access	Fee ($)	Season	Can reserve	Length of stay	Recreation
1 New Fork River			5	5		P						N	5/1-11/15		14	FT
2 Big Sandy Reservoir			D	D		V		X				N	All Year		14	FHBSR
3 Big Sandy Wilderness			12	12		P						N	6/20-9/10		14	FHW
4 Scab Creek			9	9		P						N	6/1-10/15		14	H
5 Boulder Lake			20	20		P						N	6/1-10/15		14	FBS
6 Boulder Lake North			D	D		V						N	6/1-10/15		14	FHBS
7 Boulder Lake South			D	D		V						N	6/1-10/15		14	FHBS
8 Stokes Crossing			D			P						N	6/1-10/15		14	FH
9 Fremont Lake			54	54	X	P		X				$	5/25-9/10	X	10	FHBSW
10 Half Moon Lake			18	18		P						$	6/1-9/10		14	FHBS
11 Trails End			8	8		V		X				$	6/25-9/10		14	H
12 Soda Lake				D		V						N	4/30-11/15		14	FBW
13 Willow Lake			7	7	X	P						N	6/1-10/1		14	FHBS
14 New Fork Lake			15	15		P						N	6/1-9/10		10	FHS
15 Narrows			19	19		V		X				$	6/1-9/10	X	10	FHBSW
16 Whiskey Grove			9	9		P		X				$	6/15-9/10		14	FHW
17 Green River Lake	3	14	25	42		V		X				$	6/15-9/10	X	10	FHW
18 Warren Bridge			17	17	X	V		X	X	X		$	5/1-10/15		14	FHW
19 Upper Green River				D		P						N	6/1-10/15		14	FHTW
20 Kozy			8	8		V						$	6/1-9/6		10	F
21 Granite Creek			52	52		V		X				$$	6/15-9/6		10	FHW
22 Hoback			26	26	X	V		X				$$	6/1-9/6		10	F

D=dispersed, P=pit toilets, V=vault toilets, N=none, F=fishing, H=hiking, B=boating, S=swimming, R=rockhounding, W=wildlife viewing, T=rafting

Agency: Bridger National Forest, Pinedale Ranger District, 1-307-367-4326.
Activities: Fishing, hiking, wildlife viewing.
Finding the campground: Take U.S. Highway 191 south out of Pinedale for 12 miles. Turn left onto the paved Wyoming Highway 353 and travel 16 miles. Continue on the now gravel road for another 22 miles. Turn left onto the improved-dirt access road to the Big Sandy Recreation Area and travel 10 miles.

About the campground: When we visited this spot, camping units and all possible places in between were packed with a variety of vehicles, though the better camping exists outside the actual campground along the access road. Vans, economy cars, a few pickups, and a Cadillac headed to California from

New York—not overnight campers in the developed campground, but backpackers headed into the wilderness—made the campground look like a wrecking yard. Apparently it was too far to walk from the designated parking area at the wilderness entrance. We found it strange that they would drive all that way to backpack into the wilderness and have too much trouble packing into it from outside the campground.

4 Scab Creek

Location: 26 miles southeast of Pinedale.
Facilities: Pit toilet, fire rings, tables.
Sites: 9 for tents or RVs up to 30 feet long.
Fee: None, 14-day maximum stay.
Reservations: First-come, first-served.
Agency: Bureau of Land Management, Pinedale Resource Area Office, 1-307-367-4358.
Activities: Hiking.
Finding the campground: Take U.S. Highway 191 south out of Pinedale for 12 miles. Turn left onto the paved Wyoming Highway 353 and travel 5.5 miles. Turn left onto the gravel County Road 23122 (just past the Air Force Seismic Research Center) and travel 1.5 miles. Turn left at the Scab Creek Campground sign and travel 7 miles.

About the campground: Wilderness access produces a lot of vehicles in the parking area near the campground. Camping units divide the pine forest into nonuniform but semiprivate locations. Aspen trees of different sizes grow near the entrance, helping hide the camping units even more. This is a quiet camping area with most of the visitors moving farther into the wilderness.

5 Boulder Lake

Location: 30 miles southeast of Pinedale.
Facilities: Pit toilet, fire rings, tables.
Sites: 20 for tents or RVs up to 30 feet long.
Fee: None, 14-day maximum stay.
Reservations: First-come, first-served.
Agency: Bridger National Forest, Pinedale Ranger District, 1-307-367-4326.
Activities: Fishing, boating, swimming.
Finding the campground: Take U.S. Highway 191 south out of Pinedale for 12 miles. Turn left onto the paved Wyoming Highway 353 and travel 3 miles. Turn left at the Boulder Lake sign and travel 15 miles. Bear left at the lodge to cross Boulder Creek and access the campground.

About the campground: Camping units hide quite well in this mixed forest of pine and aspen trees. After crossing the bridge, a long continuous loop provides access to nice level parking spots. No host is present here. Firewood appears to be relatively easy to gather. The very rough road accessing the campground probably produces the multiple empty spaces. There are other campgrounds nearby with much easier access and a lot more campers.

6 Boulder Lake North

Location: 18 miles southeast of Pinedale.
Facilities: Vault toilet, fire rings, tables.
Sites: Dispersed for tents or RVs up to 40 feet long.
Fee: None, 14-day maximum stay.
Reservations: First-come, first-served.
Agency: Bureau of Land Management, Pinedale Resource Area Office, 1-307-367-4358.
Activities: Fishing, hiking, boating, swimming.
Finding the campground: Take U.S. Highway 191 south out of Pinedale for 11 miles. Turn left onto the gravel Burnt Lake Road and travel 7 miles.

About the campground: This area settles onto the side hills on the north side of Boulder Lake. Boulders do in fact reside here. Between the various-sized rocks plenty of sagebrush pops up. Boulder Creek rushes down timbered ridge-sides for a change of scenery, just below the dam. The area might be designated as a forest on the map, but there are precious few trees here.

7 Boulder Lake South

Location: 23 miles southeast of Pinedale.
Facilities: Vault toilets, fire rings, tables.
Sites: Dispersed for tents or RVs up to 40 feet long.
Fee: None, 14-day maximum stay.
Reservations: First-come, first-served.
Agency: Bureau of Land Management, Pinedale Resource Area Office, 1-307-367-4358.
Activities: Fishing, hiking, boating, swimming.
Finding the campground: Take U.S. Highway 191 south out of Pinedale for 12 miles. Turn left onto the paved Wyoming Highway 353 and travel 3 miles. Turn left at the Boulder Lake sign onto the gravel County Road 23125 and travel 7 miles. Turn left at the sign and travel 1 mile.

About the campground: Access is the only difference between here and Boulder Lake North. Those that need a boat ramp would do well to consider coming here.

8 Stokes Crossing

Location: 22 miles southeast of Pinedale.
Facilities: Pit toilet, 2 tables.
Sites: Dispersed for tents or RVs up to 16 feet long.
Fee: None, 14-day maximum stay.
Reservations: First-come, first-served.
Agency: Bureau of Land Management, Pinedale Resource Area Office, 1-307-367-4358.
Activities: Fishing, hiking.
Finding the campground: Take U.S. Highway 191 south out of Pinedale for

12 miles. Turn left onto Wyoming Highway 353 and travel 3 miles. Turn left at the Boulder Lake sign onto the gravel County Road 23125 and travel 5 miles. Turn left onto the unmarked improved dirt road and travel 2 miles. NOTE: If the road is wet, do not attempt driving on it.

About the campground: There is more parking than tables here. Sagebrush outnumbers the pine trees, but there are still enough for shade. Boulder Creek wanders by, inviting angler and swimmer alike. After the frustration of trying to find this place, a cool dip works wonders.

9 Fremont Lake

Location: 8 miles north of Pinedale.
Facilities: Pit toilets, fire rings, tables, drinking water, picnic area, boat ramp.
Sites: 54 for tents or RVs up to 50 feet long.
Fee: $ per day, 10-day maximum stay.
Reservations: 1-877-444-6777.
Agency: Bridger National Forest, Pinedale Ranger District, 1-307-367-4326.
Activities: Fishing, hiking, boating, swimming, wildlife viewing.
Finding the campground: At the eastern end of Pinedale, turn at the Fremont Lake sign and travel 4 miles. Turn left at the campground sign onto the paved access road and follow signs for 4 miles.

About the campground: Legendary mountain man Jim Bridger camped here more than once with other colorful characters in the 1800s. At one point in time, seven kegs of whiskey were consumed by the group to christen the lake as Stewart Lake, in honor of Captain Stewart, a Scot who was a frequent member of the party. Unfortunately mapmakers were not aware of the previous campers' intentions, and as a result Fremont Lake became the official name. Two long paved loops wind through the forest. Aspen, rose bushes, and tall grass wall in the parking areas in the first loop. If you have allergies, this could be a real nightmare, but each unit is very well concealed. Pine trees take over in the second loop with a few places closer to the lakeshore. Jim Bridger probably didn't make reservations, but if you plan to camp here over any weekend, reservations are advised. Even during the week, as one camper pulls out of one of the more popular spots, another usually pulls right in. A host occupies one of the available spots. Firewood will need to be bought from the host or brought in. Deer forage for food and squirrels scold visitors for no apparent reason just about any time of day, so be careful when driving through. Clear water does not let the trout hide. Along the dock at the boat ramp, they can be easily seen swimming about, watching for bugs to jump at.

10 Half Moon Lake

Location: 10 miles north of Pinedale.
Facilities: Pit toilets, fire rings, tables, boat ramp.
Sites: 18 for tents or RVs up to 30 feet long.
Fee: $ per day, 14-day maximum stay.
Reservations: First-come, first-served.

Agency: Bridger National Forest, Pinedale Ranger District, 1-307-367-4326.
Activities: Fishing, hiking, boating, swimming.
Finding the campground: At the eastern end of Pinedale, turn at the Fremont Lake sign and travel 9 miles. Turn right at the Half Moon Lodge sign onto the gravel road and travel 1 mile.

About the campground: Boaters find this mountain lake worth the effort. Aspen trees and brush fill the gaps between parking units, and the campground itself looks a little overgrown. The growth may provide the sort of privacy some campers like.

Trails End

Location: 16 miles north of Pinedale.
Facilities: Vault toilet, fire rings, tables, drinking water.
Sites: 8 for tents or RVs up to 30 feet long.
Fee: $ per day, 14-day maximum stay.
Reservations: First-come, first-served.
Agency: Bridger National Forest, Pinedale Ranger District, 1-307-367-4326.
Activities: Hiking.
Finding the campground: At the eastern end of Pinedale, turn left at the Fremont Lake sign and follow directions to Elkhart Park, 16 miles away.

About the campground: Trailhead parking shares a portion of the lower part of the campground. The upper loop sneaks farther back into the pine forest with parking spots better suited for pickup campers or tents. Trees seem larger in the lower loop, but farther apart. With the possible exception of heavy traffic for the wilderness access, this spot proved lonely—a feature that you might find attractive.

Soda Lake

Location: 5 miles northwest of Pinedale.
Facilities: Vault toilets.
Sites: Dispersed for tents or RVs up to 50 feet long.
Fee: None, 14-day maximum stay.
Reservations: First-come, first-served.
Agency: Wyoming Game and Fish, Pinedale Office, 1-307-367-4353.
Activities: Fishing, boating, wildlife viewing.
Finding the campground: On the western end of Pinedale, turn at the Soda Lake Wildlife Management Area sign. Travel 5 miles down the gravel County Road 119. There are two access roads into Soda Lake. The second access road is shorter than the first.

About the campground: Parking is a matter of choice all around this lake. Most campers make use of the fishing activity. The wildlife and Wind River Mountains in the background just add that much more to the experience. Sagebrush and some grass leave plenty of open air to gaze at the mountains by day or stars on a clear night. You will need to bring your own firewood.

13 Willow Lake

Location: 11 miles northwest of Pinedale.
Facilities: Pit toilet, fire rings, tables, picnic area, boat ramp.
Sites: 7 for tents or RVs up to 40 feet long.
Fee: None, 14-day maximum stay.
Reservations: First-come, first-served.
Agency: Bridger National Forest, Pinedale Ranger District, 1-307-367-4326.
Activities: Fishing, hiking, boating, swimming.
Finding the campground: On the western end of Pinedale, turn at the Soda Lake Wildlife Management Area sign. Follow directions to and past Soda Lake on the gravel County Road 119. Bear left at Soda Lake and travel a total of 7 miles from Pinedale. At the national forest boundary, bear left just after the cattleguard and travel 4 miles. The improved dirt road gets rough and very narrow toward the end.

About the campground: Pine forest carpets the northeast mountainsides in the distance, but not the campground. Sandy beaches move up well beyond the lakeshore into the parking areas along the south shore. The high ridges surrounding this super-clear mountain lake seem to cut off the infamous Wyoming wind. This pleasant lake produces a lot of photographic opportunities with the Wind River Mountains in the background.

Sagebrush outnumbers trees at Willow Lake Campground in Bridger National Forest.

14 New Fork Lake

Location: 23 miles northwest of Pinedale.
Facilities: Pit toilets, fire rings, tables.
Sites: 15 for tents or RVs up to 20 feet long.
Fee: None, 10-day maximum stay.
Reservations: First-come, first-served.
Agency: Bridger National Forest, Pinedale Ranger District, 1-307-367-4326.
Activities: Fishing, hiking, swimming.
Finding the campground: Take U.S. Highway 191 west out of Pinedale for 6 miles. Turn right onto the paved Wyoming Highway 352 and travel 15 miles. Turn right onto the gravel New Fork Lake Road and travel 2 miles. The campground is to the right with a little dogleg sort of turn to access.

About the campground: Aspen roll up and down with no uniformity, concealing campers. Level spots must be sought, but can be found. Don't get in a hurry here. The road disappears into cavernous holes and blind corners. The lake is not within clear sight, suggesting a fair hike to its shores.

15 Narrows

Location: 26 miles northwest of Pinedale.
Facilities: Vault toilets, fire rings, tables, drinking water.
Sites: 19 for tents or RVs up to 30 feet long.
Fee: $ per day, 10-day maximum stay.
Reservations: 1-877-444-6777.
Agency: Bridger National Forest, Pinedale Ranger District, 1-307-367-4326.
Activities: Fishing, hiking, boating, swimming, wildlife viewing.
Finding the campground: Take U.S. Highway 191 west out of Pinedale for 6 miles. Turn right onto the paved Wyoming Highway 352 and travel 15 miles. Turn right onto the gravel New Fork Lake Road and travel 5 miles.

About the campground: There are so many aspen here it could almost qualify as a forest of its own. The lower loop bearing to the right at the entrance has some ups and downs with level parking. Tight turns make it a little compact. The upper loop bearing to the left at the entrance stretches out along somewhat flat ground above the lakeshore. Foot-worn paths work their way through wild roses, grass, and other shrubbery to the lake. The upper portion of New Fork Lake laps against the rocky shore below a fairly steep bank. To some extent, the Narrows Campground divides this lake into two separate bodies of water. A host occupies a unit in the campground. This is bear country, so be aware of the necessary precautions. Have your camera ready.

16 Whiskey Grove

Location: 39.5 miles northwest of Pinedale.
Facilities: Pit toilet, fire rings, tables, drinking water.
Sites: 9 for tents or RVs up to 30 feet long.
Fee: $ per day, 14-day maximum stay.

Reservations: First-come, first-served.
Agency: Bridger National Forest, Pinedale Ranger District, 1-307-367-4326.
Activities: Fishing, hiking, wildlife viewing.
Finding the campground: Take U.S. Highway 191 west out of Pinedale for 6 miles. Turn right onto the paved Wyoming Highway 352 and travel 33 miles. Turn left onto the gravel access road and travel 0.5 mile.

About the campground: The Green River runs past campers at this hidden spot, and the pine and spruce trees shading each unit are not visible from the sagebrush flats above. It is almost like someone took a great big bucketfull out of the side hill. The camping loop circles around the extent of this "dugout," and just looking from the road going past it, you'd never know it was there. Water spigots are visible, but a sign on the mobile water tank indicates that they are not functional. This little hideaway could get full quickly. Camping units are separated, with enough distance for semiprivacy. Firewood could be difficult to gather. No host was present as of our visit in late July.

17 Green River Lake

Location: 56 miles northwest of Pinedale.
Facilities: Vault toilets, fire rings, tables, drinking water.
Sites: 3 group, 14 for tents, and 25 for RVs up to 40 feet long.
Fee: $ per day, 10-day maximum stay.
Reservations: 1-877-444-6777.
Agency: Bridger National Forest, Pinedale Ranger District, 1-307-367-4326.
Activities: Fishing, hiking, wildlife viewing.
Finding the campground: Take U.S. Highway 191 west out of Pinedale for 6 miles. Turn right onto the paved Wyoming Highway 352 and travel 50 miles. The road will turn to gravel in about 33 miles. The last 17 miles are very washboardy.

About the campground: We found a good number of large pine trees on the ground in the campground; possibly it was blowdown from a fairly recent storm. None of them blocked camping units, and they could be a source of future firewood, though a good saw will be required. The campground sits above both the lake and trailhead parking, keeping the dust below. Numerous water spigots are scattered throughout. Fishing in the magnificent lakes could be difficult, but with so much mountain country to look at, you might just forget your fishing rod. Don't forget your camera, and bring lots of film. Upper Green River Lake provides a pleasant day hike and photographic opportunities. Some have claimed that the lake looks like parts of Banff National Park, in Canada. It is a long ways back here, but well worth the trip. The group areas can be reserved. Groups A and B accommodate 35 individuals each. Group C holds 70 with all three areas requiring foot access.

Square Top Mountain looms over Green River Lake Campground, northwest of Pinedale.

18 Warren Bridge

Location: 20 miles west of Pinedale.
Facilities: Vault toilets, fire rings, grills, tables, drinking water, picnic area, RV dump, pay phone.
Sites: 17 for tents or RVs up to 60-plus feet long.
Fee: $ per day, 14-day maximum stay.
Reservations: First-come, first-served.
Agency: Bureau of Land Management, Pinedale Resource Area Office, 1-307-367-4358.
Activities: Fishing, hiking, wildlife viewing.
Finding the campground: Take U.S. Highway 191 west out of Pinedale for 20 miles. The campground is on the left side of the road.

About the campground: There is no shade here, and consequently gathering firewood is not possible. The host sells wood at a very reasonable price. The gravel pull-thrus provide level parking for large RVs. At first glance you would think this to be a very hot place, but the altitude seems to make a big difference, and any shade, even sitting in a vehicle, provides plenty of relief from the sun. Ground squirrels scamper about freely, paying little attention to visitors. Moose occasionally wander by along the banks of the Green River. Big trout live in the waters, a good stone's throw away, and fishing tends to be better in early spring or late fall for the big ones, though occasional reports of impressive catches do float about all summer. Clear nights present a heavenly host of stars to gaze at. Snowcapped mountains surround the campground, though at a distance. Should you decide to taste of the pleasure of this desert camp, be sure to ask John or Norma (hopefully they will remain the hosts at this campground) about the "snow goose" on the mountain to the southwest.

19 Upper Green River

Location: 30 miles west of Pinedale.
Facilities: Pit toilets.
Sites: Dispersed. Trailers are not recommended due to steep grades.
Fee: None, 14-day maximum stay.
Reservations: First-come, first-served.
Agency: Bureau of Land Management, Pinedale Resource Area Office, 1-307-367-4358.
Activities: Fishing, hiking, rafting, wildlife viewing.
Finding the campground: Take U.S. Highway 191 west out of Pinedale for 20 miles. Just after crossing the bridge, turn right onto the improved dirt road and travel 10 miles, depending on which site you choose.

About the campground: The main access road winds along the ridgetop to 12 different access sites. Four-wheel drives are not needed if the road is dry, but forget taking a car if rain hits. There are steep grades from the main access road to the river that seem to dive directly off the ridge. Signs tend to disappear along this route, possibly taken by individuals wanting to limit the number of visitors. The first site is the most popular and has been known to host trailers. The eighth site is second in line, though it is used primarily as a take-out place for floaters. As with Warren Bridge there is no firewood here. The sagebrush clings to hilltop and sides alike with rock-filled sandy soil.

20 Kozy

Location: 55 miles west of Pinedale.
Facilities: Vault toilet, fire rings, grills, tables.
Sites: 8 for tents or RVs up to 30 feet long.
Fee: $ per day, 10-day maximum stay.
Reservations: First-come, first-served.
Agency: Teton National Forest, Jackson Ranger District, 1-307-739-5500.
Activities: Fishing.
Finding the campground: Take U.S. Highway 191 west out of Pinedale for 55 miles. The campground is on the right side of the road.

About the campground: There are water spigots at this campground, but at the time of our visit, they were turned off, so bring your own or plan to treat the water from the Hoback River, which runs alongside the sites. The highway passes close by this compact area creating some unwanted noise, and all of the available firewood has already been scrounged. A host is available at a nearby campground. This would do well as a late stopover campsite, but be careful not to be too late getting here. The other campgrounds in this area fill quickly, so if you are passing along on your way toward Jackson in the evening and notice campers already parked here, you should consider setting up in an available unit.

21 Granite Creek

Location: 65 miles west of Pinedale.
Facilities: Vault toilets, fire rings, grills, tables, drinking water.
Sites: 52 for tents or RVs up to 30 feet long.
Fee: $$ per day, 10-day maximum stay.
Reservations: First-come, first-served.
Agency: Teton National Forest, Jackson Ranger District, 1-307-739-5500.
Activities: Fishing, hiking, wildlife viewing.
Finding the campground: Take U.S. Highway 191 west out of Pinedale for 56 miles. Turn right just after crossing the bridge at the Granite Creek Recreation Area sign onto the gravel road and travel 9 miles.

About the campground: The campground loops circle around lengthwise above Granite Creek. Lodgepole pine fills the camping area, with a few units just outside the timber. Sagebrush, rocks, and a little grass take over from there. High, rocky mountains plunge into the canyon floor. Granite Falls drops off one of the outcrops almost within sight of the camping area. Farther upstream former visitors from the Civilian Conservation Corps constructed a concrete containment for the hot spring oozing out of the mountainside. This living piece of history shows its age, but still holds the water. There were not too many swimmers at the pool during our weekday visit, but few spots were vacant at the campground. It would be safe to say the weekends fill up quickly.

22 Hoback

Location: 60 miles west of Pinedale.
Facilities: Vault toilets, fire rings, grills, tables, drinking water, picnic area.
Sites: 26 for tents or RVs up to 50 feet long.
Fee: $$ per day, 10-day maximum stay.
Reservations: First-come, first-served.
Agency: Teton National Forest, Jackson Ranger District, 1-307-739-5500.
Activities: Fishing.
Finding the campground: Take U.S. Highway 191 west out of Pinedale for 60 miles. The campground is on the left side of the road.

About the campground: The paved, level parking fills quickly here. The Hoback River meanders by dividing this campground, and the 14 units across the river must be accessed by a 1-mile hike from an upstream bridge. An ice flow some 20 to 30 years ago wiped out the campground bridge, which has never been replaced. Drinking water is supplied from a well in this otherwise forgotten section. The weeds tend to take it over now. With the added interest in camping today, these units could prove useful. Spruce trees grow tall and offer some privacy with their bushy lower branches. Rose bushes fill some of the leftover space. This campground settles tightly into the canyon bottom with the Hoback River swiftly passing under the forest shade.

Alpine Area

This area lives up to its name, with seemingly countless mountain meadows from creek bank to mountain peak. Pine forests stand watch in a timeless fashion, ambassadors of the native inhabitants. A generous helping of aspen trees weaves a golden lace throughout in the late summer and fall months, making August an excellent time to visit.

The Continental Divide separates Pacific Ocean runoff from Atlantic Ocean runoff here in the waterways. Cutthroat trout entice anglers from deep pools, while rafters are dared by the sections of raging whitewater rapids. Cool, crisp, fresh air awaits campers, while echoes of river rapids and whispering pines hitch a ride on the breezes.

Campers on their way to nearby Jackson Hole find that campgrounds along the main thoroughfares fill quickly and tend to be full of activity, and many along the Snake River share facilities with raft access. For those who prefer a more relaxed pace, the less-visited "out-of-the-way" campgrounds would be best. You don't need to travel far to sense isolation. Many of the camping areas along the less-traveled gravel roads appear to have been forgotten by time and management. Pine needles from untold years have knitted together on at least one picnic table to create a natural "tablecloth" at Lynx Creek, a most appealing spot for those who like a slower rate of change.

1 Alpine

Location: 2 miles north of Alpine.
Facilities: Vault toilets, fire rings, tables, drinking water, picnic area.
Sites: 16 for tents or RVs up to 30 feet long.
Fee: $ per day, 14-day maximum stay.
Reservations: 1-877-444-6777.
Agency: Targhee National Forest, Palisades Ranger District, 1-208-523-1412.
Activities: Hiking, picnicking.
Finding the campground: Take U.S. Highway 26 north out of Alpine. The campground is on the left side of the road near the Idaho border.

About the campground: The pine forest seems a bit stunted, with a smattering of spruce trees mixed in. Rose bushes and tall grass fill the gaps between parking units. As of our visit the water required boiling before it could be used for drinking. Palisades Reservoir is visible from the campground. This area is very close to the Idaho border; only 20 percent of the lake lies in Wyoming.

2 Little Cottonwood

Location: 6 miles northeast of Alpine.
Facilities: Vault toilets, fire rings, tables, drinking water.
Sites: 5 group sites for tents or RVs up to 20 feet long.
Fee: $$ per day, 14-day maximum stay.

Alpine Area

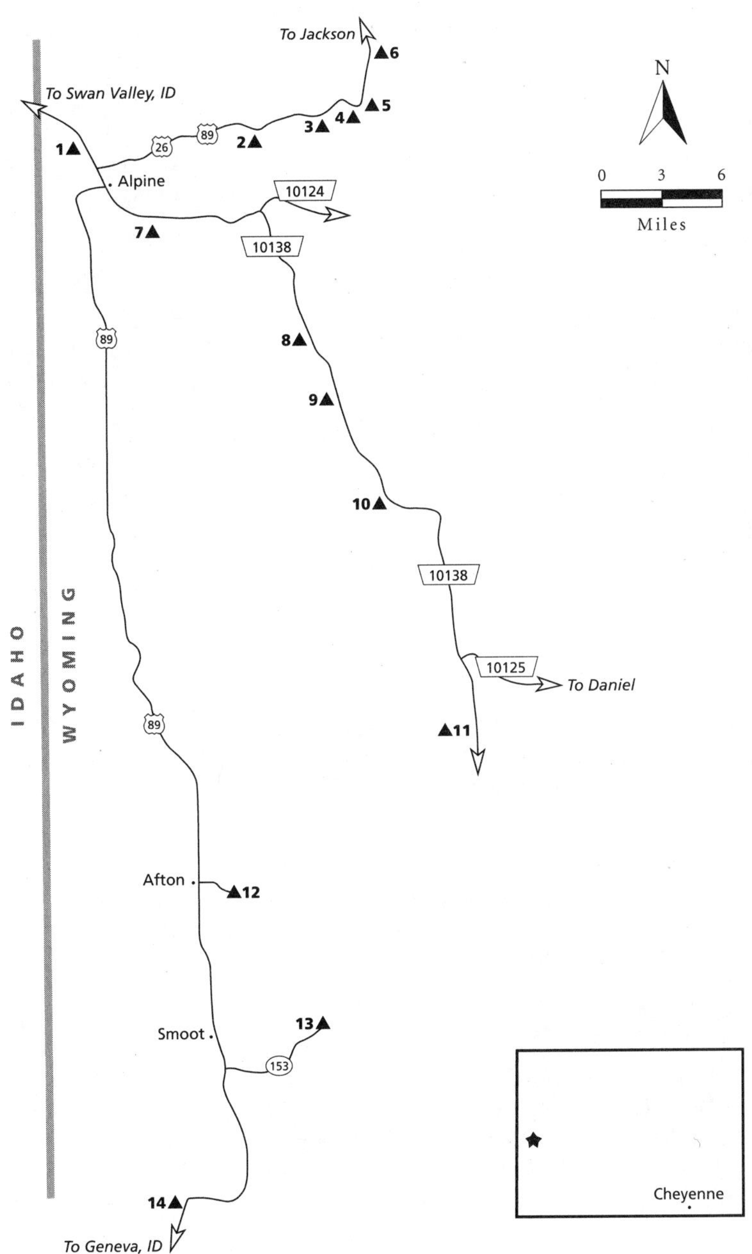

To Jackson
6
To Swan Valley, ID
N
5
4
3
89
2
26
1
0 3 6
Alpine
Miles
10124
7
10138
89
8
9
10
10138
IDAHO
WYOMING
10125
To Daniel
11
89
Afton
12
13
Smoot
153
Cheyenne
14
To Geneva, ID

	Group sites	Tents	RV sites	Total sites	Picnic area	Toilets	Showers	Drinking water	Dump station	Phone	Disabled access	Fee ($)	Season	Can reserve	Length of stay	Recreation
1 Alpine			16	16	X	V		X				$	5/25-9/5	X	14	H
2 Little Cottonwood	5			5		V		X				$$	6/10-9/10	X	14	FT
3 Station Creek			15	15		V		X				$	6/10-9/10		14	FT
4 East Table Creek			18	18	X	V		X				$	6/05-9/10		14	FT
5 Elbow			17	17		V		X				$	5/25-9/5		14	FT
6 Cabin Creek			10	10		V		X				$	5/25-9/10		14	FT
7 Bridge			5	5		V						$	6/1-9/10		16	FH
8 Lynx Creek			14	14		P						$	6/15-9/10		16	FHW
9 Murphy Creek			10	10		V		X				$	6/15-9/10		16	FHW
10 Moose Flat			10	10		V		X				$	6/1-9/10		16	FHW
11 Forest Park			13	13		V		X				$	6/1-9/10		16	FHW
12 Swift Creek			11	11		V		X				$	5/15-9/30		14	FW
13 Cottonwood Lake		10	8	18	X	V		X				$	5/15-9/10		14	FH
14 Allred Flat			32	32	X	V		X	X			$	5/25-10/31		14	FHW

V=vault toilets, P=pit toilets, F=fishing, H=hiking, T=rafting, W=wildlife viewing

Reservations: 1-877-444-6777.
Agency: Bridger National Forest, Jackson Ranger District, 1-307-739-5500.
Activities: Fishing, rafting.
Finding the campground: Take U.S. Highway 26/89 northeast out of Alpine for 6 miles. The campground is on the right side of the road.

About the campground: Lodgepole pines hug the banks of the swiftly passing Snake River just off the highway in this canyon. Fifty people can fit in this area, but 30 is the desired size. The fee varies according to the size of the group reserving the area.

3 Station Creek

Location: 11 miles northeast of Alpine.
Facilities: Vault toilets, fire rings, tables, drinking water.
Sites: 15 for tents or RVs up to 40 feet long.
Fee: $ per day, 14-day maximum stay.
Reservations: First-come, first-served.
Agency: Bridger National Forest, Jackson Ranger District, 1-307-739-5500.
Activities: Fishing, rafting.
Finding the campground: Take U.S. Highway 26/89 northeast out of Alpine for 11 miles. The campground is on the right side of the road.

About the campground: A few spruce mix with pine in this busy little place. Traffic could get noisy at times even with the raging waters of the Snake River echoing through the canyon.

4 East Table Creek

Location: 12 miles northeast of Alpine.
Facilities: Vault toilets, fire rings, tables, drinking water, picnic area.
Sites: 18 for tents or RVs up to 40 feet long.
Fee: $ per day, 14-day maximum stay.
Reservations: First-come, first-served.
Agency: Bridger National Forest, Jackson Ranger District, 1-307-739-5500.
Activities: Fishing, rafting, picnicking.
Finding the campground: Take U.S. Highway 26/89 northeast out of Alpine for 12 miles. The campground is on the right side of the road.

About the campground: This is almost a continuation of the previous campground. A day-use area attracts rafters making the run down the wild Snake River.

5 Elbow

Location: 15 miles northeast of Alpine.
Facilities: Vault toilets, fire rings, tables, drinking water.
Sites: 17 for tents or RVs up to 40 feet long.
Fee: $ per day, 14-day maximum stay.
Reservations: First-come, first-served.
Agency: Bridger National Forest, Jackson Ranger District, 1-307-739-5500.
Activities: Fishing, rafting.
Finding the campground: Take U.S. Highway 26/89 northeast of Alpine for 15 miles. The campground is on the right side of the road.

About the campground: Spruce trees take over a little more space with a greater amount of room between the highway and the Snake River.

6 Cabin Creek

Location: 17 miles northeast of Alpine.
Facilities: Vault toilets, fire rings, tables, drinking water.
Sites: 10 for tents or RVs up to 40 feet long.
Fee: $ per day, 14-day maximum stay.
Reservations: First-come, first-served.
Agency: Bridger National Forest, Jackson Ranger District, 1-307-739-5500.
Activities: Fishing, rafting.
Finding the campground: Take U.S. Highway 26/89 northeast out of Alpine for 17 miles. The campground is on the right side of the road.

About the campground: This campground seems to offer the greatest amount of space between the highway and the Snake River. Spruce trees and brush muffle a little of the traffic noise. The closer you get to the river, the less cars will be heard.

7 Bridge

Location: 3 miles southeast of Alpine.
Facilities: Vault toilet, fire rings, tables.
Sites: 5 for tents or RVs up to 16 feet long.
Fee: $ per day, 16-day maximum stay.
Reservations: First-come, first-served.
Agency: Bridger National Forest, Greys River Ranger District, 1-307-886-3166.
Activities: Hiking, fishing.
Finding the campground: In Alpine turn at the sign onto Greys River Road and travel 3 miles. Greys River Road turns to gravel and becomes Forest Road 10138 at the forest boundary. The campground is on the right side of the road.

About the campground: These close units are squeezed between the emerald green Greys River and the oil-soaked road going past it. At least the oil keeps the dust down. Lodgepole pines fill up even more space. Thick underbrush does isolate campers some. Overall, tents or pickup campers fit better here than larger RVs. Leveling will take time, but it is not too likely there will be many visitors.

Lynx Creek

Location: 11 miles southeast of Alpine.
Facilities: Pit toilets, fire rings, tables.
Sites: 14 for tents or RVs up to 25 feet long.
Fee: $ per day, 16-day maximum stay.
Reservations: First-come, first-served.
Agency: Bridger National Forest, Greys River Ranger District, 1-307-886-3166.
Activities: Hiking, fishing, wildlife viewing.
Finding the campground: In Alpine turn at the sign onto Greys River Road and travel 11 miles. Greys River Road turns to gravel and becomes Forest Road 10138 at the forest boundary. The campground is on the right side of the road.

About the campground: The weeds are taking this forgotten place over. Squirrels dine well and don't clean their leftovers off of the picnic tables, as evidenced by the piles. The ancient hand pump is surrounded by tall underbrush circled by pine trees. Don't plan on getting any water from it. Future plans for this campground do not provide for drinking water and may even result in removing this pump. The river is not too far away, but boiling is required for use. Longer trailers will need to be unhooked to make use of the parking apron. Leveling shouldn't be too hard, other than dealing with the overgrowth. Staying here might be like visiting a ghost town, but the kind of sadness that permeates could quickly evaporate with the crackling of a cheerful campfire. Echoes of past campers just might return.

9 Murphy Creek

Location: 13 miles southeast of Alpine.
Facilities: Vault toilets, fire rings, tables, drinking water.
Sites: 10 for tents or RVs up to 40 feet long.
Fee: $ per day, 16-day maximum stay.
Reservations: First-come, first-served.
Agency: Bridger National Forest, Greys River Ranger District, 1-307-886-3166.
Activities: Hiking, fishing, wildlife viewing.
Finding the campground: In Alpine turn at the sign onto Greys River Road and travel 13 miles. Greys River Road turns to gravel and becomes Forest Road 10138 at the forest boundary. The campground is on the right side of the road.

About the campground: Both the river and toilets are near the entrance to this campground. The back parking areas lack use and close access to the toilet. Lodgepole pines shelter the tables and fire rings alike. Gathering firewood might require some footwork, as none appeared in the camping area.

0 Moose Flat

Location: 22 miles southeast of Alpine.
Facilities: Vault toilets, fire rings, tables, drinking water.
Sites: 10 for tents or RVs up to 30 feet long.
Fee: $ per day, 16-day maximum stay.
Reservations: First-come, first-served.
Agency: Bridger National Forest, Greys River Ranger District, 1-307-886-3166.
Activities: Hiking, fishing, wildlife viewing.
Finding the campground: In Alpine, turn at the sign onto Greys River Road and travel 22 miles. Greys River Road turns to gravel and becomes Forest Road 10138 at the forest boundary. The campground is on the right side of the road.

About the campground: Aspen and rose bushes share the forest with pine trees in this semiactive campground. A host pleasantly greeted us on our visit. Trailers were parked in other units, as well, though the campers must have been out and about. It is far enough out here to be remote and close enough on good road to allow you to return to town for forgotten goodies. The road, as with the previous campgrounds, is liberally oiled, virtually eliminating dust.

1 Forest Park

Location: 35 miles southeast of Alpine.
Facilities: Vault toilet, fire rings, tables, drinking water.
Sites: 13 for tents or RVs up to 40 feet long.
Fee: $ per day, 16-day maximum stay.
Reservations: First-come, first-served.
Agency: Bridger National Forest, Greys River Ranger District, 1-307-886-3166.
Activities: Hiking, fishing, wildlife viewing.
Finding the campground: In Alpine turn at the sign onto Greys River Road

and travel 35 miles. Greys River Road turns to gravel and becomes Forest Road 10138 at the forest boundary. The campground is on the right side of the road.

About the campground: The forest hides this campground a short distance off of the road, almost within sight of an elk feeding ground. A host with an abundance of gallon water jugs occupied one of the units near the entrance. Lodgepole pines line the continuous meadow following the creek on the opposite side of the road. This campground showed the most activity of this group in spite of being the farthest away from the pavement. Perhaps the ability to park longer RVs brings more campers. Plentiful firewood came into sight at occupied campsites, but it was difficult to tell where it came from. The forest stretches out behind and beyond, presenting the possibility of deadfall. The main road was not oiled as it was in other places in this area, but the camping is far enough off that the dust presented no major problem.

12 Swift Creek

Location: 2 miles east of Afton.
Facilities: Vault toilets, fire rings, grills, tables, drinking water.
Sites: 11 for tents or RVs up to 20 feet long.
Fee: $ per day, 14-day maximum stay.
Reservations: First-come, first-served.
Agency: Bridger National Forest, Greys River Ranger District, 1-307-886-3166.
Activities: Fishing, wildlife viewing.
Finding the campground: In Afton turn east at the sign for the campground and travel 2 miles—watch carefully for the sign, it sneaks up with little warning. There is a short stretch of gravel road that starts at the forest boundary. The campground is on the right side across Swift Creek.

About the campground: Ancient, huge spruce trees shade most of the campground. Thick willow and cottonwood underbrush fills in the lesser-used areas, creating a sort of privacy. The crystal-clear waters of Swift Creek can be heard but not easily seen through the brush. Parking spots are designated but not leveled. A few spots would accommodate larger trailers; however, they tend to be less sheltered. A host was not present as of our visit. When a host occupies one of the sites, this is a peaceful hideaway, but as the saying goes, "When the cat's away, the mice will play." The pile of empty beer cans testified to recent weekend activity. Perhaps you would like to be a volunteer host?

13 Cottonwood Lake

Location: 12 miles southeast of Afton.
Facilities: Vault toilets, fire rings, tables, drinking water, picnic area, trailhead.
Sites: 10 for tents and 8 for RVs up to 30 feet long.
Fee: $ per day, 14-day maximum stay.
Reservations: First-come, first-served.
Agency: Bridger National Forest, Greys River Ranger District, 1-307-886-3166.

Cottonwood Lake nestles amid steep, forested mountains, creating an enchanting setting for campers.

Activities: Hiking, fishing, horseback riding.
Finding the campground: Take U.S. Highway 89 south out of Afton for 7 miles. Turn left at the sign onto the semipaved County Road 153 and travel 5 miles. About 1.5 miles from the highway, the road turns to gravel. This is where Forest Road 10208 begins.

About the campground: Three separate areas divide the campground. Seven units allow horses with tent camping, eight units accommodate tents or RVs in a fairly flat location with large spruce standing guard, and three walk-in sites require footwork to access. Steep, forested mountains wall both Cottonwood Lake and the campground secretly into this almost enchanted area. The willow brush gets high close to the water. The picnic area takes up a portion of the lakeshore, while the camping area is a short hike away. Obviously horses are a popular part of the recreation. Plenty of other activities await visitors, too.

14 Allred Flat

Location: 20 miles south Afton.
Facilities: Vault toilets, fire rings, tables, drinking water, picnic area, dump station.
Sites: 32 for tents or RVs up to 40 feet long.
Fee: $ per day, 14-day maximum stay.
Reservations: First-come, first-served.
Agency: Bridger National Forest, Greys River Ranger District, 1-307-886-3166.
Activities: Hiking, fishing, wildlife viewing.
Finding the campground: Take U.S. Highway 89 south out of Afton for 20 miles. The campground is on the right side of the highway.

About the campground: Both pull-thru and back-in sites are stretched out in this mixed forest. Lodgepole pines and aspens of various ages share the sun with rose bushes and other grasses. Salt Creek meanders past on the opposite side of the highway, enticing anglers.

Green River Area

Brilliant colored badlands and dynamic fishing abundantly adorn the countryside. Much of the terrain shows little, if any, change from when wagon trains lumbered across. Reaching forested mountains takes some travel time, but rewards the seeker in a typical wonderful Wyoming way. So many of the hidden treasures defy a cynical belief that anywhere so beautiful could not exist in the midst of such stark contrast.

Fossils and agates abound all through this vast expanse, to the delight of rockhounds. In fact, some fossils and petrified wood have been agatized over the course of time, making them very collectible. Most can be found on the surface, with a semipolish making them easy to identify.

1 Meeks Cabin

Location: 25 miles southwest of Mountain View.
Facilities: Vault toilets, fire rings, tables, drinking water.
Sites: 24 for tents or RVs up to 40 feet long.
Fee: $ per day, 14-day maximum stay.
Reservations: First-come, first-served.
Agency: Wasatche-Cache National Forest, Evanston Ranger District, 1-307-789-3194.
Activities: Fishing, hiking, boating, swimming.
Finding the campground: Take Wyoming Highway 410 south and west out of Mountain View for 13 miles. Bear left on the gravel Meeks Cabin Access Road and travel 12 miles.

About the campground: Evergreen trees and sandstone surround this reservoir at almost 9,000 feet above sea level. A host occupies one of the units. Most are back-in sites of different lengths. Fishing is not always the best, but the water offers a cool way of dealing with the heat.

2 Firehole Canyon

Location: 29 miles southeast of Green River.
Facilities: Comfort stations, grills, sheltered tables, drinking water, picnic area, boat ramp.
Sites: 40 for tents or RVs up to 40 feet long.
Fee: $$ per day, 14-day maximum stay.
Reservations: 1-877-444-6777.
Agency: Ashley National Forest, Flaming Gorge National Recreation Area, 1-801-784-3448.
Activities: Fishing, hiking, boating, swimming.
Finding the campground: Take Interstate 80 east of Green River for 8 miles. At exit 99 turn right onto U.S. Highway 191 and travel 13 miles. At the Firehole Recreation Area sign, turn right onto the paved road and travel 8 miles.

Green River Area

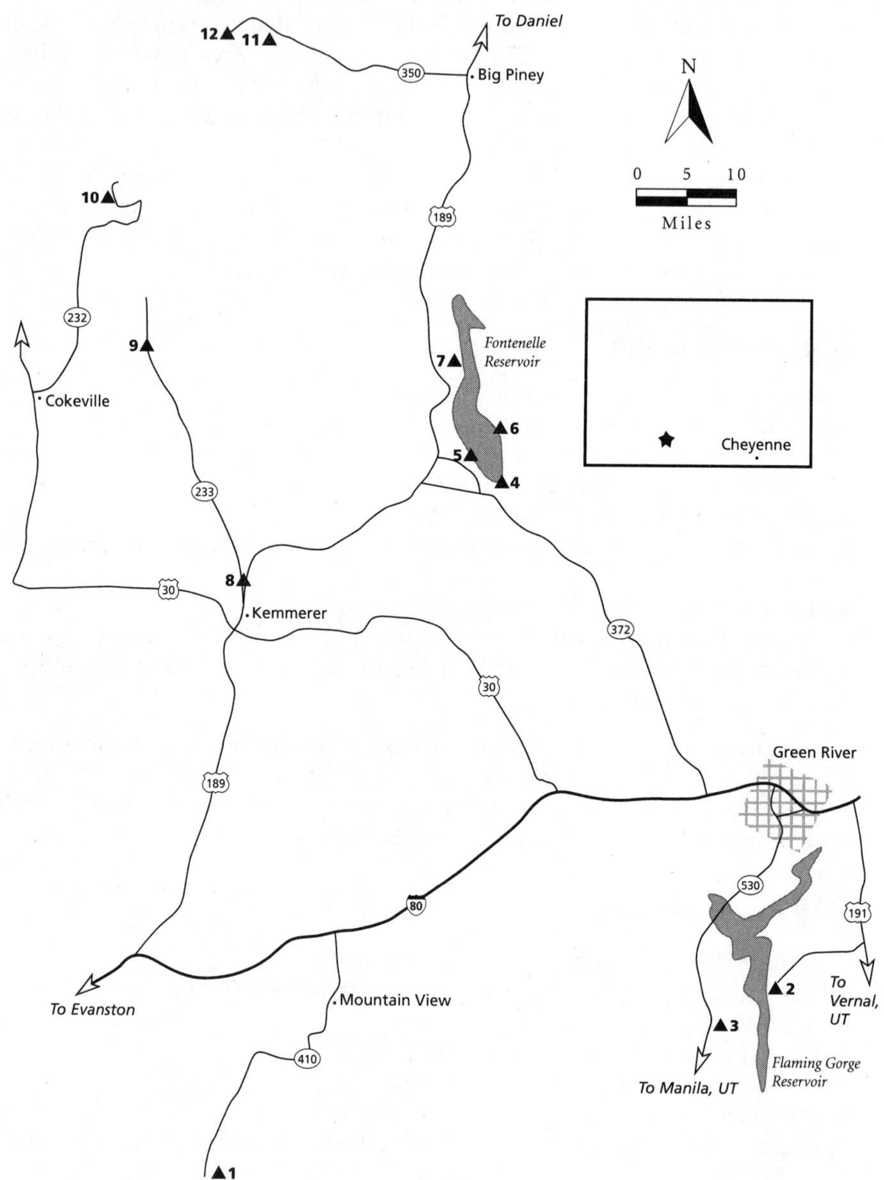

	Group sites	Tents	RV sites	Total sites	Picnic area	Toilets	Showers	Drinking water	Dump station	Phone	Disabled access	Fee ($)	Season	Can reserve	Length of stay	Recreation
1 Meeks Cabin			24	24		V		X				$	May-June		14	FHBS
2 Firehole Canyon			40	40	X	F		X			X	$$	Apr-Oct	X	14	FHBS
3 Buckboard Crossing			68	68		F		X	X		X	$$	Apr-Oct	X	14	FHBS
4 Slate Creek				D		V						N	Summer		14	FWR
5 Weeping Rock				D		V						N	Summer		14	FW
6 Tailrace				D		V						N	Summer		14	F
7 Fontenelle Creek			55	55		F		X	X			$	Summer	X	14	FBSR
8 Kemmerer Tent Park		5		5		P						$	Summer		3	
9 Hams Fork			13	13		V		X				$	5/25-10/31		14	FH
10 Hobble Creek			18	18		V		X				$	7/1-10/31		14	FH
11 Sacajawea			26	26		V		X				$	6/15-9/30		14	FH
12 Middle Piney Lake			4	4		V						N	7/1-9/30		10	FHBS

D=dispersed, F=flush toilets, V=vault toilets, P=pit toilets, N=none, F=fishing, H=hiking, B=boating, S=swimming, W=wildlife viewing, R=rockhounding

About the campground: Sagebrush, cedar trees, and dramatic rock formations provide a scenic drive to the campground. The cedar trees tend to disappear at the camping area, but the rock formations make up for the absence. The paved road continues all the way through the camping area, including the parking aprons. Long trailers could fit, but they will need to be unhooked. The comfort station includes flush toilets, showers, sinks, and electrical outlets. Willow trees don't provide a lot of shade yet. The sturdy shelters built over the tables grant welcome relief for lunchtime picnickers.

3 Buckboard Crossing

Location: 25 miles southwest of Green River.
Facilities: Comfort stations, grills, tables, drinking water, RV dump.
Sites: 68 for tents or RVs up to 50 feet long.
Fee: $$ per day, 14-day maximum stay.
Reservations: 1-877-444-6777.
Agency: Ashley National Forest, Flaming Gorge National Recreation Area, 1-801-784-3448.
Activities: Fishing, hiking, boating, swimming.
Finding the campground: Take Wyoming Highway 530 south out of Green River for 23 miles. Turn left at the sign onto the paved access road and travel 2 miles. The campground is on the right side of the access road.

About the campground: You might think of a desert oasis on first sight of this campground. Willow trees pop up out of the desert in stark contrast to

Unusual rock formations provide a dramatic backdrop for the campground at Firehole Canyon.

their arid surroundings. These trees are watered from a manmade system—they don't drink from a lakeshore. Two loops hold 34 parking units apiece, with comfort stations centrally located. The older willow trees offer more shade than the younger ones at Firehole Canyon, and individual shelters cover the tables for more relief on hot, sunny days. At times the wind can be a real blessing. Only a few spaces were still available on our visit, testifying to the popularity of the area. The biggest attraction seemed to be the fairly easily accessible water recreation—boats, jet skis, and so forth. Reportedly this is the first year that Firehole Canyon has had a paved access. As knowledge of this new feature becomes known, there could be a shift of campers from here to there.

4 Slate Creek

Location: 35 miles northeast of Kemmerer.
Facilities: Vault toilet, fire rings, tables.
Sites: Dispersed for tents or RVs up to 60-plus feet long.
Fee: None, 14-day maximum stay.
Reservations: First-come, first-served.
Agency: Bureau of Land Management, Kemmerer District, 1-307-877-3933.
Activities: Fishing, wildlife viewing, rockhounding.
Finding the campground: Take U.S. Highway 189 northeast out of Kemmerer for 25 miles. Turn right onto Wyoming Highway 372 and travel about 9 miles. Continue dead ahead at the Fontenelle store on the gravel road for 1

mile. The campground is on the left side of the road along the banks of the Green River.

About the campground: Parking outnumbers tables in this stretched-out camping area. About 40 RVs could park in here with some forethought, but your neighbors would be closer than they are in most suburbs. The majority of the units follow the Green River below the Fontenelle Reservoir. When the large trout start moving into these waters to spawn, there will likely be very few vacant spots. A large fenced area holds huge cottonwood logs for those that want campfires. A good saw and sweat is required. Keep in mind that wood is supplied as it becomes available. If you must have a campfire for your needs, it would be best to pack some wood along. Shade can be found under the large cottonwoods still alive and standing, though the better spots fill first.

Weeping Rock

Location: 37 miles northeast of Kemmerer.
Facilities: Vault toilet, fire rings, tables.
Sites: Dispersed for tents or RVs up to 50 feet long.
Fee: None, 14-day maximum stay.
Reservations: First-come, first-served.
Agency: Bureau of Land Management, Kemmerer District, 1-307-877-3933.
Activities: Fishing, wildlife viewing.
Finding the campground: Take U.S. Highway 189 northeast out of Kemmerer for 30 miles. Turn right onto County Road 313 and travel about 6 miles. Turn left at the sign onto the gravel access road and travel 1 mile.

About the campground: About 20 RVs would be the limit for this tight little river corner. Cottonwoods offer shade and, when they die, some firewood. This campground is somewhat concealed and therefore tends to have more activity.

Tailrace

Location: 36 miles northeast of Kemmerer.
Facilities: Vault toilet, tables.
Sites: Dispersed for tents or RVs up to 40 feet long.
Fee: None, 14-day maximum stay.
Reservations: First-come, first-served.
Agency: Bureau of Land Management, Kemmerer District, 1-307-877-3933.
Activities: Fishing.
Finding the campground: Take U.S. Highway 189 northeast out of Kemmerer for 30 miles. Turn right onto County Road 313 and travel about 6 miles. Continue on the access road across the dam. Don't take the first right turn on the dam. After completely crossing the dam, bear right onto the gravel road and travel to the river.

About the campground: Parking along the riverbank might hold 10 RVs with some forethought, though a rainstorm would make life very miserable and possibly make an exit impossible. There is better ground up away from the bank, but one of the other campgrounds would offer closer access.

7 Fontenelle Creek

Location: 36 miles north of Kemmerer.
Facilities: Comfort stations, grills, drinking water, sheltered tables, dump station.
Sites: 55 for tents or RVs up to 50 feet long.
Fee: $ per day, 14-day maximum stay.
Reservations: 1-877-444-6777.
Agency: Bureau of Land Management, Kemmerer District, 1-307-877-3933.
Activities: Fishing, boating, swimming, rockhounding.
Finding the campground: Take U.S. Highway 189 northeast out of Kemmerer for 36 miles. The campground is on the right side of the road.

About the campground: Parking is paved in two loops, with sheltered tables on this gumbo soil. Firewood does not exist, but there are no fire rings anyway. The comfort stations have running water for sinks and flush toilets, along with electrical outlets. Sagebrush and wind seem to be permanent parts of the area, and a small hike is required to reach the water. A site is set aside for a host, though as of our visit there wasn't one.

8 Kemmerer Tent Park

Location: Kemmerer.
Facilities: Pit toilets, fire rings, tables.
Sites: 5 for tents.
Fee: $ per day, 3-day maximum stay.
Reservations: First-come, first-served.
Agency: City of Kemmerer, 1-307-877-9761.
Activities: Camping.
Finding the campground: Take Wyoming Highway 233 north out of Kemmerer for 0.25 mile.

About the campground: Firewood gathering is not allowed here, so if you want a fire, bring your own wood. Cottonwood trees line the rectangular gravel parking, with tables and fire rings on either side. The toilets stand noticeably at the end of the parking.

9 Hams Fork

Location: 44 miles northwest of Kemmerer.
Facilities: Vault toilets, fire rings, tables, drinking water.
Sites: 13 for tents or RVs up to 20 feet long.
Fee: $ per day, 14-day maximum stay.
Reservations: First-come, first-served.

A ranger station typical of those built around 1900.

Agency: Bridger National Forest, Kemmerer Ranger District, 1-307-877-4415.
Activities: Fishing, hiking.
Finding the campground: Take Wyoming Highway 233 north out of Kemmerer for 44 miles. This paved road will turn to gravel in 17 miles and change to Forest Road 10062.

About the campground: A well-preserved log cabin sits along the road near the campground, which originally was the Elk Creek Ranger Station. This station is typical of those built around 1900. The road divides this campground, and the toilets and water are found in the main camping area on the east. Three units sit under the pine trees, with less distance to the Hams Fork River, which is more of a creek here. Tall willow brush shades the cool waters, inviting anglers and hot feet alike. Firewood appeared easy to gather from the forest sheltering the main campground. This is a very pleasant place to spend some time.

10 Hobble Creek

Location: 35 miles north of Cokeville.
Facilities: Vault toilets, fire rings, tables, drinking water, trailhead.
Sites: 18 for tents or RVs up to 16 feet long.
Fee: $ per day, 14-day maximum stay.

Reservations: First-come, first-served.
Agency: Bridger National Forest, Kemmerer Ranger District, 1-307-877-4415.
Activities: Fishing, hiking.
Finding the campground: Take Wyoming Highway 232 north out of Cokeville for 13 miles to the end of the pavement. Bear right at the fork onto what will become Forest Road 10062. It is a steady climb from here on a single-lane dirt road with small, narrow pullouts. Continue on Forest Road 10062 for about 8 miles. Bear left onto Forest Road 10066, following the signs to Lake Alice. The road signs get scarce, so continue following directions to Lake Alice for about 14 miles. The single-lane narrow portion with hairpin turns clinging to the mountainside is not a place you would want to meet a trailer. A river ford is also required near the last 1.5 miles of access.

About the campground: This is not the place to arrive only to discover you forgot the matches, or anything else for that matter. The road goes from pavement to what I would call primitive access. The last 1.5 miles of the road must be reached by fording Hobble Creek. As of our visit it appeared to be around 5 feet deep for about 8 feet through the middle. We chose not to continue the journey. The water could have been higher and swifter than normal for the time of year we were there, but whether it gets lower or not does not change the fact that to use this campground, you must ford it. Upon leaving, we stopped to view the majestic mountain beauty far above on the single lane switchbacks accessing the canyon. As we contemplated what might have been beyond our turnaround, a vehicle came bouncing out of the campground area far below. They did not ford the creek as we anticipated, but instead pulled off into one of the many meadows. This assured us that campers do in fact use the facilities. We were more than a mile away from the campers, so exactly what kind of rig they were in was open for debate. It definitely displayed a high profile, with the qualities of a Blazer or Bronco of an older make.

11 Sacajawea

Location: 27 miles west of Big Piney.
Facilities: Vault toilets, fire rings, tables, drinking water.
Sites: 26 for tents or RVs up to 30 feet long.
Fee: $ per day, 14-day maximum stay.
Reservations: First-come, first-served.
Agency: Bridger National Forest, Big Piney Ranger District, 1-307-276-3375.
Activities: Fishing, hiking.
Finding the campground: Take Wyoming Highway 350 west out of Big Piney for 10 miles. Continue dead ahead on the gravel road for 17 miles. The campground is on the left side of the road.

About the campground: Middle Piney Creek rushes past the pine forest housing these well-placed units. Nestled comfortably in the bottom of this forested canyon, you wouldn't know the campground existed if you weren't looking for it. Signs posted all over advise visitors that the water and other services are only for paying campers. Some thinning of the surrounding forest appeared to be in process, leaving large logs conveniently located near fire rings. Even with the abundance of cut trees, plentiful shade shrouded the tables. Fishing could be challenging, with the thick willow brush choking the banks. Don't forget the bug spray, especially if your visit occurs during late June or early July.

12 Middle Piney Lake

Location: 30 miles west of Big Piney.
Facilities: Vault toilet, fire rings, tables.
Sites: Dispersed (4 with tables) for tents.
Fee: None, 10-day maximum stay.
Reservations: First-come, first-served.
Agency: Bridger National Forest, Big Piney Ranger District, 1-307-276-3375.
Activities: Fishing, hiking, boating, swimming.
Finding the campground: Take Wyoming Highway 350 west from Big Piney for 10 miles. Continue dead ahead on the gravel road for 20 miles. Follow the signs to the end of the road. The last 2 miles of this road are very treacherous, if not impassable, when wet.

About the campground: Pickup campers might make the grade to this campground only to wonder why. Precious little level ground can be found on this lakeshore, and pine trees grow between rock outcrops and grassy meadows. Middle Piney Lake definitely presents quality photo opportunities, with snow-capped mountains nodding approval in the background. Steep, forested mountains on each side crowd the lake, making a canoe exploration of the wilderness above appealing. A few more campers could have fit when we visited, but even with the tight quarters, a very short hike would leave a person very isolated. Keep in mind that the last 2 miles of the access road should not be traveled when wet. Even if you make it up the grade, which is highly unlikely, it only makes travel harder for those who follow.

Sheridan Area

Stagecoaches of Old West fame opened the roadway leading to the majority of campgrounds in the northern Bighorns. Classic western trout streams are abundant, with plenty of room for exploring.

Multiple dynamic canyons beckon to the adventuresome to discover the beauties resting in their shadows. A glimpse of their glory can be found near Shell, along the highway at the spectacular Shell Creek Falls. Campers can choose between camping along the roar of mountain snowmelt crashing over defiant boulders or having a placid ice-cold lake within walking distance. In more than a few places, the lakes are in view of camping areas and make for a beautiful site opposite an evening campfire.

1 Connor Battlefield

Location: 12 miles northwest of Sheridan.
Facilities: Vault toilets, fire rings, grills, tables, drinking water, picnic area.
Sites: 10 for tents or RVs up to 60 feet long.
Fee: $ per day, 14-day maximum stay.
Reservations: First-come, first-served.
Agency: Wyoming State, 1-307-777-6323.
Activities: Fishing.
Finding the campground: Take Interstate 90 north out of Sheridan for 10 miles to the Ranchester Exit/exit 9. Turn left onto U.S. Highway 14 and travel for 1 mile to Ranchester. In Ranchester turn left onto Gillette Street and travel 1 mile. The campground will be on the left.

About the campground: Previous campers at this historic site were the Arapaho, led by Chief Black Bear. Camping duties changed on August 29, 1865, when Jim Bridger guided General Patrick E. Connor and his troops to the campsite. The Arapaho suffered, but prevailed and forced Connor's troops to retreat. Ranchester sits peacefully across the Tongue River from this former battle. Anglers test their skill along the mowed grassy banks, and children noisily play under the huge cottonwood trees. Under the noise of occasional traffic and a boom box, one can almost hear the echoes of Arapaho children running, jumping, and splashing in the water. Starving mosquitoes anxiously await your arrival, so take plenty of bug spray. If your hour is getting late and your "tin tepee" pulls hard on a mountain grade, this would be an excellent place to spend the night and reflect on the history of the area.

2 Tongue River

Location: 20 miles northwest of Sheridan.
Facilities: Vault toilets, fire rings.
Sites: Dispersed, dependent on size.
Fee: None, 14-day maximum stay.
Reservations: First-come, first-served.

SHERIDAN AREA

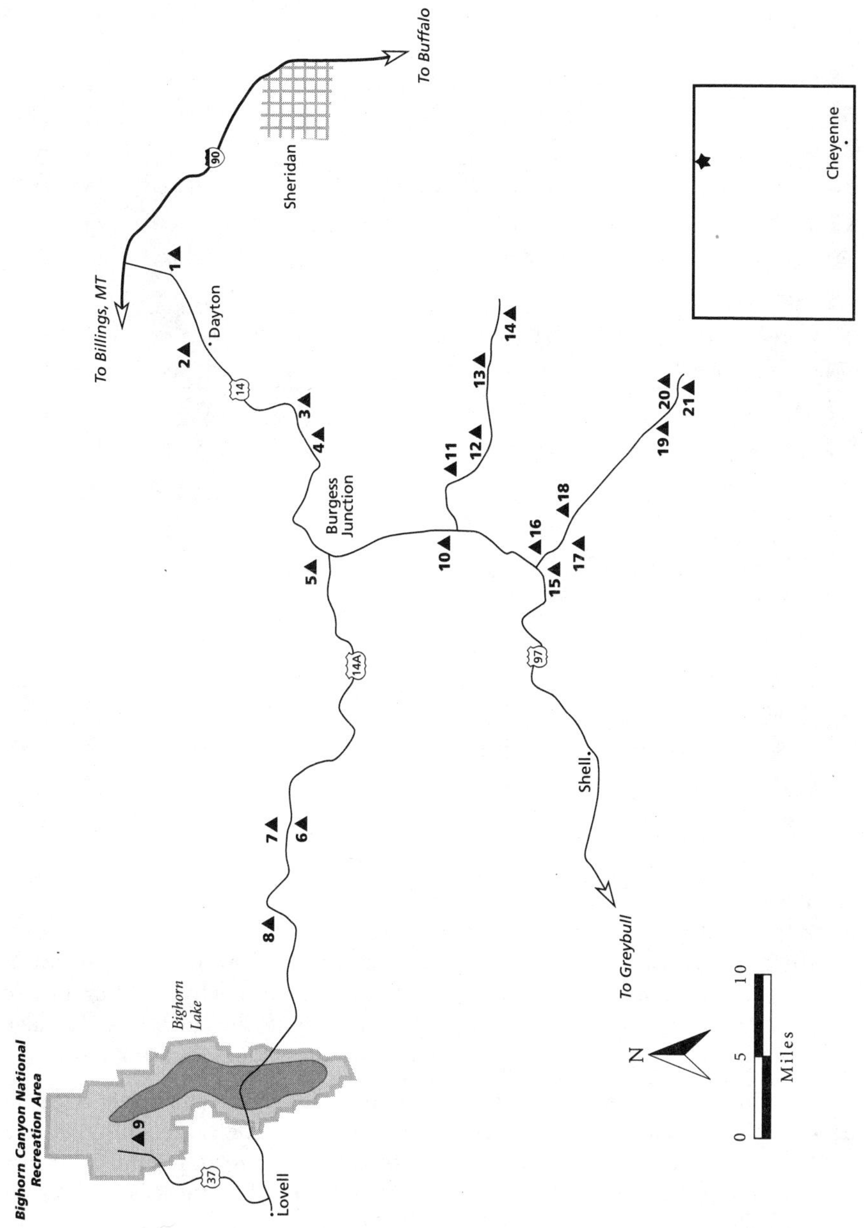

	Group sites	Tents	RV sites	Total sites	Picnic area	Toilets	Utilities	Drinking water	Dump station	Phone	Disabled access	Fee ($)	Season	Can reserve	Length of stay	Recreation
1 Connor Battlefield			10	10	X	V		X				$	All Year		14	F
2 Tongue River			D	D		V						N	5/1-11/17		14	FHW
3 Sibley Lake			25	25		V	E	X				$	6/15-10/31	X	14	FHBS
4 Prune Creek			21	21		V		X				$	6/15-10/31	X	14	FH
5 North Tongue			12	12		V		X				$	6/15-10/31		14	FH
6 Bald Mountain			15	15		V		X				$	6/15-10/31		14	H
7 Porcupine			15	15		V		X				$	6/15-10/31	X	14	FH
8 Five Springs		3		3		V						N	Summer		14	HC
9 Horseshoe Bend			128	128		F		X	X		X	$	All Year		14	FHBSR
10 Owen Creek			7	7		V		X				$	6/15-10/31		14	FH
11 Tie Flume			25	25		V		X				$	6/15-10/31		14	FH
12 Dead Swede			22	22	X	V		X				$	6/15-10/31		14	FH
13 Ranger Creek			11	11		V		X				$	6/15-10/31		14	FH
14 East Fork			11	11	X	V		X				$	6/15-10/31		14	FH
15 Cabin Creek			4	4		V		X				$	6/1-10/31		14	FH
16 Cabin Creek TP			26	26		V		X				$	6/1-10/31	X	30	H
17 Shell Creek			11	11		V		X				$	5/30-10/31		14	FH
18 Ranger Creek (SC)			10	10		V		X				$	5/30-10/31	X	14	FH
19 Medicine Lodge Lake			8	8		V		X				$	5/30-10/31	X	14	FHBS
20 Upper Paint Rock Lake			5	5		V						$	5/30-10/31		14	FHS
21 Lower Paint Rock Lake			4	4		V		X				$	5/30-10/31		14	FH

D=dispersed, F=flush toilets, V=vault toilets, N=none, E=electricity, F=fishing, H=hiking, B=boating, S=swimming, C=rock climbing, W=wildlife viewing, R=rockhounding

Agency: Wyoming Game and Fish Department, 1-307-672-7418.
Activities: Fishing, hiking, wildlife viewing.
Finding the campground: Take Interstate 90 north out of Sheridan for 10 miles to the Ranchester exit/exit 9. Turn left onto U.S. Highway 14 and travel 6 miles. At Dayton turn right at the Amsden Creek Wildlife Habitat Management Area access sign. Follow this gravel road for 4 miles, bearing left.

About the campground: Huge cottonwood trees shade the river, with unusual limestone cliff formations towering far above. The single-lane dirt road leading to the turnaround at the main campsite is not recommended for long RVs or trailers. Tents and pickup campers are more suited for this secret hideaway. Trailers and larger units have made the journey, but it can be a very trying experience. Both the cottonwoods and larger than average willow brush cling tightly to the boulder-filled shoreline. There are no developed sites, which means leveling a camper will take extra effort.

3 Sibley Lake

Location: 33 miles west of Sheridan.
Facilities: Vault toilets, fire rings, tables (with lamp holders), drinking water, boat ramp, electricity in 15 units.
Sites: 25 for tents or RVs up to 50 feet long.
Fee: $ per day, with an extra charge for electricity, 14-day maximum stay.
Reservations: 1-877-444-6777.
Agency: Bighorn National Forest, Tongue Ranger District, 1-307-672-0751.
Activities: Fishing, hiking, boating, swimming.
Finding the campground: Take Interstate 90 north out of Sheridan for 10 miles to the Ranchester exit/exit 9. Turn left onto U.S. Highway 14 and travel 23 miles. The campground is on the left side of the highway.

About the campground: Laughter and pleasant echoes of recreation associated with cold water on a hot day replace war cries and gunfire. Chief White Antelope of the Cheyenne was killed here during an attack on July 7, 1876. Lt. Frederick W. Sibley led a scouting party into this area, resulting in the subsequent attack. Members of the 2nd Cavalry were forced to abandon their horses and supplies. Hiking through the surrounding country reveals how difficult the soldiers found retreat out of the mountains with no supplies. Wind whispers through the needles of the slender, tall lodgepole pine forest that envelops both lake and campground with stories left to your imagination. Gathering firewood takes extra effort as the immediate area has been picked clean. A host is available, and there is access for the disabled for fishing and at other facilities. Reservations well in advance of your trip are a must if you want to spend time here.

4 Prune Creek

Location: 35 miles west of Sheridan.
Facilities: Vault toilets, fire rings, grills, tables (with lamp holders), drinking water.
Sites: 21 for tents or RVs up to 50 feet long.
Fee: $ per day, 14-day maximum stay.
Reservations: 1-877-444-6777.
Agency: Bighorn National Forest, Tongue Ranger District, 1-307-672-0751.
Activities: Fishing, hiking.
Finding the campground: Take Interstate 90 north out of Sheridan for 10 miles to the Ranchester exit/exit 9. Turn left onto U.S. Highway 14 and travel 25 miles. The campground is on the left side of the highway.

About the campground: Easy access and refreshing water recreation make this a popular place and one that fills quickly. Prune Creek rushes through the campground with willow brush and lodgepole pine sharing the bank. Pools captured by downfall and large boulders in the creek tempt angler and wader alike. Firewood will involve some footwork to gather. A host is available at this campground. The paved highway alongside the campground does not produce any dust, but traffic can be heavy during the day. As with other campgrounds along the roadways, the traffic generally dies off after dark. Any noise is soon forgotten with s'mores roasted over a crackling fire under a clear, star-filled night. The two loops have a turnaround at the end for easy trailer access and exit.

5 North Tongue

Location: 44 miles west of Sheridan.
Facilities: Vault toilets, fire rings, grills, tables (with lamp holders), drinking water.
Sites: 12 (including 2 pull-thrus) for tents or RVs up to 24 feet long.
Fee: $ per day, 14-day maximum stay.
Reservations: First-come, first-served.
Agency: Gallatin Canyon Campgrounds, 1-406-587-9054.
Activities: Fishing, hiking.
Finding the campground: Take Interstate 90 north out of Sheridan for 10 miles to the Ranchester exit/exit 9. Turn left onto U.S. Highway 14 and travel 33 miles. Turn right onto U.S. Highway 14 Alternate and travel 0.5 mile. Turn right onto the gravel Forest Road 15 and travel 1 mile. The campground is on the left.

About the campground: The main attraction to this area is the prime fishing in close by streams. Douglas-fir close in on the units here with lodgepole pine crowding up behind them on the ridges. A happy little creek is hard to see but easy to hear bouncing over rocks and logs; it pleasantly gurgles peacefully through the campground, quenching the thirst of tall grass and willow brush alike. A host is available at a nearby site. Firewood will take some footwork to gather. Trailers can enter and exit either of the two loops easily with a turnaround at the end. Traffic creates a whole lot of dust that can be very annoying on a busy weekend; however, as the sun drops, so does the dust, making for a pleasant evening. This area fills quickly so don't put off obtaining a unit.

6 Bald Mountain

Location: 70 miles west of Sheridan.
Facilities: Vault toilets, fire rings, tables, drinking water.
Sites: 15 for tents or RVs up to 30 feet long.
Fee: $ per day, 14-day maximum stay.
Reservations: First-come, first-served.
Agency: Bighorn National Forest, Medicine Wheel Ranger District, 1-307-548-6541.
Activities: Hiking.
Finding the campground: Take Interstate 90 north out of Sheridan for 10 miles to the Ranchester exit/exit 9. Turn left onto U.S. Highway 14 and travel 33 miles. Turn right onto US 14 Alternate and travel 27 miles. Turn left at the Bald Mountain Campground sign and travel 0.25 mile.

About the campground: Willow brush and a thick stand of fir trees share this camping area in the wide-open alpine meadow typical of the Bighorn Mountains. Gathering firewood will be difficult, though a short drive will take you to available deadfall. The wind cuts with a steely cold after sliding over any one of the remaining snow piles above. The vast meadows surrounding the area display plenty of wildflowers from late June to early July in an average year. Wildlife can be seen frequently, especially early in the evening. The highway is close enough to be convenient and far enough away for the campground to seem isolated.

7 Porcupine

Location: 70 miles west of Sheridan.
Facilities: Vault toilets, fire rings, grills, tables, drinking water.
Sites: 15 for tents or RVs up to 22 feet long.
Fee: $ per day, 14-day maximum stay.
Reservations: 1-877-444-6777.
Agency: Bighorn National Forest, Medicine Wheel Ranger District, 1-307-548-6541.
Activities: Fishing, hiking.
Finding the campground: Take Interstate 90 north out of Sheridan for 10 miles to the Ranchester exit/exit 9. Turn left onto U.S. Highway 14 and travel 33 miles. Turn right onto U.S. Highway 14 Alternate and travel 27 miles. Turn right at the sign onto the gravel road and travel for 1 mile. The campground is on the left.

About the campground: The shade from the fir trees, which snag the incoming sun with no apologies, is almost unwelcome in this high altitude. Extra clothing and/or coats are a must in this mountain country where the fresh mountain air bites with a hard cold. Porcupine Creek is a short walk from the campground. Nearby trails lead the adventurous into some very rugged canyon country complete with torrential rapids and a waterfall. Depending upon the weather, this campground may not be open until the first part of July. Even on the fourth of July, holiday piles of snow stubbornly hide in the shadows.

8 Five Springs

Location: 79 miles west of Sheridan.
Facilities: Vault toilets, fire rings, tables.
Sites: 3 walk-in sites for tents.
Fee: None, 14-day maximum stay.
Reservations: First-come, first-served.
Agency: Bureau of Land Management, Cody Resource Area Office, 1-307-587-2216.
Activities: Hiking, rock climbing.
Finding the campground: Take Interstate 90 west out of Sheridan for 10 miles to the Ranchester exit/exit 9. Turn left onto U.S. Highway 14 and travel 33 miles. Turn right onto US 14 Alternate and travel 34 miles. Turn right at the

Five Springs Campground sign and travel 2 miles. NOTE: Vehicles more than 30 feet long are not recommended. The old highway here is very steep with literal hairpin curves that require use of the whole road for longer rigs to go around.

About the campground: Steep vertical cliffs hide forest and campground alike. Five Springs Creek rages through the combined camping-picnicking area, seemingly trying to be one of the big boys, but there just is not enough water. There is one parking spot that could be used for a pickup camper unit; you will have to share the rest of the parking area with those who access their tents. All in all, this seems to be a forgotten refuge. Five Springs Falls is a short hike up the narrowing canyon and well worth the time. Good photographs of the falls are hard to get. Most visitors don't know this waterfall exists.

9 Bighorn Canyon National Recreation Area: Horseshoe Bend

Location: 107 miles west of Sheridan.
Facilities: Comfort stations, fire rings, tables, drinking water, RV dump.
Sites: 128 for tents or RVs up to 60-plus feet long.
Fee: $ per day, 14-day maximum stay.
Reservations: First-come, first-served.
Agency: National Park Service, 1-406-666-2412.
Activities: Fishing, hiking, boating, swimming, rockhounding.
Finding the campground: Take Interstate 90 north out of Sheridan for 10 miles to the Ranchester exit/exit 9. Turn onto U.S. Highway 14 and travel 33 miles. Turn right onto U.S. 14 Alternate and travel 52 miles. Turn right at the

Shade structures dot the Horseshoe Bend Campground in Bighorn Canyon National Recreation Area.

sign onto Wyoming Highway 37 and travel 10 miles. Turn right at the Horseshoe Bend sign and travel 2 miles.

About the campground: There are no trees here. The comfort stations offer running water and electricity. Parking spaces are well separated, with shade structures scattered about. Driftwood is collected over the year and placed in an access area; inquire at the ranger station across from the campground entrance. There is really no size limit, and that makes this an excellent place to park your trailer or RV and cruise the Bighorns. Bright stars in an unobstructed, warm badlands sky can be extremely refreshing after the freezing mountain air is left behind. Over the fourth of July, there were many empty units, and a whole loop was closed due to lack of campers. Reportedly this striking, colorful campground has yet to be filled.

0 Owen Creek

Location: 50 miles west of Sheridan.
Facilities: Vault toilets, fire rings, tables, drinking water.
Sites: 7 for tents or RVs up to 30 feet long.
Fee: $ per day, 14-day maximum stay.
Reservations: First-come, first-served.
Agency: Bighorn National Forest, Tongue Ranger District, 1-307-672-0751.
Activities: Fishing, hiking.
Finding the campground: Take Interstate 90 north out of Sheridan for 10 miles to the Ranchester exit/exit 9. Turn left onto U.S. Highway 14 and travel 40 miles. Turn right at the Owen Creek Campground sign and travel 0.5 mile.

About the campground: A few Douglas-fir trees share the area with lodgepole pines, shading the camping units. Owen Creek meanders through the grassy rolling meadow, with willow brush hugging the banks. A host is present in 1 of the 7 available units. Gathering firewood requires some effort and may be done much more effectively by taking a drive. This campground is far enough off the highway to be quiet and close enough for easy access. If time is an issue, this may be the place to check in the early afternoon.

1 Tie Flume

Location: 52 miles west of Sheridan.
Facilities: Vault toilets, fire rings, tables, drinking water.
Sites: 25 (3 pull-thrus) for tents or RVs up to 50 feet long.
Fee: $ per day, 14-day maximum stay.
Reservations: First-come, first-served.
Agency: Bighorn National Forest, Tongue Ranger District, 1-307-672-0751.
Activities: Fishing, hiking.
Finding the campground: Take Interstate 90 north out of Sheridan for 10 miles to the Ranchester exit/exit 9. Turn left onto U.S. Highway 14 and travel 40 miles. Turn left onto the gravel Forest Road 26 and travel 2 miles. Bear left onto Forest Road 16 and travel 0.25 mile.

About the campground: These somewhat-level units sit in a fairly thick pine forest. There are few branches on the lower reaches of the lodgepole pines, probably due to previous campfires. A lush grassy meadow runs along the bottom loop. The cool shade can be a precious commodity on a hot day, but when the sun goes down, don't have your coats very far away. Deadfall is within a short distance. A host is available at another nearby campground. Weekends get active, though the campground is usually not full. Crystal-clear water in nearby South Tongue River makes catching trout very challenging. It might be more fun to join them.

12 Dead Swede

Location: 56 miles west of Sheridan.
Facilities: Vault toilets, fire rings, tables, drinking water, picnic area.
Sites: 22 for tents or RVs up to 22 feet long.
Fee: $ per day, 14-day maximum stay.
Reservations: First-come, first-served.
Agency: Bighorn National Forest, Tongue Ranger District, 1-307-672-0751.
Activities: Fishing, hiking.
Finding the campground: Take Interstate 90 north out of Sheridan for 10 miles to the Ranchester exit/exit 9. Turn left onto U.S. Highway 14 and travel 40 miles. Turn left onto Forest Road 26 and travel 6 miles. The campground is on the left side.

About the campground: The upper loop nestles into the lodgepole pine forest well away from the East Fork South Tongue River. The lower loop clings to the banks along with taller-than-usual willow brush. This campground gets a lot of company, both for overnight and day use. Trailers up to 22 feet long require being unhooked for leveling. Larger ones have made the journey, but extra effort is required. Not all of the sites accommodate larger RVs, narrowing the odds of finding a spot. A host is available at another nearby campground. Gathering firewood requires little effort at the present time. The increasing popularity of this prime spot will no doubt decrease the supply. You might want to scrounge some of the deadfall along the way in. Be sure to do it safely—park well out of the way of traffic.

13 Ranger Creek

Location: 69 miles west of Sheridan.
Facilities: Vault toilets, fire rings, grills, tables, drinking water.
Sites: 11 for tents or RVs up to 32 feet long.
Fee: $ per day, 14-day maximum stay.
Reservations: First-come, first-served.
Agency: Bighorn National Forest, Tongue Ranger District, 1-307-672-0751.
Activities: Fishing, hiking.
Finding the campground: Take Interstate 90 north out of Sheridan for 10 miles to the Ranchester exit/exit 9. Turn left onto U.S. Highway 14 and travel

40 miles. Turn left onto the gravel Forest Road 26 and travel 19 miles. Turn left at the Ranger Creek Campground sign.

About the campground: The lodgepole pines have been thinned out here, leaving more meadow than forest. Gathering firewood is fairly easy, with plenty of deadfall close by. The main road passes close by, creating a very dusty atmosphere. Traffic, as with most places, tends to die down after dark. Nearby East Fork Campground might be a better choice to avoid the dust; however, plenty of other visitors are aware of the option, so you will likely have plenty of company.

14 East Fork

Location: 70 miles west of Sheridan.
Facilities: Vault toilets, fire rings, tables, drinking water, picnic area.
Sites: 11 for tents or RVs up to 20 feet long.
Fee: $ per day, 14-day maximum stay.
Reservations: First-come, first-served.
Agency: Bighorn National Forest, Tongue Ranger District, 1-307-672-0751.
Activities: Fishing, hiking.
Finding the campground: Take Interstate 90 north out of Sheridan for 10 miles to the Ranchester exit/exit 9. Turn left onto U.S. Highway 14 and travel 40 miles. Turn left onto Forest Road 26 and travel 20 miles. Turn right at the East Fork Campground sign and travel 0.25 mile.

About the campground: Willow brush is scattered out along the banks of the adjacent East Fork Big Goose Creek. Lodgepole pines line the single-lane road entering the campground. Grassy meadows with sagebrush surround the camping area, with bunches of pine holding the fort. The dust and wind have a tough time reaching this little hollow, making it more appealing than the nearby Ranger Creek. Gathering firewood will take some forethought and work. No host is available at this campground. It is a long dusty road to get here, so you want to plan on spending some time.

15 Cabin Creek

Location: 60 miles west of Sheridan.
Facilities: Vault toilets, fire rings, tables, drinking water.
Sites: 4 for tents or RVs up to 20 feet long.
Fee: $ per day, 14-day maximum stay.
Reservations: First-come, first-served.
Agency: Bighorn National Forest, Paintrock Ranger District, 1-307-765-4435.
Activities: Fishing, hiking.
Finding the campground: Take Interstate 90 north out of Sheridan for 10 miles to the Ranchester exit/exit 9. Turn left onto U.S. Highway 14 and travel 50 miles. Turn left onto the gravel Forest Road 17 and travel 0.25 mile bearing to the right.

About the campground: Tall fir trees and short aspens crowd these compact units, with willow brush lining the small stream bubbling through it. The highway is close, though traffic is not usually heavy. If you have a large RV or trailer, the Cabin Creek Trailer Park would be a better choice. One of the campgrounds farther up Forest Road 17 might be more appealing for those with tents or pickup campers. Firewood is not readily available, though bundles are advertised for sale on the sign at the entrance to the campground. A host is available at a nearby camping area.

16 Cabin Creek Trailer Park

Location: 60 miles west of Sheridan.
Facilities: Vault toilets, fire rings, drinking water.
Sites: 26 for RVs up to 50 feet long.
Fee: $ per day, 30-day maximum stay.
Reservations: 1-877-444-6777.
Agency: Bighorn National Forest, Paintrock Ranger District, 1-307-765-4435.
Activities: Hiking.
Finding the campground: Take Interstate 90 north out of Sheridan for 10 miles to the Ranchester exit/exit 9. Turn left onto U.S. Highway 14 and travel 50 miles. Turn left onto the gravel Forest Road 17 and travel 0.25 mile bearing to the left.

About the campground: One side of this large, hidden draw offers a rocky slope complete with grass and a healthy amount of sagebrush. On the opposite side a lodgepole pine forest is lined with mature aspen trees. There are no tables in this area. Firewood is not readily available to gather. This is a good area to drop your trailer, which allows you to access other viewing areas. A host is located at the entrance.

17 Shell Creek

Location: 61 miles west of Sheridan.
Facilities: Vault toilets, fire rings, tables, drinking water.
Sites: 11 for tents or RVs up to 40 feet long.
Fee: $ per day, 14-day maximum stay.
Reservations: First-come, first-served.
Agency: Bighorn National Forest, Paintrock Ranger District, 1-307-765-4435.
Activities: Fishing, hiking.
Finding the campground: Take Interstate 90 north out of Sheridan for 10 miles to the Ranchester exit/exit 9. Turn left onto U.S. Highway 14 and travel 50 miles. Turn left onto the gravel Forest Road 17 and travel 1 mile. The campground is on the right.

About the campground: Forest meets grassy ridge along the crashing waters of Shell Creek. The tables and fire rings are tucked away just inside the fir and aspen groves. A host is available at another nearby camping area. As the night sky lights up, you can steal away from the crackling fire and study the heavens just past the forest boundary. On the full moon, the stars are not easily seen, but other features of the surrounding nature are presented in a unique fashion. Shell Creek roars its complaint to all within hearing, seemingly not wanting to move out into the thirsty desert badlands below. If you like listening to powerful rapids with occasional interruptions due to passing wind, this is the place.

18 Ranger Creek (Shell Creek)

Location: 62 miles west of Sheridan.
Facilities: Vault toilets, fire rings, tables, drinking water.
Sites: 10 for tents or RVs up to 22 feet long.
Fee: $ per day, 14-day maximum stay.
Reservations: 1-877-444-6777.
Agency: Bighorn National Forest, Paintrock Ranger District, 1-307-765-4435.
Activities: Fishing, hiking.
Finding the campground: Take Interstate 90 north out of Sheridan for 10 miles to the Ranchester exit/exit 9. Turn left onto U.S. Highway 14 and travel 50 miles. Turn left onto Forest Road 17 and travel 2 miles.

About the campground: The road divides this campground, with 8 sites on the right side. A small stream struggles past these units on its way to join the raging Shell Creek. Short aspen trees take shelter in the shadows of Douglas-fir. The compact parking areas will accommodate trailers up to 22 feet long, but they must be unhooked. Leveling takes forethought and effort. A host is available at another nearby campground. Gathering firewood will take some scouting. This is a cool area to be when the temperature climbs in the late summer. Keep your coat handy; when the sun goes behind the mountains overlooking this canyon, the heat goes with it. If you have longer RVs, the previous Shell Creek Campground or even Cabin Creek Trailer Park would be a much better choice.

19 Medicine Lodge Lake

Location: 85 miles west of Sheridan.
Facilities: Vault toilets, fire rings, tables, drinking water, boat ramp.
Sites: 8 for tents or RVs up to 40 feet long.
Fee: $ per day, 14-day maximum stay.
Reservations: 1-877-444-6777.
Agency: Bighorn National Forest, Paintrock Ranger District, 1-307-765-4435.
Activities: Fishing, hiking, boating, swimming.
Finding the campground: Take Interstate 90 north out of Sheridan for 10 miles to the Ranchester exit/exit 9. Turn left onto U.S. Highway 14 and travel 50 miles. Turn left onto the gravel Forest Road 17 and travel 25 miles. Turn right at the campground sign.

About the campground: Douglas-fir mixed with aspen march right up the shoreline at Medicine Lodge Lake, which has 65 surface acres of trout-infested mountain water to invite anglers. Hikers can explore deep rugged canyons or high alpine meadows, depending on individual desires. The camping units settle in among the shade of the thick forest, providing a sort of seclusion from any passersby. The long gravel road leading to the end of the road does not see a lot of traffic, but those that do go by would not know of any campers here without actually driving through the camping area. This is a very good place to spend more than a few days; however, be sure to have all your needed supplies. It is a long way to any store, and it is especially difficult to find one still open after dark.

20 Upper Paint Rock Lake

Location: 86 miles west of Sheridan.
Facilities: Vault toilets, fire rings, tables.
Sites: 5 for tents or RVs up to 19 feet long.
Fee: $ per day, 14-day maximum stay.
Reservations: First-come, first-served.
Agency: Bighorn National Forest, Paintrock Ranger District, 1-307-765-4435.
Activities: Fishing, hiking, swimming.
Finding the campground: Take Interstate 90 north out of Sheridan for 10 miles to the Ranchester exit/exit 9. Turn left onto U.S. Highway 14 and travel 50 miles. Turn left onto the gravel Forest Road 17 and travel 25.7 miles. Turn left at the campground sign and travel 0.25 mile.

About the campground: Large Douglas-fir are scattered throughout this cramped, bumpy little draw. Trailers were present when we visited, but the trees showed signs of some difficult maneuvering. A small creek bubbles between boulders past one side of the campground, though the main attraction is Upper Paint Rock Lake. The trout-infested waters offer anglers a pleasant time, and on a hot day youngsters cool off quickly. This is a very pleasant area. You want to consider staying here for more than a single night after traveling the long, dusty, trying road. Trailers do make it back here on a regular basis, but there are stretches of road that turn into deeply rutted, nerve-racking trails. A host is available at the Cabin Creek Trailer Park.

21 Lower Paint Rock Lake

Location: 86 miles west of Sheridan.
Facilities: Vault toilets, fire rings, tables, drinking water.
Sites: 4 for tents or RVs up to 45 feet long.
Fee: $ per day, 14-day maximum stay.
Reservations: First-come, first-served.
Agency: Bighorn National Forest, Paintrock Ranger District, 1-307-765-4435.
Activities: Fishing, hiking.
Finding the campground: Take Interstate 90 north out of Sheridan for 10 miles to the Ranchester exit/exit 9. Turn left onto U.S. Highway 14 and travel 50 miles. Turn left onto the gravel Forest Road 17 and travel 26 miles. The campground is at the end of the road.

About the campground: Longer RVs and trailers take extra effort to level because of the obvious slope of the parking area. Douglas-fir trees shade the tables in most spots, with a grassy slope down to the small but trout-inhabited Lower Paint Rock Lake. Firewood is within a short distance. The road leading into this area can be very trying, especially a private section of dirt that gets heavily rutted after any amount of moisture. This is a jumping-off place for entering the Cloud Peak Wilderness, complete with a loading/unloading area for horses. It is a quiet place that you want to spend some time at; if you need to be on the move the following morning, the long painstaking drive would not be worth it. This is one of those hideouts where you would want to forget about the calendar. A host is available at Cabin Creek Trailer Park.

Buffalo Area

Both Native Americans and outlaws took refuge in this area, which has changed little since the days of the Wild West. The "Wild Bunch," which included Butch Cassidy and the Sundance Kid, used Outlaw Caves near Hole-in-the-Wall as a hide-out. The difficult access still discourages more than a few travelers. The desertlike prairie dominating the Hole-in-the-Wall area rapidly develops into alpine meadows with thick evergreen forests of Douglas-fir and lodgepole pine in the Bighorn Mountains. Outlaws were not the only contributors to the scattered artifacts of the vicinity. Chief Red Cloud of the Sioux effectively drove the U.S. Cavalry out of the area in 1858, and you can see abandoned forts and headstones along the eastern slope. Further evidence of the Native Americans who camped in the area lives on along the western slope of the Bighorn Mountains—the town of Ten Sleep was so named for the ten sleeps it took to arrive in the area from across the mountains. The beauty and uniqueness of this area will undoubtedly create a desire to spend more time exploring the region.

Mountain lakes reflect snowy peaks contrasted against blue skies, and massive canyons hold the echoes of voices and whitewater rapids alike. Excellent fishing awaits anglers in this relatively unknown portion of Wyoming. Classic western trout streams with unforgettable mountain scenery for a background place travelers in a difficult situation. It is impossible to keep this wonderful area a secret, and yet the majority of its beauty lies in the fact that few know of it, making more of a wilderness area outside of the boundaries of the Cloud Peak Wilderness than inside.

1 Outlaw Caves

Location: 81 miles south of Buffalo.
Facilities: Vault toilet, fire rings, tables, picnic area.
Sites: 10 to 15 for tents.
Fee: $ per day, 14-day maximum stay.
Reservations: First-come, first-served.
Agency: Bureau of Land Management, Buffalo District, 1-307-684-1100.
Activities: Hiking, fishing.
Finding the campground: Take Interstate 25 south out of Buffalo for 45 miles to Kaycee. Take Wyoming Highway 191 west for 1 mile. Turn left onto Wyoming Highway 190 and travel 15 miles. Bear left following the BLM access signs and travel 13 miles. High-profile vehicles are strongly recommended for the steep, heavily tilted last 7 miles. A two-wheel drive will make it, but when stormy weather rolls in, even a four-wheel drive will be hard pressed to move around.

About the campground: Wind roars aggressively through ancient pine trees and sagebrush on this cliff edge. Every now and then an echo from the tumbling Middle Fork of the Powder River sneaks in between wind blasts. Tables and fire rings find shade part of the day a short distance from the cliff edge. The cave, some 800 to 1,000 feet below, at one time hosted such infamous

BUFFALO AREA

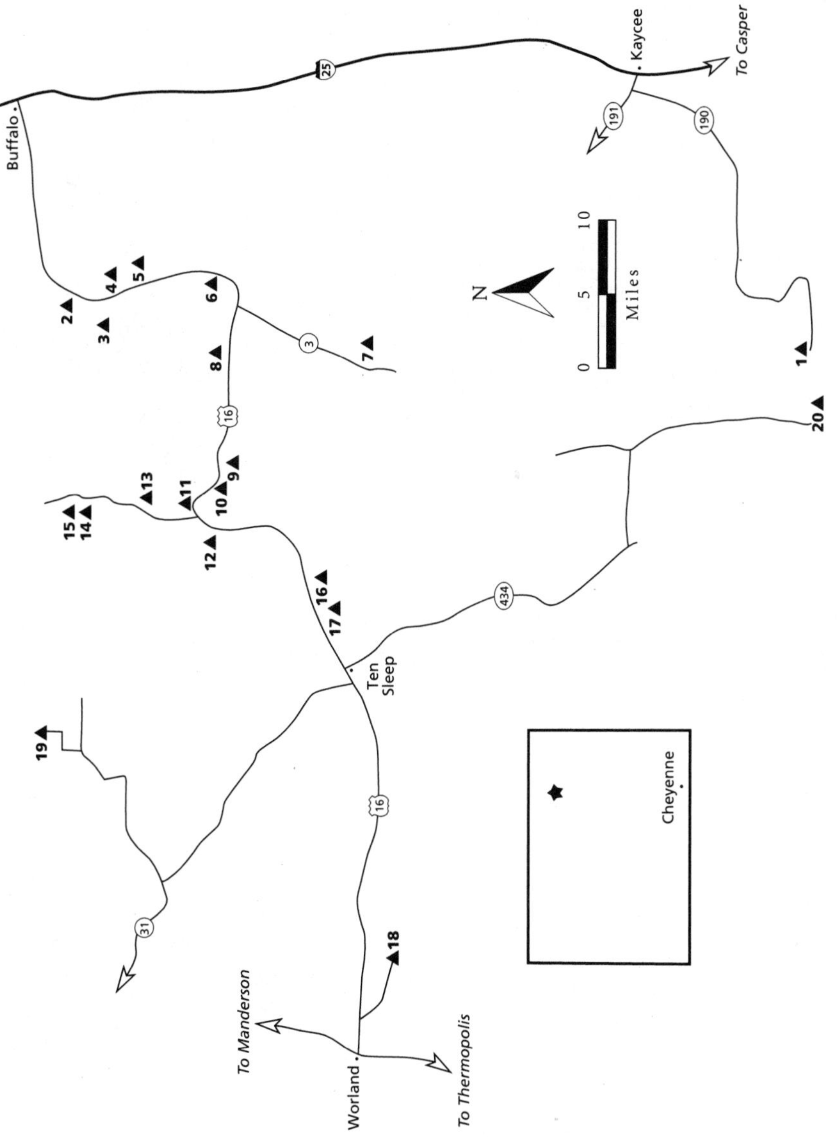

	Group sites	Tents	RV sites	Total sites	Picnic area	Toilets	Showers	Drinking water	Dump station	Phone	Disabled access	Fee ($)	Season	Can reserve	Length of stay	Recreation
1 Outlaw Caves		15		15	X	V						$	4/16-11/16		14	FH
2 Middle Fork			10	10		V		X				$	5/15-10-31	X	14	FH
3 Circle Park			10	10		V		X				$	5/15-10-31		14	FH
4 Tie Hack			20	20	X	V		X				$	5/15-10-31	X	14	FHBS
5 South Fork		5	10	15		V		X				$	5/15-10-31	X	14	FH
6 Crazy Woman			6	6		V		X				$	5/15-10-31		14	FH
7 Doyle			19	19		V						$	5/15-10-31		14	FH
8 Lost Cabin			18	18		V		X				$	5/15-10-31		14	FH
9 Bull Creek			10	10		V						$	6/15-10/31		14	FHBS
10 Lake View		5	6	11	X	V		X				$	6/15-9/30	X	14	FHBS
11 Sitting Bull			42	42		V		X				$	6/15-9/30	X	14	FHM
12 Boulder Park			37	37		V		X				$	6/15-9/30	X	30	FH
13 Island Park			10	10		V		X				$	6/15-9/30		14	FHM
14 Deer Park			7	7		V		X				$	6/15-9/30		14	FH
15 West Tensleep Lake			10	10		V		X				$	6/15-9/30	X	14	FHB
16 Leigh Creek		5	6	11		V		X				$	5/15-10/31		14	F
17 Tensleep Creek			5	5		V		X				$	6/1-10/31		14	F
18 Castle Gardens			8	8	X	V						N	6/1-10/31		14	HP
19 Medicine Lodge	1		30	30	X	V		X				$	5/1-11/4		14	FH
20 Middle Fork (PR)			6	6		V		X				$	Summer		14	FHW

V=vault toilets, N=none, F=fishing, H=hiking, B=boating, S=swimming, M=mountain biking, P=photography, W=wildlife viewing

outlaws as Butch Cassidy and the Sundance Kid. Before them Native Americans left evidence of their presence in the form of petroglyphs. Trout fishing is excellent in the stair-stepped pools of the Middle Fork of the Powder River, which appears to be the forming force of this awesome canyon. This is an excellent place to pitch a tent and explore, listening to the sounds of ghosts of past campers that echo off the colorful limestone walls. This point of interest cannot be accessed easily, but neither can the full impact of its meaning be understood in a whirlwind visit.

2 Middle Fork

Location: 14 miles west of Buffalo.
Facilities: Vault toilets, fire rings, tables, drinking water.
Sites: 10 for tents or RVs up to 25 feet long.
Fee: $ per day, 14-day maximum stay.

Butch Cassidy and the Sundance Kid once made camp in the vicinity of Outlaw Caves Campground.

Reservations: 1-877-444-6777.
Agency: Bighorn National Forest and Bureau of Land Management, Buffalo Ranger District, 1-307-684-1100.
Activities: Fishing, hiking.
Finding the campground: Take U.S. Highway 16 west out of Buffalo for 14 miles. The campground is on the right.

About the campground: Middle Fork Clear Creek stops to visit at various pools, inviting angler and wader alike. Small aspen and willow brush compete with aged Douglas-fir for drinks of the crystal-clear ice water. Lodgepole pines take over the steep rocky sides of the draw, hiding this pleasant place. Backing skills are required to put your trailer here. A host is available at another nearby campground. This campground has been here some time, so all the easy firewood is gone. Deer and elk generally come out early in the evening, so in your search for firewood, keep an open eye on the timberline along the upper alpine meadows.

3 Circle Park

Location: 17 miles west of Buffalo.
Facilities: Vault toilets, fire rings, grills, tables, drinking water.
Sites: 10 for tents or RVs up to 30 feet long.
Fee: $ per day, 14-day maximum stay.
Reservations: First-come, first-served.
Agency: Bighorn National Forest and Bureau of Land Management, Buffalo Ranger District, 1-307-684-1100.
Activities: Fishing, hiking.
Finding the campground: Take U.S. Highway 16 west out of Buffalo for 15 miles. Turn right onto the gravel Forest Road 20 and travel 2 miles.

About the campground: The access road passes through an ancient aspen grove, and when the wind tears through these aspen leaves, it sounds like rapids of a mountain river. It's almost as if the leaves are defiantly trying to deny the blasts a right of passage. Lodgepole pine and younger aspen shade the tables along the fire line of a relatively recent forest fire—a very vivid reminder to be careful of your own sparks. Trailers up to 22 feet long will have to be unhooked for proper parking, and the parking units are not all that level. Tents, small trailers, and pickup campers would be more suited for this area. A host is available at another nearby campground. Gathering firewood is not difficult with the adjacent fire-dead timber. Granite pokes out in multiple areas, challenging young and old explorers alike. Some of the higher outcrops are excellent places to wait for the local residents to emerge from the timber toward evening. A pair of binoculars enhances viewing the plentiful deer and elk, though they are not necessary.

4 Tie Hack

Location: 16 miles west of Buffalo.
Facilities: Vault toilets, fire rings, tables, drinking water, picnic area.

Sites: 20 for tents or RVs up to 50-plus feet long.
Fee: $ per day, 14-day maximum stay.
Reservations: 1-877-444-6777.
Agency: Bighorn National Forest, Buffalo Ranger District, 1-307-684-1100.
Activities: Fishing, hiking, boating (gas-powered boats not allowed), swimming.
Finding the campground: Take U.S. Highway 16 west out of Buffalo for 15 miles. Turn left onto Forest Road 21 and travel 1 mile.

About the campground: A new campground was under construction as of our visit; it was scheduled to open in 2000. The former campground now sits at the bottom of a small reservoir. This crystal-clear addition makes a desirable spot even more so. Lodgepole pine forest surrounds the lake on mountain ridges beckoning to young and old explorers alike. No doubt this will be a very popular place. In fact, the current picnic facilities are already extremely active. The new parking aprons will stretch out to a total of 70 feet, which is quite enough room for about any size RV on the road. If you have a longer unit, it will be tougher to get through some of Wyoming's town streets than to park it here.

South Fork

Location: 16 miles west of Buffalo.
Facilities: Vault toilets, fire rings, tables, drinking water.
Sites: 5 for tents and 10 for RVs up to 35 feet long.
Fee: $ per day, 14-day maximum stay.
Reservations: 1-877-444-6777.
Agency: Bighorn National Forest, Buffalo Ranger District, 1-307-684-1100.
Activities: Fishing, hiking.
Finding the campground: Take U.S. Highway 16 west out of Buffalo for 16 miles. The campground is on the left side of the highway.

About the campground: The almost whitewater rapids of South Fork Clear Creek take up a good portion of this tight draw. Granite cliffs confine fir and aspen trees as well as directing the complaining creek. A host occupies one of the available units. Gathering firewood is best left to young adventure-seekers in need of spending energy. Bundles of wood are advertised for sale for those of us with no "slaves" present.

Crazy Woman

Location: 25 miles west of Buffalo.
Facilities: Vault toilets, fire rings, grills, tables, drinking water.
Sites: 6 for tents or RVs up to 20 feet long.
Fee: $ per day, 14-day maximum stay.
Reservations: First-come, first-served.
Agency: Bighorn National Forest, Buffalo Ranger District, 1-307-684-1100.
Activities: Fishing, hiking.

Finding the campground: Take U.S. Highway 16 west out of Buffalo for 25 miles. Turn right at the Crazy Woman Campground sign and travel 0.5 mile.

About the campground: Crazy Woman Creek meanders through large willow brush with tall pine trees along an unyielding granite outcrop directing flow. Trailers up to 16 feet long will fit but require excellent backing skills and unhooking. Just getting parked is only half the job. Leveling takes forethought and blocking. A host occupies one of the available units. Firewood is reasonably close by, though most will require cutting.

7 Doyle

Location: 32 miles west and south of Buffalo.
Facilities: Vault toilets, fire rings, grills, tables.
Sites: 19 for tents or RVs up to 30 feet long.
Fee: $ per day, 14-day maximum stay.
Reservations: First-come, first-served.
Agency: Bighorn National Forest, Buffalo Ranger District, 1-307-684-1100.
Activities: Fishing, hiking.
Finding the campground: Take U.S. Highway 16 west out of Buffalo for 26 miles. Turn left onto Johnson County Road 3 and travel 6 miles. Turn left at the Doyle Campground sign and travel 0.25 mile. CR 3 will turn to gravel within 3.5 miles.

About the campground: Lodgepole pine forest houses these units, offering plenty of shade. A large meadow separates Doyle Creek from the campsites. The lack of drinking water and a very rough road for the last 0.25 mile make this peaceful place less desirable. If you have plenty of drinking water and time, this would be an excellent place for rest and relaxation. A bucket would provide enough water from the lazy crystal-clear Doyle Creek for other needs. A host is available at another nearby campground. Firewood is fairly accessible.

8 Lost Cabin

Location: 27 miles west of Buffalo.
Facilities: Vault toilets, fire rings, grills, tables, garbage service, drinking water.
Sites: 18 (10 pull-thrus) for tents or RVs up to 50 feet long.
Fee: $ per day, 14-day maximum stay.
Reservations: First-come, first-served.
Agency: Bighorn National Forest, Buffalo Ranger District, 1-307-684-1100.
Activities: Fishing, hiking.
Finding the campground: Take U.S. Highway 16 west out of Buffalo for 27 miles. Turn right at the Lost Cabin Campground sign onto the gravel road and travel 0.5 mile.

About the campground: Thick lodgepole pines and a noticeable number of mature aspen dominate this quiet place. The grass and underbrush is green and thick with plenty of water oozing from the ground within the central part, so hiking can get wet in the campground proper. There is plenty of hiking territory to explore in the adjacent forest, with plenty of downed timber for roasting marshmallows. The drinking water is provided by way of a hand pump that can add to the exercise agenda or keep young ones occupied at least for a little time. A host is available.

9 Bull Creek

Location: 42 miles west and south of Buffalo.
Facilities: Vault toilets, fire rings, tables.
Sites: 10 for tents or RVs up to 20 feet long, trailers are not recommended.
Fee: $ per day, 14-day maximum stay
Reservations: First-come, first-served.
Agency: Bighorn National Forest, Tensleep Ranger District, 1-307-684-1100.
Activities: Fishing, hiking, boating, swimming.
Finding the campground: Take U.S. Highway 16 west out of Buffalo for 42 miles. Turn left onto the gravel Forest Road 426 and travel 0.5 mile.

About the campground: Douglas-fir choke the banks of a small gurgling brook as it pounds its way toward Meadowlark Lake in this draw. The camping sites are not all that close, but the parking is tight and short. Tents would be more suited for this area. High campers could find the tree branches a problem. Firewood is close by, and Meadowlark Lake is in sight, though some footwork is still required. The host is located at another nearby campground. If you do try taking a trailer into this area, be aware that there is no turnaround. The parking spaces are at 90-degree angles to the access road. If all the units are occupied, you will have to back out for no small distance with some tricky obstacles to overcome.

10 Lake View

Location: 49 miles west of Buffalo.
Facilities: Vault toilets, fire rings, tables, drinking water, picnic area.
Sites: 5 for tents and 6 for RVs up to 25 feet long.
Fee: $ per day, 14-day maximum stay.
Reservations: 1-877-444-6777.
Agency: Bighorn National Forest, Tensleep Ranger District, 1-307-684-1100.
Activities: Fishing, hiking, boating, swimming, picnicking.
Finding the campground: Take U.S. Highway 16 west out of Buffalo for 49 miles. The campground is on the left.

About the campground: Meadowlark Lake is a short hike down the ridge in plain sight from the camping sites. The tables and parking areas are all located within the shade of Douglas-fir with tall grass in the open areas along the edge. The tent sites are the farthest ones to get to but the closest to the highway. To park a trailer in one of the remaining units will require unhooking. The host is located at another nearby campground. This is a popular spot for those who like water sports, so weekends find this campground full.

11 Sitting Bull

Location: 43 miles west and south of Buffalo.
Facilities: Vault toilets, fire rings, grills, tables (with lantern hooks), drinking water.
Sites: 42 for tents or RVs up to 65 feet long.
Fee: $ per day, 14-day maximum stay.
Reservations: 1-877-444-6777.
Agency: Bighorn National Forest, Tensleep Ranger District, 1-307-684-1100.
Activities: Fishing (Meadowlark Lake is reasonably close), hiking, mountain biking.
Finding the campground: Take U.S. Highway 16 west out of Buffalo for 42 miles. Turn right onto Forest Road 432 and travel 1 mile.

About the campground: Willow brush and mountain meadows line the banks of Lake Creek as it passes by this campground. Tall lodgepole pines populate the camping area along with a pleasant mixture of Douglas-fir. Inviting trails take off into the surrounding area. Four-wheel-drive roads are present, though many have been gated, limiting use to bikes, horses, and feet. Mountain biking is not allowed in wilderness areas, but this campground has some distance between it and the Cloud Peak Wilderness, if you want to bring your knobby tires. There is a host at the site.

Sitting Bull Campground hides in the trees to the left of this forest road in Bighorn National Forest.

12 Boulder Park

Location: 52 miles west of Buffalo.
Facilities: Vault toilets, fire rings, tables, drinking water.
Sites: 37 for tents or RVs up to 45 feet long.
Fee: $ per day, 30-day maximum stay.
Reservations: 1-877-444-6777, 6 sites are available on a first-come, first-served basis.
Agency: Bighorn National Forest, Tensleep Ranger District, 1-307-684-1100.
Activities: Fishing, hiking.
Finding the campground: Take U.S. Highway 16 west out of Buffalo for 52 miles. Turn right onto the gravel Forest Road 27 and travel 0.2 mile. The campground is on the left.

About the campground: This campground is well named for the boulders that defiantly try to keep the raging Tensleep Creek from going any farther down the canyon. The irritated waters voice their disapproval loudly enough to echo off the nearby majestic limestone cliffs. Douglas-fir line the banks, with a narrow strip of grassy meadow centered in the camping area. Firewood is within a short walk, though most of the smaller pieces have been used up. A campground host occupies one spot, and the Deerhaven Lodge is just across the creek.

13 Island Park

Location: 48 miles west of Buffalo.
Facilities: Vault toilets, fire rings, tables, drinking water.
Sites: 10 for tents or RVs, the largest unit is 22 feet long.
Fee: $ per day, 14-day maximum stay.
Reservations: First-come, first-served.
Agency: Bighorn National Forest, Tensleep Ranger District, 1-307-684-1100.
Activities: Fishing, hiking, mountain biking.
Finding the campground: Take U.S. Highway 16 west out of Buffalo for 45 miles. Turn right onto Forest Road 27 and travel 3.5 miles.

About the campground: Tents, trailers, or RVs can park directly on the bank of West Tensleep Creek. Lodgepole pine, spruce, and Douglas-fir shade the tables and fire pits while willow brush bordered by aspen trees outlines the crystal-clear, trout-infested creek. Firewood appeared relatively easy to gather from nearby deadfall.

14 Deer Park

Location: 52 miles west and south of Buffalo.
Facilities: Vault toilets, fire rings, tables, drinking water.
Sites: 7 for tents or RVs up to 20 feet long.
Fee: $ per day, 14-day maximum stay.
Reservations: First-come, first-served.

Agency: Bighorn National Forest, Tensleep Ranger District, 1-307-684-1100.
Activities: Fishing, hiking.
Finding the campground: Take U.S. Highway 16 west out of Buffalo for 45 miles. Turn right onto Forest Road 27 and travel 7 miles.

About the campground: A classic western trout stream sleepily passes by this little place in a lush grassy meadow. Douglas-fir inhabit the camping area proper, with firewood within walking distance. The gravel road leading to and past the campground can get busy, creating a dusty situation. Deer and moose are frequently seen in the area, and an assortment of wildflowers is present in late June through early July. A campground host is available at a nearby camping area. This is an excellent area to sit in the shade next to a campfire and scout the meadows for native inhabitants.

15 West Tensleep Lake

Location: 52 miles west and south of Buffalo.
Facilities: Vault toilets, fire rings, tables, drinking water.
Sites: 10 for tents or RVs up to 45 feet long.
Fee: $ per day, 14-day maximum stay.
Reservations: 1-877-444-6777.
Agency: Bighorn National Forest, Tensleep Ranger District, 1-307-684-1100.
Activities: Fishing, hiking, boating (nonmotorized).
Finding the campground: Take U.S. Highway 16 west out of Buffalo for 45 miles. Turn right onto Forest Road 27 and travel 7 miles.

About the campground: This compact place is well situated on the shores of the postcard quality West Tensleep Lake. Mature fir trees are well spaced, with some willow brush and grass in between. Snowcapped mountains often reflect off of the lake surface, and trout shatter the image in airborne attempts to eat lunch. There is some contention over reserving sites. Locals reportedly dislike the extra fee to reserve units, and as a result others fill the camping area. The campground can get crowded at times, with a waiting line at the restroom. The inconvenience is quickly forgotten with the first breath of mountain fresh air and whisper of the wind in the trees.

16 Leigh Creek

Location: 58 miles west of Buffalo.
Facilities: Vault toilets, fire rings, tables, drinking water.
Sites: 5 for tents and 6 for RVs up to 20 feet long.
Fee: $ per day, 14-day maximum stay.
Reservations: First-come, first-served.
Agency: Bighorn National Forest, Tensleep Ranger District, 1-307-684-1100.
Activities: Fishing.
Finding the campground: Take U.S. Highway 16 west out of Buffalo for 57 miles. Turn left onto Forest Road 18 and travel 1 mile.

About the campground: Cottonwood, willow brush, some aspen, and a few cedar trees are crunched together in this confined place. Roaring Tensleep Creek drowns out any sounds from the nearby highway, providing a smashing orchestra for those who relish nature's unashamed revelation of power. A host is available nearby (directions are noted on the sign at the campground entrance). Firewood is not readily available.

7 Tensleep Creek

Location: 59 miles west of Buffalo.
Facilities: Vault toilets, fire rings, tables, drinking water.
Sites: 5 for tents or RVs up to 40 feet long.
Fee: $ per day, 14-day maximum stay.
Reservations: First-come, first-served.
Agency: Bighorn National Forest, Tensleep Ranger District, 1-307-684-1100.
Activities: Fishing.
Finding the campground: Take U.S. Highway 16 west out of Buffalo for 57 miles. Turn left onto Forest Road 18 and travel 2 miles.

About the campground: Tensleep Creek rushes through this campground, with ancient cottonwood trees and willow brush clutching tightly to its banks. In fact, the brush grows everywhere except on the roadways and well-used trails. For those who like the sound of powerful water flows, this is the place. Firewood is not readily available. Trailers and RVs require forethought and skill because of the crowding vegetation.

8 Castle Gardens

Location: 8 miles east of Worland.
Facilities: Vault toilet, fire rings, tables, picnic area.
Sites: 8 for tents or RVs up to 20 feet long.
Fee: None, 14-day maximum stay.
Reservations: First-come, first-served.
Agency: Bureau of Land Management, Worland District, 1-307-684-1100.
Activities: Hiking, photography.
Finding the campground: Take U.S. Highway 16 east out of Worland for 2 miles. Turn right at the Castle Gardens sign onto the gravel road and travel about 6 miles.

About the campground: "Hot" describes this desert badlands setting. Early spring proves the most inviting time to camp, especially when snow keeps the upper mountain campgrounds closed. The unusual white sandstone formations give the campground its name.

The badlands in the Worland area present a stark beauty all their own.

19 Medicine Lodge

Location: 33 miles north of Ten Sleep.
Facilities: Vault toilets, fire rings, tables, drinking water, picnic area, playground.
Sites: 1 group site, 30 for tents or RVs up to 40 feet long.
Fee: $ per day, 14-day maximum stay.
Reservations: First-come, first-served.
Agency: Medicine Lodge State Archaeological Site, 1-307-469-2234.
Activities: Fishing, hiking, picnicking.
Finding the campground: Ten Sleep is 65 miles west of Buffalo. Just past Ten Sleep turn right onto the paved Lower Nowood Road and travel 20 miles. Turn right onto the paved Wyoming Highway 31 and travel 7 miles. Turn left onto the paved Wyoming Highway 31 and travel 4 miles. Stay to the left, following the sign to Medicine Lodge Archaeological Site and travel 2 miles down this gravel road.

About the campground: The group area accommodates large numbers of people. The exact number is a function of how much room the vehicles and related material take up. Large, mowed grassy fields surrounded by ancient cottonwood trees offer a variety of ways to park. The ice-cold mountain water of Medicine Lodge Creek offers a cool retreat in this desertlike setting. At the upper camping area, the creek undercuts limestone cliffs, with the tables and fire rings adjacent to the opposite shore. A visitor center is present for those desiring to investigate the history of the area.

20 Middle Fork (Powder River)

Location: 35 miles southeast of Ten Sleep.
Facilities: Vault toilet, fire rings, tables, drinking water.
Sites: 6 for tents or RVs up to 30 feet long.
Fee: $ per day, 14-day maximum stay.
Reservations: First-come, first-served.
Agency: Bureau of Land Management, Worland District, 1-307-347-5100.
Activities: Fishing, hiking, wildlife viewing.
Finding the campground: At Ten Sleep take Wyoming Highway 434 south for 21 miles. Just before the pavement ends, turn left onto the rough gravel road and travel 8 miles. Turn right onto the gravel Hazelton Road and travel 6 miles.

About the campground: The Middle Fork Powder River runs clear and cold up here, unlike the muddy mass passing by the rest area west of Gillette. Fir trees mingle with the lodgepole pine along the banks. Firewood gathering takes some effort, as previous campers have cleaned up the smaller pieces. Good drinking water surfaces from a hand pump outside the main campground.

Black Hills North

History hides in seemingly every draw and canyon in these hills. Many tales and log cabins of the Old West are shared among the ponderosa pine trees blanketing the hillsides. Such colorful characters as "Wild Bill" Hickok and "Calamity Jane," among others, rest in peace at Deadwood.

Wary trout can often be viewed in the crystal-clear waters, many of which are within very short distances from camping areas. When fishing is frustrating, it is most refreshing to pull off your boots and roll up your pants for an old-fashioned wading spree. The ice-cold water, combined with pine-scented fresh air, puts a different perspective on life instantly.

Sandwiched between the limestone cliffs, Little Spearfish Creek uniquely conceals Roughlock Falls. Wading is required to obtain the full view of this impressive site. The Homestake Mining Company has developed and continues to maintain a very pleasant picnic area that in spite of the large numbers of visitors seems to always have an available table. Upstream from the falls a scene from *Dances With Wolves* was shot.

Legends live on the Black Hills of the Wyoming side. Native Americans once gathered in the shadow of a most impressive mountain and danced. The dance has in fact left its mark on both the mountain and the name of the town now occupying the area. Sundance also boasts of outlaw tales, such as the escape of the "Sundance Kid" from the local jail. Not too far away from Sundance, Devils Tower snuggles up against the western edge of the Black Hills in Wyoming. This ancient geological wonder is reported by Native American legend to have been created when a monolithic bear attacked seven girls. To protect these girls the ground rose under them while the bear clawed at the sides attempting to reach them; the credibility of this tale increases with your visit.

1 Beaver Creek (South Dakota)

Location: 6 miles east of Four Corners.
Facilities: Vault toilets, fire rings, tables, drinking water.
Sites: 8 for tents or RVs up to 45 feet long.
Fee: $ per day, 14-day maximum stay.
Reservations: First-come, first-served.
Agency: Black Hills National Forest, Custer Ranger District, 1-605-673-4853.
Activities: Fishing, hiking.
Finding the campground: Four Corners is about 20 miles north of Newcastle, Wyoming, or about 34 miles southwest of Lead, South Dakota. Follow the signs to Mallo Camp for 4.5 miles; it's just across from the Four Corners Store. Turn right to enter the Mallo Camp and follow the road past the motel and later the lodge to the Wyoming/South Dakota border for 1.5 miles. Continue on this otherwise unmarked gravel road for 0.5 mile to the campground.

About the campground: Spruce trees and high banks offer plenty of shade for the trout in Beaver Creek. The tables and fire rings are located close to the

BLACK HILLS NORTH

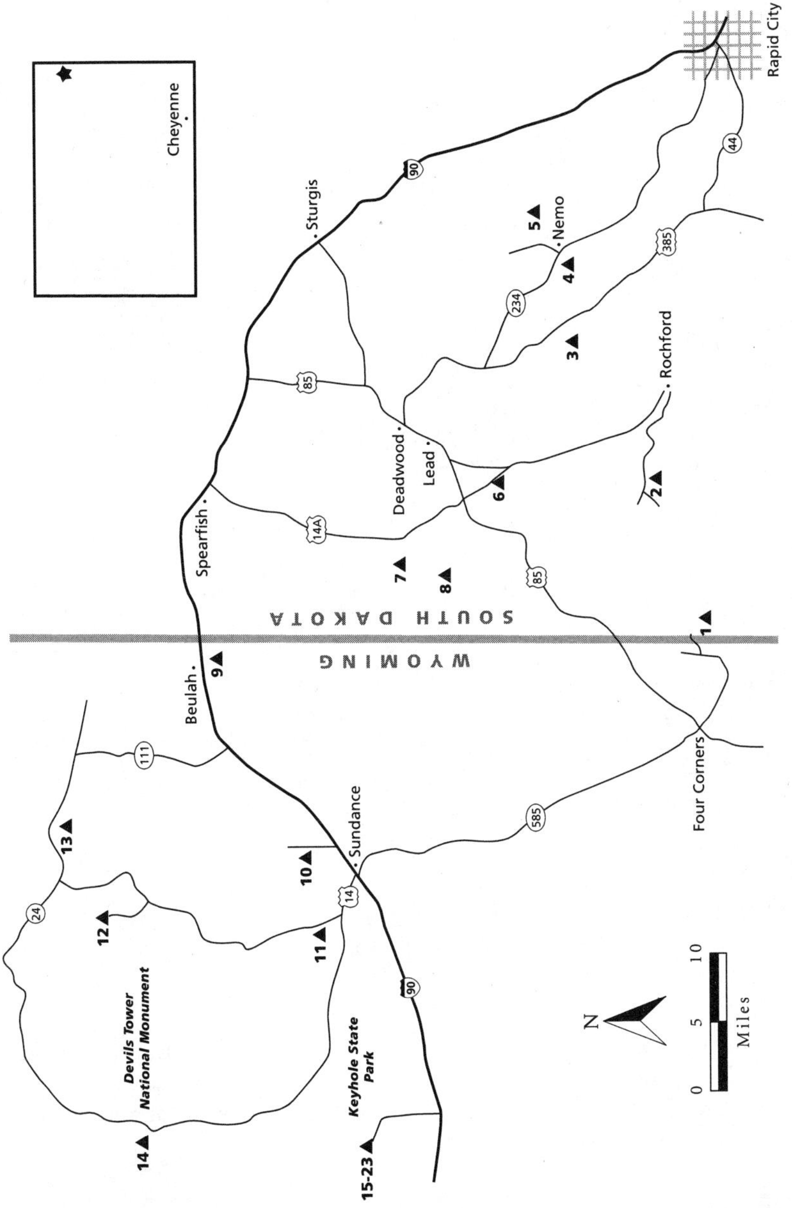

	Group sites	Tents	RV sites	Total sites	Picnic area	Toilets	Showers	Drinking water	Dump station	Phone	Disabled access	Fee ($)	Season	Can reserve	Length of stay	Recreation
1 Beaver Creek			8	8		V		X				$	All Year		14	FH
2 Black Fox			9	9		V						D	All Year		14	FH
3 Robaix Lake		16	37	53	X	F		X		X		$$	Partial	X	14	FBS
4 Boxelder Forks			13	13		V		X				$	Partial		14	FH
5 Dalton Lake			11	11	X	V		X				$	All Year		14	FHS
6 Hanna		6	7	13		V		X				$	Apr-Nov		10	FH
7 Rod and Gun			7	7		V		X				$	Apr-Nov	X	14	FH
8 Timon			7	7		V		X				$	Apr-Nov	X	14	FH
9 Sand Creek			D	D		V						N	All Year		5	F
10 Sundance Trails			10	10		V		X				$	Apr-Nov	X	14	H
11 Reuter			24	24		V		X				$	All Year	X	14	HM
12 Cook Lake		13	20	33	X	V		X				$$	All Year	X	14	FHB
13 Bearlodge			8	8		V						D	All Year			H
14 Devils Tower			50	50		F		X				$$	May-Sep			HWP
Keyhole State Park													**All Year**		**14**	
15 Pat's Point	1		36	36	X	V		X				$	All Year		14	FBSPW
16 Beach			3	3	X	V		X				$	All Year		14	FBSPW
17 Arch Rock			11	11		V						$	All Year		14	FBSPW
18 Homestead			50	50		V		X				$	All Year		14	FBSPW
19 Pronghorn			37	37	X	V		X			X	$	All Year		14	FBSPW
20 Cottonwood	1		29	29	X	V		X				$	All Year		14	FBSPW
21 Rocky Point			27	27	X	V						$	All Year		14	FBSPW
22 Coulter Bay	1		25	25	X	V						$	All Year		14	FBSPW
23 Wind Creek			20	20	X	V						$	All Year		14	FBSPW

F=flush toilets, V=vault toilets, D=donation, N=none, F=fishing, H=hiking, B=boating, S=swimming, M=mountain biking, P=photography, W=wildlife viewing

creek, with parking a bit of a walk. Aspen appear at different places, with granite outcrops defining the water flow. Directions to this campground are not well posted, which probably helps promote a sense of remoteness. The road is narrow and steep in places, so take your time.

2 Black Fox (South Dakota)

Location: 49 miles south of Spearfish.

Facilities: Vault toilets, fire rings, tables.

Sites: 9 for tents or RVs up to 45 feet long.
Fee: Donation, 14-day maximum stay.
Reservations: First-come, first-served.
Agency: Black Hills National Forest, Pactola Ranger District, 1-605-343-1567.
Activities: Fishing, hiking.
Finding the campground: Take U.S. Highway 14 Alternate south out of Spearfish for 20 miles. Turn left onto U.S. Highway 85 and travel 5 miles. Turn right onto the paved Forest Road 17 and travel 15 miles to Rochford. Stay to the right in Rochford and follow Forest Road 231 for 9 miles. Turn left onto Forest Road 233 and travel 0.5 mile. The campground is along the road on the left side.

About the campground: There is likely little traffic along the road where the majority of the parking units are. The ancient hand pump is no longer used to provide water, so be sure to bring plenty. Rapid Creek meanders past spruce trees and willow brush with semideep pools inviting anglers and hot feet alike. The trout spook easily, making for a greater challenge and offering evidence of continued use of this seemingly forgotten refuge.

Robaix Lake (South Dakota)

Location: 45 miles northwest of Rapid City.
Facilities: Vault and flush toilets, fire rings, tables, drinking water, picnic area, pay phone.
Sites: 16 for tents and 37 for RVs up to 45 feet long.
Fee: $$ per day, 14-day maximum stay.
Reservations: 1-877-444-6777.
Agency: Black Hills National Forest, Nemo Ranger District, 1-605-578-2744.
Activities: Swimming, fishing, boating (nonmotorized).
Finding the campground: Take U.S. Highway 44 south out of Rapid City for 24 miles. Turn right onto U.S. Highway 385 and travel 23 miles. Turn left onto Forest Road 255 and travel 0.5 mile. The campground is on the left.

About the campground: The refreshing waters of this small lake lure picnickers, anglers, and swimmers from near and far. All three of the camping loops are a short hike from the lake. The units are scattered among tall ponderosa pine. The sandy beaches along these 5 acres of mountain water have a specially designated swimming area with no lifeguard. A campground host is present. Firewood should be purchased or obtained elsewhere.

Boxelder Forks (South Dakota)

Location: 25 miles northwest of Rapid City.
Facilities: Vault toilets, fire pits, tables, drinking water.
Sites: 13 for tents or RVs up to 45 feet long.
Fee: $ per day, 14-day maximum stay.
Reservations: First-come, first-served.
Agency: Black Hills National Forest, Nemo Ranger District, 1-605-578-2744.

Activities: Fishing, hiking.
Finding the campground: Take U.S. Highway 44 south out of Rapid City. Turn right onto U.S. Highway 385. Turn right onto Nemo Road/County Road 234. At Nemo turn right onto Forest Road 140 (going past the Nemo Store) and travel for 2 miles. Note: The more traveled Ford Road just past the Nemo Store bears dead ahead, but it is not the road you want. Look for the bridge crossing the creek.

About the campground: The campground is nestled quietly within the pines, with Boxelder Creek bubbling through the shadows. Spruce and large ponderosa pine block out the burning sun's rays for most of the units. Where the shade is not too thick, the tall grass is. The fairly swift creek cuts the campground in two, with a footbridge shortcut to the toilets. A host stays at the campground. Firewood could take some energy and climbing, unless you purchase it from the host.

5 Dalton Lake (South Dakota)

Location: 25 miles northwest of Rapid City.
Facilities: Vault toilets, fire rings, tables, drinking water, picnic area.
Sites: 11 for tents or RVs up to 45 feet long.
Fee: $ per day, 14-day maximum stay.
Reservations: First-come, first-served.
Agency: Black Hills National Forest, Nemo Ranger District, 1-605-578-2744.
Activities: Fishing, hiking, swimming.
Finding the campground: Take U.S. Highway 44 south out of Rapid City. Turn right onto U.S. Highway 385 and travel 29 miles. Turn right onto Nemo Road/County Road 234 and travel 11 miles. Turn left onto Forest Road 26 and travel 4 miles. Turn right at the campground sign onto the otherwise unmarked gravel road and travel 4 miles.

About the campground: A rustic pole fence designates parking and units alike. Large spruce trees share the ground with younger aspen, resulting in plenty of shade. An old log structure shelters a huge fireplace to keep rain off any picnickers. Plenty of trout live in little Dalton Lake, but the water is a little cloudy. Between the moss and muddy-looking water, swimming might not be to your liking. Gathering firewood shouldn't be too difficult, but you will need a saw or axe. Most of the smaller pieces have already crackled away for previous visitors. This area does have a reputation for weekend parties, so during the week would be a better time to visit this pleasant spot.

6 Hanna (South Dakota)

Location: 20 miles south of Spearfish.
Facilities: Vault toilets, tables, fire pits, grills, drinking water.
Sites: 6 for tents and 7 for RVs up to 55 feet long.
Fee: $ per day, 10-day maximum stay.
Reservations: First-come, first-served.

Agency: Black Hills National Forest, Spearfish Ranger District, 1-605-642-4622.
Activities: Fishing, hiking.
Finding the campground: Take U.S. Highway 14 Alternate south out of Spearfish for 18 miles. Turn right onto U.S. Highway 85 and travel a short distance (the turn is almost in sight). At the Hanna Campground sign turn left and travel 2 miles.

About the campground: The crystal-clear waters of Spearfish Creek make their way past grassy meadows and tall spruce trees. Ponderosa pines blanket the mountains overlooking this peaceful place. The six tent sites require crossing the creek via a footbridge, creating a little more isolation. The longer units are in the sun. This out-of-the-way place seems to get less traffic than do other nearby campgrounds.

7 Rod and Gun (South Dakota)

Location: 15 miles south of Spearfish.
Facilities: Vault toilets, fire rings, tables, drinking water.
Sites: 7 for tents or RVs up to 50 feet long.
Fee: $ per day, 14-day maximum stay.
Reservations: 1-877-444-6777.
Agency: Black Hills National Forest, Spearfish Ranger District, 1-605-642-4622.
Activities: Fishing, hiking.
Finding the campground: Take U.S. Highway 14 Alternate south out of Spearfish for 12 miles. At Savoy turn right onto Forest Road 222 and travel 3 miles.

About the campground: The grass gets high here and the temperature can, too. The spruce and aspen trees hug the banks of the crystal-clear Little Spearfish Creek rushing past. Roughlock Falls is an attraction you will pass by on your way, and is well worth taking some time to explore. The falls are quite well hidden and require wading in the ice-cold, almost knee-deep water for a full view. A developed trail leads to the water's edge, where you must continue on ancient stones positioned with seekers and photographers in mind. Homestake Mining Company maintains the Roughlock Falls Picnic Area. Before embarking on this little adventure, it would be a good idea to secure your site. The campgrounds just past the falls fill quickly any time of the week.

8 Timon (South Dakota)

Location: 16 miles south of Spearfish.
Facilities: Vault toilets, fire rings, tables, drinking water.
Sites: 7 for tents or RVs up to 60 feet long.
Fee: $ per day, 14-day maximum stay.
Reservations: 1-877-444-6777.
Agency: Black Hills National Forest, Spearfish Ranger District, 1-605-642-4622.

Activities: Fishing, hiking.
Finding the campground: Take U.S. Highway 14 Alternate south out of Spearfish for 12 miles. At Savoy turn right onto Forest Road 222 and travel 4 miles.

About the campground: Shade is plentiful but room is not. Huge spruce trees and tall grass crowd the units even more. Don't get in a hurry. Deadfall is nearby, making the gathering of firewood less work than at other areas. This campground tends to fill first, possibly due to the better shade on hot days. If you prefer to have isolation and inactivity, this is not the best choice. Spectacular Spearfish Canyon and Roughlock Falls draw plenty of visitors, almost creating an overworked appearance. No doubt there will be quiet moments, but there is plenty of activity between.

9 Sand Creek

Location: 3 miles south of Beulah.
Facilities: Vault toilets.
Sites: Dispersed.
Fee: None, 5-day maximum stay.
Agency: Wyoming Game and Fish, 1-800-225-5996.
Activities: Fishing.
Finding the campground: Take the Ranch A exit, number 205, on Interstate 90 just west of the South Dakota border. Travel 3 miles south on the gravel Sand Creek Road.

About the campground: Camping is more allowed here than promoted. Elm trees spread shade and a sense of secrecy over grassy hollows scattered throughout. Crystal-clear Sand Creek still cuts away at the defiant banks. Ponderosa pines pepper the agreeable ground anywhere they can find it along the colorful limestone cliffs. Anglers from near and far frequent this blue-ribbon trout stream and tend to fill it to capacity on holidays. Exactly how many campers get to utilize this area is dependent upon the size and what kind of forethought individuals use. Most of the available firewood is gone, and private land surrounding the area requires that wood be brought in.

10 Sundance Trails

Location: 2 miles north of Sundance.
Facilities: Vault toilets, fire rings, tables, drinking water.
Sites: 6 for tents or RVs up to 25 feet long and 4 for longer units, primarily for horse trailers.
Fee: $ per day, 14-day maximum stay.
Reservations: 1-877-444-6777.
Agency: Black Hills National Forest, Bearlodge Ranger District, 1-307-283-1361.
Activities: Hiking, horseback riding (horses not provided).
Finding the campground: Leave Interstate 90 at the Port of Entry exit, number 189, and go north. Turn left toward Sundance and travel a short distance to

the Government Valley Road, where you'll find a large, commercial black-on-yellow camping sign to help you spot it. Turn right onto Government Valley Road and travel 2 miles. The campground is on the left side.

About the campground: Firewood and shade are in short supply here. The pine forest climbs up and away on the hill behind the parking areas with no attempt to interfere with the intense heat of the summer sun. This area is more of a jump-off point for horse riders to explore the backcountry of the Bearlodge. Unless you have horses or just don't like trees, it would be best to move on to another campground.

11 Reuter

Location: 4 miles west of Sundance.
Facilities: Vault toilets, fire rings, tables, drinking water.
Sites: 24 for tents or RVs up to 45 feet long.
Fee: $ per day, 14-day maximum stay.
Reservations: 1-877-444-6777.
Agency: Black Hills National Forest, Bearlodge Ranger District, 1-307-283-1361.
Activities: Hiking, mountain biking.
Finding the campground: Take U.S. Highway 14 at exit 185 on Interstate 90 for 1 mile west of Sundance. Turn right onto the paved Forest Road 838 and travel about 3 miles.

About the campground: Huge ponderosa pine trees are spaced just right so that too much sun can't get in. Chipmunks, scolding pine squirrels, and multiple birds share their home with an occasional whitetail deer. Please keep in mind that this is truly their home, and we are the visitors. This campground rarely fills up because of nearby Cook Lake. The long and somewhat tricky road back to the lake suggests you stay here at Reuter and take advantage of the excellent picnic area on the lakeshore via access in a more compact vehicle, assuming you have that option.

12 Cook Lake

Location: 21 miles north of Sundance.
Facilities: Vault toilets, fire rings, tables, drinking water, picnic area.
Sites: 13 for tents and 20 for tents or RVs up to 45 feet long.
Fee: $$ per day, 14-day maximum stay.
Reservations: 1-877-444-6777.
Agency: Black Hills National Forest, Bearlodge Ranger District, 1-307-283-1361.
Activities: Fishing, hiking, boating.
Finding the campground: Take U.S. Highway 14 at exit 185 on Interstate 90 west of Sundance for 1 mile. At the Cook Lake Recreation Area sign, turn right onto Forest Road 838 and travel 13 miles. Forest Road 838 turns to gravel in about 7 miles. Turn right onto Forest Road 843 and travel about 2.5 miles. Bear

left to continue on FR 843 and travel 3.5 miles. Turn left onto Forest Road 842 and travel 1 mile to Cook Lake.

About the campground: Cost is dependent upon which of the two loops you choose. The more modern Loop B costs the most, though it is the farthest from the lake. As of this writing, a notice posted on the hand pump for drinking water advised that it had not been tested. Tall ponderosa pines are far apart between cut grass. The Cliff Swallow Trail takes off from this area and offers 3.5 miles of backcountry exploration. Loop A houses the tents-only units for less cost and the few units that get close to the lakeshore. Beaver lodges and big pine trees share the shoreline, with the picnic area between the two loops. Aspen sneak between pine and grass at different places along the 30 acres of Cook Lake. A host is present at Loop A. Gathering firewood could involve some effort unless you choose to purchase it from the host. This area fills fast on weekends, so reservations are recommended. If you plan on only one night of camping, this would not be the best place. The road leading here can be tricky, with large trucks making it almost treacherous. If you plan to stay awhile, then by all means the hazards are worth enduring.

13 Bearlodge

Location: 24 miles north of Sundance.
Facilities: Vault toilets, fire rings, tables.
Sites: 8 for tents or RVs up to 20 feet long.

A picnic area lies along the shore of Cook Lake, while campsites can be found at either end.

Fee: Donation.
Reservations: First-come, first-served.
Agency: Black Hills National Forest, Bearlodge Ranger District, 1-307-283-1361.
Activities: Hiking.
Finding the campground: Take Interstate 90 east out of Sundance for 8 miles to the Alladin exit/exit 199. Turn left onto Wyoming Highway 111 and travel 9 miles. Turn left onto Wyoming Highway 24 and travel 7 miles. The campground is on the left side of the road.

About the campground: Even without water this forgotten campground is a real prize for those who want to avoid the "herd." The grass and brush grow unhindered by many feet. Deadfall is plentiful, though be careful to clear away weeds and dry grass from the unused fire rings. The back road to Devils Tower offers wildlife viewing and a side of the monument few will see. If you have a taste for the unique or unusual, with respect to discovering the life beyond billboards and fast-food places, this is a good option.

14 Devils Tower National Monument

Location: 26 miles northwest of Sundance.
Facilities: Flush toilets, fire rings, tables, drinking water.
Sites: 50 for tents or RVs up to 30 feet long.
Fee: $$ per day (including entrance fee).

Even from its backside, Devils Tower is a distinctive landmark in northeastern Wyoming.

Reservations: First-come, first-served.
Agency: Devils Tower National Monument, 1-307-467-5283.
Activities: Hiking, wildlife viewing, photography.
Finding the campground: Take U.S. Highway 14 at exit 185 on Interstate 90 west of Sundance for 20 miles. Turn right onto Wyoming Highway 24 and travel 6 miles. The monument is on the left side of the road.

About the campground: Legend states that seven Native American girls took refuge from a bear on a rock at this site long ago. As the aggressive bear clawed at the rock, it shot upward, keeping the girls from its grasp. The claw marks are still very visible today. Huge cottonwood trees shade the paved road of the campground. Pullouts accommodate RVs up to 30 feet long, though it can get cramped. Parking in the summer has limitations. Visitors pulling trailers must unhook them in special parking areas before proceeding to the end of the park road. Campers should find a spot and set up first. The second week of August is very crowded.

Keyhole State Park

15 Keyhole State Park: Pat's Point

Location: 7 miles north of Interstate 90, near Moorcroft.
Facilities: Vault toilets, fire rings, tables, drinking water, boat ramp, picnic area, playground, group shelter.
Sites: 36 for tents or RVs up to 40-plus feet long.
Fee: $ per day (including entrance fee), 14-day maximum stay.
Agency: Keyhole State Park, 1-307-756-3596.
Activities: Fishing, boating, swimming, picnicking, photography, bird watching.
Finding the campground: The park can be accessed by either of two ways: 1) Take the Keyhole State Park exit on Interstate 90 at exit 165, and drive north for 7 miles; or 2) leave Interstate 90 at either exit 153 or exit 154 and enter Moorcroft. Drive into town and turn north onto U.S. Highway 14. This road will go under the interstate between these two exits with no on or off-ramp access. Drive 5 miles north to the Pine Haven Road/Wyoming Highway 113. Turn right onto this paved road and drive 5 miles east to the Pine Haven turnoff. Turn left onto this paved road and drive about 2 miles to Pine Haven.

About the campground: Devils Tower, more than 200 types of birds, and large fish await you at this beautiful park. Sandstone outcrops poke out of the rolling pine hills that house the camping areas. The Wind Creek and Coulter Bay areas tend to be a bit more flat with less shade. Water recreation is the major attraction, providing a refreshing relief from the intense summer sun.

16 Keyhole State Park: Beach Area

Location: 7 miles north of Interstate 90, near Moorcroft.
Facilities: Vault toilets, fire rings, tables, drinking water, picnic area.
Sites: 3 for tents or RVs up to 40-plus feet long.
Fee: $ per day (including entrance fee), 14-day maximum stay.
Agency: Keyhole State Park, 1-307-756-3596.
Activities: Fishing, boating, swimming, picnicking, photography, bird watching.
Finding the campground: The park can be accessed by either of two ways: 1) Take the Keyhole State Park exit on Interstate 90 at the Pine Ridge Road/exit 165 and drive north for 7 miles; or 2) leave Interstate 90 at either exit 153 or exit 154 and enter Moorcroft. Drive into town and turn north onto U.S. Highway 14. This road will go under the interstate between these 2 exits with no on or off ramp access. Drive 5 miles north to the Pine Haven Road/Wyoming Highway 113. Turn right onto this paved road and drive 5 miles east to the Pine Haven turnoff. Turn left onto this paved road and drive about 2 miles to Pine Haven.

About the campground: Devils Tower, more than 200 types of birds, and large fish await you at this beautiful park. Sandstone outcrops poke out of the rolling pine hills that house the camping areas. The Wind Creek and Coulter Bay areas tend to be a bit more flat with less shade. Water recreation is the major attraction, providing a refreshing relief from the intense summer sun.

17 Keyhole State Park: Arch Rock

Location: 7 miles north of Interstate 90, near Moorcroft.
Facilities: Vault toilets, fire rings, tables.
Sites: 11 for tents or RVs up to 40 plus feet long.
Fee: $ per day (including entrance fee), 14-day maximum stay.
Agency: Keyhole State Park, 1-307-756-3596.
Activities: Fishing, boating, swimming, picnicking, photography, bird watching.
Finding the campground: The park can be accessed by either of two ways: 1) Take the Keyhole State Park exit on Interstate 90 at the Pine Ridge Road/exit 165, and drive north for 7 miles; or 2) leave Interstate 90 at either exit 153 or exit 154 and enter Moorcroft. Drive into town and turn north onto U.S. Highway 14. This road will go under the interstate between these 2 exits with no on or off ramp access. Drive 5 miles north to the Pine Haven Road/Wyoming Highway 113. Turn right onto this paved road and drive 5 miles east to the Pine Haven turnoff. Turn left onto this paved road and drive about 2 miles to Pine Haven.

About the campground: See Pat's Point Campground (above).

18 Keyhole State Park: Homestead

Location: 7 miles north of Interstate 90, near Moorcroft.
Facilities: Vault toilets, fire rings, tables, drinking water.
Sites: 50 for tents or RVs up to 40-plus feet long.
Fee: $ per day (including entrance fee), 14-day maximum stay.
Agency: Keyhole State Park, 1-307-756-3596.
Activities: Fishing, boating, swimming, picnicking, photography, bird watching.
Finding the campground: The park can be accessed by either of two ways: 1) Take the Keyhole State Park exit on Interstate 90 at the Pine Ridge Road/exit 165, and drive north for 7 miles; or 2) leave Interstate 90 at either exit 153 or exit 154 and enter Moorcroft. Drive into town and turn north onto U.S. Highway 14. This road will go under the interstate between these 2 exits with no on or off ramp access. Drive 5 miles north to the Pine Haven Road/Wyoming Highway 113. Turn right onto this paved road and drive 5 miles east to the Pine Haven turnoff. Turn left onto this paved road and drive about 2 miles to Pine Haven.

About the campground: Devils Tower, more than 200 types of birds, and large fish await you at this beautiful park. Sandstone outcrops poke out of the rolling pine hills that house the camping areas. The Wind Creek and Coulter Bay areas tend to be a bit more flat with less shade. Water recreation is the major attraction, providing a refreshing relief from the intense summer sun.

19 Keyhole State Park: Pronghorn

Location: 7 miles north of Interstate 90, near Moorcroft.
Facilities: Vault toilets, fire rings, tables, drinking water, picnic area, playground.
Sites: 37 for tents or RVs up to 40-plus feet long.
Fee: $ per day (including entrance fee), 14-day maximum stay.
Agency: Keyhole State Park, 1-307-756-3596.
Activities: Fishing, boating, swimming, picnicking, photography, bird watching.
Finding the campground: The park can be accessed by either of two ways: 1) Take the Keyhole State Park exit on Interstate 90 at the Pine Ridge Road/exit 165, and drive north for 7 miles; or 2) leave Interstate 90 at either exit 153 or exit 154 and enter Moorcroft. Drive into town and turn north onto U.S. Highway 14. This road will go under the interstate between these 2 exits with no on or off ramp access. Drive 5 miles north to the Pine Haven Road/Wyoming Highway 113. Turn right onto this paved road and drive 5 miles east to the Pine Haven turnoff. Turn left onto this paved road and drive about 2 miles to Pine Haven.

About the campground: Devils Tower, more than 200 types of birds, and large fish await you at this beautiful park. Sandstone outcrops poke out of the rolling pine hills that house the camping areas. The Wind Creek and Coulter Bay areas tend to be a bit more flat with less shade. Water recreation is the major attraction, providing a refreshing relief from the intense summer sun.

20 Keyhole State Park: Cottonwood Area

Location: 7 miles north of Interstate 90, near Moorcroft.
Facilities: Vault toilets, fire rings, tables, drinking water, picnic area, playground, group shelter.
Sites: 29 for tents or RVs up to 40-plus feet long.
Fee: $ per day (including entrance fee), 14-day maximum stay.
Agency: Keyhole State Park, 1-307-756-3596.
Activities: Fishing, boating, swimming, picnicking, photography, bird watching.
Finding the campground: The park can be accessed by either of two ways: 1) Take the Keyhole State Park exit on Interstate 90 at the Pine Ridge Road/exit 165, and drive north for 7 miles; or 2) leave Interstate 90 at either exit 153 or exit 154 and enter Moorcroft. Drive into town and turn north onto U.S. Highway 14. This road will go under the interstate between these 2 exits with no on or off ramp access. Drive 5 miles north to the Pine Haven Road/Wyoming Highway 113. Turn right onto this paved road and drive 5 miles east to the Pine Haven turnoff. Turn left onto this paved road and drive about 2 miles to Pine Haven.

About the campground: Devils Tower, more than 200 types of birds, and large fish await you at this beautiful park. Sandstone outcrops poke out of the rolling pine hills that house the camping areas. The Wind Creek and Coulter Bay areas tend to be a bit more flat with less shade. Water recreation is the major attraction, providing a refreshing relief from the intense summer sun.

21 Keyhole State Park: Rocky Point

Location: 7 miles north of Interstate 90, near Moorcroft.
Facilities: Vault toilets, fire rings, tables, picnic area, boat ramp.
Sites: 27 for tents or RVs up to 40-plus feet long.
Fee: $ per day (including entrance fee), 14-day maximum stay.
Agency: Keyhole State Park, 1-307-756-3596.
Activities: Fishing, boating, swimming, picnicking, photography, bird watching.
Finding the campground: The park can be accessed by either of two ways: 1) Take the Keyhole State Park exit on Interstate 90 at the Pine Ridge Road/exit 165 and drive north for 7 miles; or 2) leave Interstate 90 at either exit 153 or exit 154 and enter Moorcroft. Drive into town and turn north onto U.S. Highway 14. This road will go under the interstate between these 2 exits with no on or off ramp access. Drive 5 miles north to the Pine Haven Road/Wyoming Highway 113. Turn right onto this paved road and drive 5 miles east to the Pine Haven turnoff. Turn left onto this paved road and drive about 2 miles to Pine Haven.

About the campground: Devils Tower, more than 200 types of birds, and large fish await you at this beautiful park. Sandstone outcrops poke out of the rolling pine hills that house the camping areas. The Wind Creek and Coulter Bay areas tend to be a bit more flat with less shade. Water recreation is the major attraction, providing a refreshing relief from the intense summer sun.

22 Keyhole State Park: Coulter Bay

Location: 7 miles north of Interstate 90, near Moorcroft.
Facilities: Vault toilets, fire rings, tables, picnic area, group shelter, boat ramp.
Sites: 25 for tents or RVs up to 40-plus feet long.
Fee: $ per day (including entrance fee), 14-day maximum stay.
Agency: Keyhole State Park, 1-307-756-3596.
Activities: Fishing, boating, swimming, picnicking, photography, bird watching.
Finding the campground: The park can be accessed by either of two ways: 1) Take the Keyhole State Park exit on Interstate 90 at the Pine Ridge Road/exit 165, and drive north for 7 miles; or 2) leave Interstate 90 at either exit 153 or exit 154 and enter Moorcroft. Drive into town and turn north onto U.S. Highway 14. This road will go under the interstate between these 2 exits with no on or off ramp access. Drive 5 miles north to the Pine Haven Road/Wyoming Highway 113. Turn right onto this paved road and drive 5 miles east to the Pine Haven turnoff. Turn left onto this paved road and drive about 2 miles to Pine Haven.

About the campground: Devils Tower, more than 200 types of birds, and large fish await you at this beautiful park. Sandstone outcrops poke out of the rolling pine hills that house the camping areas. The Wind Creek and Coulter Bay areas tend to be a bit more flat with less shade. Water recreation is the major attraction, providing a refreshing relief from the intense summer sun.

23 Keyhole State Park: Wind Creek

Location: 7 miles north of Interstate 90, near Moorcroft.
Facilities: Vault toilets, fire rings, tables, picnic area, boat ramp.
Sites: 20 for tents or RVs up to 40-plus feet long.
Fee: $ per day (including entrance fee), 14-day maximum stay.
Agency: Keyhole State Park, 1-307-756-3596.
Activities: Fishing, boating, swimming, picnicking, photography, bird watching.
Finding the campground: The park can be accessed by either of two ways: 1) Take the Keyhole State Park exit on Interstate 90 at the Pine Ridge Road/exit 165, and drive north for 7 miles; or 2) leave Interstate 90 at either exit 153 or exit 154 and enter Moorcroft. Drive into town and turn north onto U.S. Highway 14. This road will go under the interstate between these 2 exits with no on or off ramp access. Drive 5 miles north to the Pine Haven Road/Wyoming Highway 113. Turn right onto this paved road and drive 5 miles east to the

Pine Haven turnoff. Turn left onto this paved road and drive about 2 miles to Pine Haven.

About the campground: Devils Tower, more than 200 types of birds, and large fish await you at this beautiful park. Sandstone outcrops poke out of the rolling pine hills that house the camping areas. The Wind Creek and Coulter Bay areas tend to be a bit more flat with less shade. Water recreation is the major attraction, providing a refreshing relief from the intense summer sun.

Black Hills South

Lakes and reservoirs dominate this section, which also holds popular, more recently built attractions. The Mount Rushmore National Monument and the Crazy Horse Monument are obvious destinations, but for the more inquisitive there are numerous other treasures to discover. Before his defeat at the Battle of the Little Bighorn in 1876, Lieutenant Colonel George Armstrong Custer camped in various places throughout this area, and members of his party discovered gold here, opening the area up to exploration and settlement.

Water sports abound in the many reservoirs with scenic pine-forested hills for a background. In the evenings, crackling fires and cool breezes make an excellent setting for roasted marshmallows. The gentle lapping of waves along the shoreline can be a soothing addition to a brilliantly starlit night as well.

Custer State Park presents camping and abundant wildlife in the midst of spectacular geologic formations. Narrow tunnels push through adequately named needle spires of hard granite with countless cubbyholes to explore. An old fire lookout tower invites visitors to hike up Harney Peak, the highest point in the Black Hills, for the chance to see five states from one spot. Naturally the weather conditions must smile favorably on the endeavor. All the same, a moderately difficult hike rewards the conquerors.

Campers at Horsethief Lake need drive only a couple of miles to view the imposing faces of Mount Rushmore.

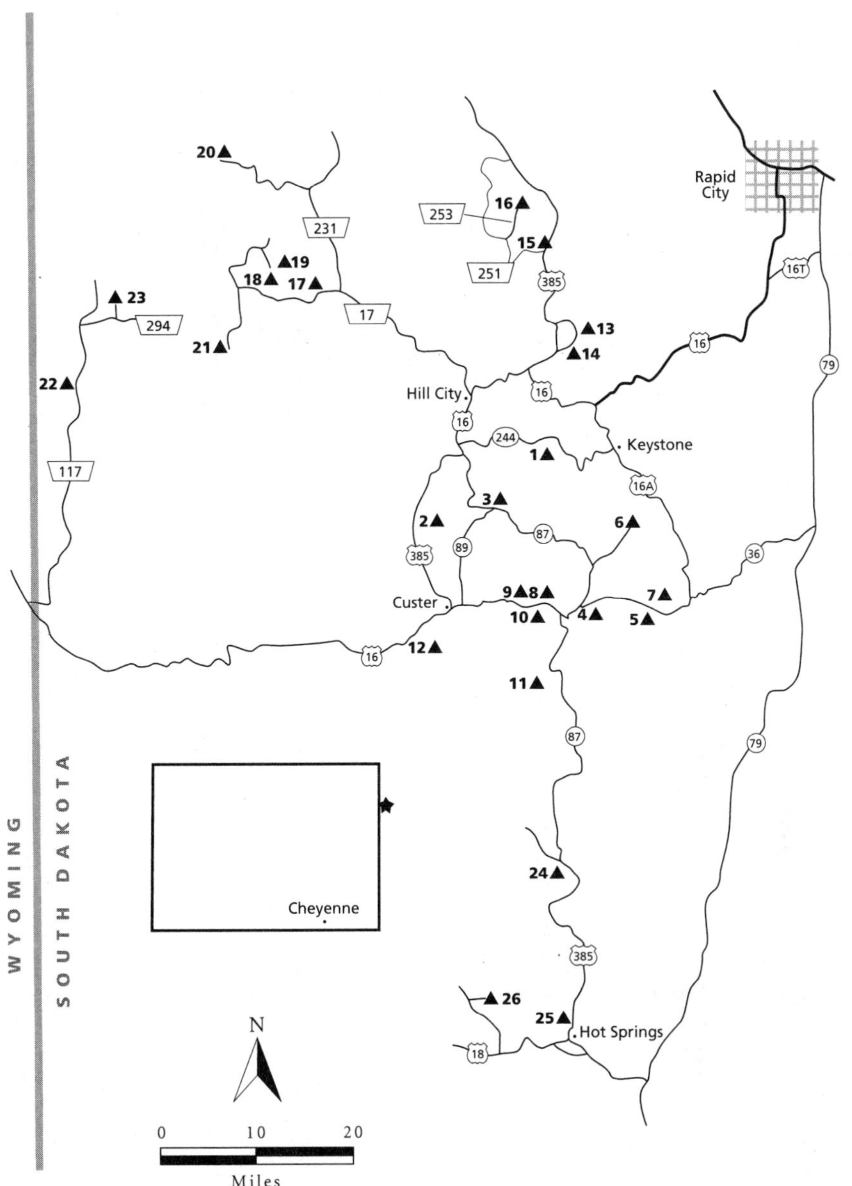

Rapid City
Hill City
Keystone
Custer
Hot Springs
Cheyenne
WYOMING
SOUTH DAKOTA
N
0
10
20
Miles
1
2
3
4
5
6
7
8
9
10
11
12
13
14
15
16
17
18
19
20
21
22
23
24
25
26
16
16A
16T
18
17
36
79
87
89
117
231
244
251
253
294
385

	Group sites	Tents	RV sites	Total sites	Picnic area	Toilets	Showers	Drinking water	Dump station	Phone	Disabled access	Fee ($)	Season	Can reserve	Length of stay	Recreation
1 Horsethief Lake		8	18	26		F		X				$$	Summer	X	14	FHB
2 Oreville			25	25		F		X		X		$$	Summer	X	14	FH
3 Sylvan Lake			39	39		F	X	X			X	$$	Apr-Oct	X		FHS
4 Legion Lake			25	25		F	X	X				$$	Apr-Oct	X		FHBS
5 Game Lodge			57	57		F	X	X	X	X	X	$$	Apr-Oct	X		FHSC
6 Center Lake		5	66	71		F	X	X				$$	Apr-Oct	X		FHBS
7 Grace Coolidge		4	22	26		F	X	X		X	X	$$	Apr-Oct			FHW
8 Bismark Lake			23	23	X	V		X				$$	Part Year	X	14	FB
9 Stockade Lake North			43	43		C	X	X		X		$$	Apr-Oct	X		FHB
10 Stockade Lake South			23	23		C	X	X				$$	Apr-Oct			FHB
11 Blue Bell		4	29	33		F		X				$$	Apr-Oct	X		H
12 Comanche Park		7	26	33		V		X				$	Part Year	X	14	HW
13 North Cove	5			5		V		X				$$$$	Part Year	X		FHBS
14 Sheridan South			126	126	X	F		X			X	$$	Part Year	X	14	FHBS
15 Pactola		39	45	84		F		X			X	$$	Summer	X	14	FHBS
16 Bear Gulch	1		8	9		V		X				$$$$	Summer	X	14	FHBS
17 Dutchman			45	45		V		X				$	Part Year	X	14	FHBSM
18 Whitetail			17	17		V		X				$	All Year	X	14	FHBS
19 Custer Trails		9	16	25	X	V		X				$	Summer		14	FHBS
20 Castle Peak			9	9		V						D	All Year		14	FH
21 Ditch Creek			13	13		V		X				$	All Year		14	FH
22 Moon			3	3		V						D	All Year		14	H
23 Redbank Spring			4	4		V						D	All Year		14	HW
24 Elk Mountain		21	53	74		C						$	Apr-Oct		14	HW
25 Cold Brook Reservoir			11	11		V						$			14	FS
26 Cotton Wood Springs			18	18		C		X				$			14	FH

C=comfort station, F=flush toilets, V=vault toilets, D=donation, F=fishing, H=hiking, B=boating, S=swimming, C=rock climbing, M=mountain biking, W=wildlife viewing

1 Horsethief Lake (South Dakota)

Location: 35 miles southwest of Rapid City.
Facilities: Flush toilets, fire rings, grills, tables, drinking water.
Sites: 8 for tents and 18 for tents or RVs up to 45 feet long.
Fee: $$ per day, 14-day maximum stay.
Reservations: 1-877-444-6777.

Agency: Black Hills National Forest, Harney Ranger District, 1-605-574-2534.
Activities: Fishing, hiking, boating (gas-powered motorboats are not allowed).
Finding the campground: Take U.S. Highway 16 south out of Rapid City for 29 miles, passing through Hill City. Turn left onto South Dakota Highway 244 and travel 6 miles (toward Mount Rushmore). The campground is on the right side of the road.

About the campground: Granite formations unique to the Black Hills look out over old and high ponderosa pine trees. Ten-acre Horsethief Lake is reportedly stocked twice a day with better-than-average trout. Local anglers and visitors alike compete for a tight line. Reservations should be made well in advance; reports have indicated that this campground can fill up a year in advance. Mount Rushmore is about 2 miles from this popular campground, just north of wildlife-rich Custer State Park. A host stays in the campground and firewood is for sale.

2 Oreville (South Dakota)

Location: 28 miles southwest of Rapid City.
Facilities: Flush toilets, fire rings, grills, tables, drinking water, pay phone.
Sites: 25 for tents or RVs up to 50 feet long.
Fee: $$ per day, 14-day maximum stay.
Reservations: 1-877-444-6777.
Agency: Black Hills National Forest, Harney Ranger District, 1-605-574-2534.
Activities: Fishing, hiking.
Finding the campground: Take U.S. Highway 16 south out of Rapid City for 28 miles, passing through Hill City. The campground is on the left side of the road.

About the campground: The units have plenty of space between pine trees, with aspen thickets sprinkled haphazardly about. Granite outcrops invite young and old explorers alike. The forest quietly hides special formations from passersby. Spring Creek sneaks past this area just across the highway out of sight, and as a result the trout here have far less pressure than other spots. Be very careful when crossing the highway; traffic is very active and has a reputation for going well over the speed limit. This campground is centrally located for most points of interest in the Black Hills. If you want to stay here, reservations must be made well in advance. Firewood can be purchased from the host present at the campground. Gathering deadfall will require some extra work.

3 Custer State Park: Sylvan Lake (South Dakota)

Location: 41 miles southwest of Rapid City.
Facilities: Vault and flush toilets, fire rings, tables, drinking water, warm showers.
Sites: 39 for tents or RVs up to 20 feet long.
Fee: $$ per day.

Reservations: 1-800-710-2267.
Agency: Custer State Park, 1-605-255-4515.
Activities: Fishing, hiking, swimming, scenic drives.
Finding the campground: Take U.S. Highway 16 south out of Rapid City for 32 miles. In Custer turn left onto Alternate U.S. Highway 16 and travel 2 miles. Turn left onto South Dakota Highway 89 and travel 7 miles.

About the campground: Spruce trees separate the compact sites and also provide a green curtain for isolation. Parking units accommodate tents and cab-over campers best. Shower facilities add to the desire for a longer stay, but reservations are advised if you want to stay here at all. Generally as one camper pulls out, another is waiting to pull in. Sylvan Lake is a short distance away. A very active picnic area clings to the shoreline, with backcountry trails beckoning those who want to temporarily escape the crowd. The spectacular Needles Highway is a must. Keep in mind that very narrow, low tunnels do not accommodate large vehicles. Take your time and camera when traveling this stretch.

4 Custer State Park: Legion Lake (South Dakota)

Location: 42 miles southwest of Rapid City.
Facilities: Flush toilets, fire rings, tables, drinking water, warm showers.
Sites: 25 for tents or RVs up to 50 feet long.

Sandy beaches lure campers, picnickers, and swimmers to Sylvan Lake.

Fee: $$ per day.
Reservations: 1-800-710-2267.
Agency: Custer State Park, 1-605-255-4515.
Activities: Fishing, hiking, boating, swimming.
Finding the campground: Take South Dakota Highway 79 south out of Rapid City for 18 miles. Turn right onto South Dakota Highway 36 and travel 9 miles. Turn left onto Alternate U.S. Highway 16 and travel 15 miles.

About the campground: These units are well spaced, with huge ponderosa pines scattered between the two sections. Legion Lake is just across the highway along with a store. The picnic area is closer to the lake, offering a pleasant place for a sandwich. This is a good place to set up a central base camp for large trailers and RVs. A host is present, but does not offer firewood.

Custer State Park: Game Lodge (South Dakota)

Location: 28 miles southwest of Rapid City.
Facilities: Vault and flush toilets, fire rings, tables, drinking water, public telephone, RV dump, warm showers.
Sites: 57 for tents or RVs up to 60 feet long.
Fee: $$ per day.
Reservations: 1-800-710-2267.
Agency: Custer State Park, 1-605-255-4515.
Activities: Fishing, hiking, swimming, rock climbing.
Finding the campground: Take South Dakota Highway 79 south out of Rapid City for 18 miles. Turn right onto South Dakota Highway 36 and travel 9 miles. Turn left onto Alternate U.S. Highway 16 and travel 9 miles.

About the campground: Ash trees are liberally planted among the paved parking units. Short grass testifies to the use of mowers for upkeep. Cold water is available for a refreshing dip in the small pool near the entrance. The pine forest borders one side of the campground, offering some shade though most units are in the sun.

Custer State Park: Center Lake (South Dakota)

Location: 40 miles south of Rapid City.
Facilities: Vault and flush toilets, fire rings, tables, drinking water, warm showers.
Sites: 5 for tents and 66 for tents or RVs up to 40 feet long.
Fee: $$ per day.
Reservations: 1-800-710-2267.
Agency: Custer State Park, 1-605-255-4515.
Activities: Fishing, hiking, boating, swimming.
Finding the campground: Take South Dakota Highway 79 south out of Rapid City for 18 miles. Turn right onto South Dakota Highway 36 and travel 9 miles. Turn left onto Alternate U.S. Highway 16 and travel 9 miles. Turn right onto the Needles Highway and travel 3 miles. Turn right at the Center Lake sign and travel 1 mile.

The low, narrow tunnels along the spectacular Needles Highway were not made to accommodate RVs.

About the campground: Upper and Lower Center Lake Campgrounds are separated from the tent area. Shade is plentiful under the thick ponderosa pine. The hike from the upper campground can seem fairly long, but the shock of cold water on hot feet will drown the memory. The extremely scenic drive along the Needles Highway is a must, but be advised of very narrow, short tunnels.

Custer State Park: Grace Coolidge (South Dakota)

Location: 31 miles southwest of Rapid City.
Facilities: Vault and flush toilets, fire rings, grills, tables, drinking water, public telephone, warm showers.
Sites: 4 for tents or 22 for tents or RVs up to 45 feet long.
Fee: $$ per day.
Reservations: First-come, first-served.
Agency: Custer State Park, 1-605-255-4515.
Activities: Fishing, hiking, wildlife viewing.
Finding the campground: Take South Dakota Highway 79 south out of Rapid City for 18 miles. Turn right onto South Dakota Highway 36 and travel 9 miles. Turn left onto Alternate U.S. Highway 16 and travel 4 miles.

About the campground: Four tent sites are located across the highway in a secluded area. The shower offers a very refreshing place to visit after hiking all day. Oak trees dominate the area.

Bismark Lake (South Dakota)

Location: 48 miles southwest of Rapid City.
Facilities: Vault toilets, fire rings, tables, drinking water, picnic area, boat ramp.
Sites: 23 for tents or RVs up to 55 feet long.
Fee: $$ per day, 14-day maximum stay.
Reservations: 1-877-444-6777.
Agency: Black Hills National Forest, Custer Ranger District, 1-605-673-4853.
Activities: Fishing, boating, scenic drives.
Finding the campground: Take South Dakota Highway 79 south out of Rapid City for 18 miles. Turn right onto South Dakota Highway 36 and travel 9 miles. Turn left onto Alternate U.S. Highway 16 and travel 20 miles. At the sign turn right and travel 0.5 mile.

About the campground: Old ponderosa pine trees and granite outcrops collide, with resulting rough terrain. An occasional aspen grove appears at random. There are three loops of parking to choose from. Units 18 through 23 are closest to the lake and boat ramp. Canoeing is the activity of choice; however, electric motors are allowed. A picnic area shares the boat ramp for a daily-use fee. A host occupies one of the available units. Firewood would best be bought or brought, depending on your capacity. This is a pleasant area to spend some time exploring.

9 Custer State Park: Stockade Lake North (South Dakota)

Location: 38 miles southwest of Rapid City.
Facilities: Comfort station, vault toilets, fire rings, tables, drinking water, public telephone, warm showers.
Sites: 43 for tents or RVs up to 60 feet long.
Fee: $$ per day.
Reservations: 1-800-710-2267.
Agency: Custer State Park, 1-605-255-4515.
Activities: Fishing, hiking, boating.
Finding the campground: Take South Dakota Highway 79 south out of Rapid City for 18 miles. Turn right onto South Dakota Highway 36 and travel 9 miles. Turn left onto Alternate U.S. Highway 16 and travel 20 miles. Follow the signs to Stockade Lake North.

About the campground: Sites must be reserved if you want to stay here, though if there is a cancellation a stay of one night is allowed with no guarantee of another. A host is present at the campground. The pine forest housing this campground appears to have been thinned, but not enough to lose any shade. Juniper pops up here and there among the rock outcrops. Larger RVs may have some work involved in leveling up in this uneven terrain. Members of Custer's expedition reported finding gold on their way through here. As a result John Gordon illegally led a group of gold seekers here in the fall of 1874. The group eluded army patrols assigned to keep "white men" out of the Black Hills. Seven cabins and the stockade walls were constructed in three weeks. A bitter winter and little gold found many of the original party leaving the following year. The Gordon party was eventually evicted and escorted to Fort Laramie in an attempt to honor the treaty allowing the Native Americans to possess the Black Hills. All too soon, however, gold fever infected more people than the army could dissuade. The stockade has been rebuilt and is standing at its original place a short distance from the lake named for it.

10 Custer State Park: Stockade Lake South (South Dakota)

Location: 47 miles southwest of Rapid City.
Facilities: Comfort station, fire rings, tables, drinking water, warm showers.
Sites: 23 for tents or RVs up to 45 feet long.
Fee: $$ per day.
Reservations: First-come, first-served.
Agency: Custer State Park, 1-605-255-4515.
Activities: Fishing, hiking, boating, waterskiing.
Finding the campground: Take South Dakota Highway 79 south out of Rapid City for 18 miles. Turn right onto South Dakota Highway 36 and travel 9 miles. Turn left onto Alternate U.S. Highway 16 and travel 20 miles. Follow the signs to Stockade Lake South.

About the campground: Fireplaces built by the Civilian Conservation Corps of the 1930s both fit in this historic place and pleasantly add a striking contrast to the wild surroundings. At first glance, you might think these stone structures are left over from a cabin burning down. Yellow-bellied marmots willingly share their home with ever-changing visitors and scurry from one place to another stopping now and then for a picture. The heated comfort station becomes a popular meeting place on a chilly day.

Custer State Park: Blue Bell (South Dakota)

Location: 45 miles southwest of Rapid City.
Facilities: Flush toilets, fire rings, grills, tables, drinking water.
Sites: 4 for tents and 29 for tents or RVs up to 50 feet long.
Fee: $$ per day.
Reservations: 1-800-710-2267.
Agency: Custer State Park, 1-605-255-4515.
Activities: Hiking, horseback riding.
Finding the campground: Take South Dakota Highway 79 south out of Rapid City for 18 miles. Turn right onto South Dakota Highway 36 and travel 9 miles. Turn left onto Alternate U.S. Highway 16 and travel 12 miles. Turn left onto South Dakota Highway 87 and drive 6 miles.

About the campground: Cut grass fills the long distance between towering ponderosa pines. These sites are only available on a reservation basis, with a requirement of two days advance notice—and you may need to make them several months in advance for a summer stay. Firewood is sold at the store across the highway. A host is available at the campground.

Comanche Park (South Dakota)

Location: 51 miles southwest of Rapid City.
Facilities: Vault toilets, fire pits, tables, drinking water.
Sites: 7 for tents and 26 for RVs up to 45 feet long.
Fee: $ per day, 14-day maximum stay.
Reservations: 1-877-444-6777.
Agency: Black Hills National Forest, Custer Ranger District, 1-605-673-4853.
Activities: Hiking, wildlife viewing.
Finding the campground: Take U.S. Highway 16 south out of Rapid City for 46 miles. Continue on U.S. Highway 16 west out of Custer for 5 miles. The campground is on the left side of the highway.

About the campground: Tall pines populate this campground, with grassy spaces between. This campground is named for a horse named Comanche, the only survivor of Lieutenant Colonel George Armstrong Custer's 7th Cavalry, defeated at the Battle of the Little Bighorn. Captain Keogh captured this horse from the Comanches previously, and it camped near here with Custer's expedition during the winter of 1874. The tent sites are separated from the RVs by a fair distance; however, they are located close to the highway. If you have tents to break away from reminders of modern conveniences, a different campground could be more appealing. A host is available.

North Cove (South Dakota)

Location: 25 miles southwest of Rapid City.
Facilities: Vault toilets, fire rings, drinking water.
Sites: 5 group areas: Beaver (25 sites), Deer (30), Otter (60), Ranger (100), Squirrel (55).
Fee: $$$$ plus depending upon group size.
Reservations: 1-877-444-6777.
Agency: Black Hills National Forest, Pactola Ranger District, 1-605-343-1567.
Activities: Fishing, hiking, boating, swimming, waterskiing.
Finding the campground: Take U.S. Highway 16 south out of Rapid City for 22 miles. Turn right onto U.S. Highway 385 and travel 3 miles. Turn right onto Sheridan Lake Road and travel 0.5 mile, following the signs to North Cove.

About the campground: There are five sites scattered among the pines within a short distance to a sandy beach and marina. These are popular areas. Reservations are recommended.

Sheridan South (South Dakota)

Location: 25 miles southwest of Rapid City.
Facilities: Vault and flush toilets, fire rings, grills, tables, drinking water, picnic area, boat ramp.
Sites: 126 for tents or RVs up to 60 feet long.
Fee: $$ per day, 14-day maximum stay.
Reservations: 1-877-444-6777.
Agency: Black Hills National Forest, Pactola Ranger District, 1-605-343-1567.
Activities: Fishing, hiking, boating, swimming, waterskiing.
Finding the campground: Take U.S. Highway 16 south out of Rapid City for 22 miles. Turn right onto U.S. Highway 385 and travel 2 miles. Turn right at the Sheridan South sign onto Forest Road 392 and travel 1 mile.

About the campground: This campground offers water access for those who want to get wet and is large enough for those who want isolation. Noise levels go up closer to the water. Wide, grassy open areas are sheltered by well-thinned ponderosa pines. The paved access roads make driving up and down the hillsides much easier. Level gravel parking spaces accommodate units up to 50 feet long. Gathering firewood will take time and work. Picking some of the deadfall up on one of your tours to other parts of the Black Hills might be considered. Firewood is advertised for sale as an additional convenience. Campground hosts are available at various locations. Sheridan Lake holds 383 acres of refreshing water, especially on a hot day. The elevation, as a rule, is high enough for cool evenings and chilly mornings. The chill burns off quickly on a late summer afternoon, however. With so many visitors discovering the beauty of the Black Hills, this would be an excellent starting place. In the course of your tours, other camping spots could be investigated. Reportedly over the Fourth of July and Labor Day holidays, all of the campgrounds fill up. If you will be traveling here during these holidays, reservations must be made well in advance.

5 Pactola (South Dakota)

Location: 31 miles west of Rapid City.
Facilities: Vault and flush toilets, fire pits, grills, tables, drinking water, boat ramp.
Sites: 39 for tents and 45 for RVs up to 60 feet long.
Fee: $$ per day, 14-day maximum stay.
Reservations: 1-877-444-6777.
Agency: Black Hills National Forest, Pactola Ranger District, 1-605-343-1567.
Activities: Fishing, hiking, boating, swimming.
Finding the campground: Take U.S. Highway 16 south out of Rapid City for 22 miles. Turn right onto U.S. Highway 385 and travel 8 miles. Turn left at the sign (near Black Forest Inn) onto Forest Road 258 and travel 0.5 mile. Turn left onto Forest Road 545 and travel 0.5 mile.

About the campground: This wooded campground is nestled quietly along the shores of the 640-acre Pactola Reservoir. There are wheelchair-accessible toilets. The sandy beaches beckon invitingly on hot summer days, with rainbow trout, brown trout, kokanee salmon, largemouth bass, yellow perch, and rock bass calling to anglers. A campground host is present.

6 Bear Gulch (South Dakota)

Location: 37 miles west of Rapid City.
Facilities: Vault toilets, fire rings, tables, drinking water.
Sites: 8 for tents or RVs up to 45 feet long.
Fee: Group rate, 14-day maximum stay.
Reservations: 1-877-444-6777.
Agency: Black Hills National Forest, Pactola Ranger District, 1-605-343-1567.
Activities: Fishing, hiking, boating, swimming.
Finding the campground: Take U.S. Highway 16 south out of Rapid City for 22 miles. Turn right onto U.S. Highway 385 and travel 8 miles. Turn left at the sign (near Black Forest Inn) onto Forest Road 258 and travel 0.25 mile. Turn left onto the gravel Forest Road 251 and travel 4 miles. Turn left onto Forest Road 253 and travel 3 miles. The campground is at the end of the road.

About the campground: Pactola Lake backs up into this narrow forested canyon a long ways away from anyone. The dead-end road leading to the water's edge tends to isolate campers. Firewood is relatively close by, though you might want to pick up some deadfall on the way in. This quiet little haven is a good area for a family reunion. Reservations need to be made well in advance for a holiday weekend.

17 Dutchman (South Dakota)

Location: 40 miles west of Rapid City.
Facilities: Vault toilets, tables, fire pits, boat ramp, drinking water.
Sites: 45 for tents or RVs up to 55 feet long.
Fee: $ per day, 14-day maximum stay.

Reservations: 1-877-444-6777.
Agency: Black Hills National Forest, Harney Ranger District, 1-605-574-2534.
Activities: Fishing, hiking, boating, swimming, mountain biking.
Finding the campground: Take U.S. Highway 16 south out of Rapid City for 24 miles to Hill City. In Hill City turn right onto the paved Forest Road 17 and travel 14 miles. Turn right at the Dutchman Campground sign and travel 2 miles on this gravel road. The camping area is on the right side.

About the campground: Spruce and aspen are sprinkled within the pine forest housing these moderately spaced units. Both the boat ramp and the lake are no short distance from the camping area. If you were planning on a lakeside table, this is not the place. There is really no firewood to gather in the campground proper; however, it is advertised for sale. You might want to bring your own. A host occupies one of the available units. Keep in mind that this is a no-wake lake.

18 Whitetail (South Dakota)

Location: 40 miles west of Rapid City.
Facilities: Vault toilets, fire rings, tables, drinking water.
Sites: 17 for tents or RVs up to 45 feet long.
Fee: $ per day, 14-day maximum stay.
Reservations: 1-877-444-6777.
Agency: Black Hills National Forest, Harney Ranger District, 1-605-574-2534.
Activities: Fishing, hiking, boating, swimming.
Finding the campground: Take U.S. Highway 16 south out of Rapid City for 24 miles. In Hill City turn right onto the paved Forest Road 17 and travel 15 miles. Turn right at the sign onto the gravel road and travel 1 mile.

About the campground: Ponderosa pines stand along the shoreline of the 414-acre Deerfield Reservoir. The divided campground does not. Ten units are across the road and the farthest from the lake. The remaining units are still some distance from the water, though it is in sight. A host occupies one of the available spaces. Leveling trailers or campers requires some work, and tents have the upper hand here. Firewood is available for purchase unless you pick up some deadfall along the way. No-wake boating is allowed on Deerfield Lake, though there is no ramp here. Most of these sites can be reserved. If you gamble on obtaining one of the other spots, the odds are against winning.

19 Custer Trails (South Dakota)

Location: 47 miles west of Rapid City.
Facilities: Vault toilets, fire rings, drinking water, picnic area, boat ramp.
Sites: 9 for tents and 16 for RVs up to 50 feet long.
Fee: $ per day, 14-day maximum stay.
Reservations: First-come, first-served.
Agency: Black Hills National Forest, Harney Ranger District, 1-605-574-2534.
Activities: Fishing, hiking, boating, swimming.

Finding the campground: Take U.S. Highway 16 south out of Rapid City for 24 miles. In Hill City turn right onto the paved Forest Road 17 and travel for 19 miles. Continue on this road after it turns to gravel for 2.5 miles. A sign for County Road 306 appears, though it is still known as Forest Road 17. Turn right at the Custer Trails Campground sign onto Forest Road 417 and travel 1.25 miles.

About the campground: Tent campers are the only ones with fire rings, and no one gets a table on this windswept part of the lake. The 16 RV spaces are just that, so be careful when you open your door if anyone else does manage to join you. Firewood appears to be within a little bit of a hike up the ridge, or you can, with some difficulty, acquire it from the host available at another campground. This might be the place to stay if you are one of the unlucky ones who gambled and lost on getting a space at one of the other areas. There is an unconfirmed report that this campground will be reconstructed. Hopefully this is true.

20 Castle Peak (South Dakota)

Location: 45 miles west of Rapid City.
Facilities: Vault toilets, fire rings, tables.
Sites: 9 for tents or pickup campers.
Fee: Donation, 14-day maximum stay.
Reservations: First-come, first-served.
Agency: Black Hills National Forest, Pactola Ranger District, 1-605-343-1567.
Activities: Fishing, hiking.
Finding the campground: Take U.S. Highway 16 south out of Rapid City for 24 miles. In Hill City turn right onto the paved Forest Road 17 and travel for 8 miles. Bear right onto the gravel Mystic Road/Forest Road 231 and travel for 5 miles. Turn left at the Castle Peak Campground sign onto the improved dirt road and travel for 8 miles. Do not attempt this road if it is wet.

About the campground: The Old West is not alive here anymore, but little has changed since the miners left. The old cabins, buildings, and other scattered remnants add a perfect touch to this forgotten treasure. The gold might be gone, but the pot at the end of the rainbow is still here. Moss droops off of the spruce trees, making them look like old men of the mountains. Rust-stained Castle Creek pleasantly clashes with the vertical granite cliffs further sheltering the sun. The water pump, like the nearby abandoned equipment, no longer produces water, so be sure to pack plenty of drinking water. A short-wheelbase vehicle navigates the two parallel ruts leading back here the best, unless it rains. If the weather looks threatening, you would be well advised to have extra supplies. Firewood and mosquitoes are plentiful. This remote little place offers a lot of history to investigate. It is not the sort of place that can be fully appreciated with a one-night stay. Trailers might make the journey; however, it is going to be a test of equipment and nerves. There are some very appealing places to camp along the way, however. Fire rings make this historical campground even more inviting.

21 Ditch Creek (South Dakota)

Location: 46 miles west of Rapid City.
Facilities: Vault toilets, tables, fire pits, drinking water.
Sites: 13 for tents or RVs up to 50 feet long.
Fee: $ per day, 14-day maximum stay.
Reservations: First-come, first-served.
Agency: Black Hills National Forest, Harney Ranger District, 1-605-574-2534.
Activities: Fishing, hiking.
Finding the campground: Take U.S. Highway 16 south out of Rapid City for 24 miles. In Hill City turn right onto the paved Forest Road 17 and travel 17 miles. Turn left onto the gravel Ditch Creek Road and travel 4.5 miles.

About the campground: Spruce trees and willow brush compete for space on the banks of Ditch Creek. Lush grass flourishes where the sun can find its way through. A large shade-free meadow takes up one side of the campground, which also contains the best units for larger RVs. Tents and pickup campers are better suited for the opposite side. The ice-cold waters of Ditch Creek are equally close to all of the units. Pools ranging from knee- to waist-deep offer refreshment for waders and fish for anglers. For the adventurous the limestone cliffs above the campground provide a place to explore. Gathering firewood is not too difficult, though the better stuff is found farther out. A host is available at another nearby campground. This is an excellent hideaway to drink in a portion of the Black Hills that is for the most part untouched by civilization.

22 Moon (South Dakota)

Location: 73 miles southwest of Rapid City.
Facilities: Vault toilets, fire rings, tables.
Sites: 3 for tents or RVs up to 30 feet long.
Fee: Donation, 14-day maximum stay.
Reservations: First-come, first-served.
Agency: Black Hills National Forest, Custer Ranger District, 1-605-673-4853.
Activities: Hiking.
Finding the campground: Take U.S. Highway 16 south out of Rapid City for 59 miles. Just past the Wyoming/South Dakota border (about 0.75 mile) take the first right turn and travel 14 miles. (This will be Forest Road 817, which will change to Forest Road 117 at South Dakota.) The campground is on the left side of the road.

About the campground: The wind whispers stories of days gone by around the log cabins and the smoke-stained fire grates. When we visited the area, logging trucks made things dusty, but by the time this is written, that work should be finished. This is an old campground. Privately owned, ancient log houses share the pine forest with the campground. Weekends find the wind echoing with the smell of fresh smoke and the sounds of campers. As with other old campgrounds, it is very likely that persistent use keeps them open. During the week is the best time to drop in here. If you listen closely, the wind may tell of former residents.

23 Redbank Spring (South Dakota)

Location: 83 miles southwest of Rapid City.
Facilities: Vault toilets, fire rings, tables.
Sites: 4 for tents or RVs up to 40 feet long.
Fee: Donation, 14-day maximum stay.
Reservations: First-come, first-served.
Agency: Black Hills National Forest, Custer Ranger District, 1-605-673-4853.
Activities: Hiking, wildlife viewing.
Finding the campground: Take U.S. Highway 16 south out of Rapid City for 59 miles. Just past the Wyoming/South Dakota border (about 0.75 mile) take the first right turn and travel 22 miles. (This will be Forest Road 817, which will change to Forest Road 117 at South Dakota.) Turn right onto Forest Road 294 and travel 1 mile. Turn left at the sign and travel 1 mile. The campground is at the end of the road.

About the campground: Rolling meadows lined with pine forest seem to never end in this area, where the large pine trees leave plenty of room for grass and a few aspen. This is an old campground that used to have water and garbage service, and the persistent campers that tend to fill the area probably keep the campground on the map. It is a very popular spot on weekends and holidays. The roads leading away from here go a long distance before encountering human habitation. Firewood is within a reasonable distance. If you like remote places and isolation, this is a good place during the week.

24 Wind Cave National Park: Elk Mountain (South Dakota)

Location: 13 miles north of Hot Springs, South Dakota.
Facilities: Comfort stations, flush toilets, fire rings, tables, amphitheater.
Sites: 21 for tents and 53 for tents or RVs up to 60 feet long.
Fee: $ per day, 14-day maximum stay.
Reservations: First-come, first-served.
Agency: National Park Service, 1-605-745-4600.
Activities: Guided hikes, wildlife viewing.
Finding the campground: Take U.S. Highway 385 north out of Hot Springs for 12 miles. Turn left at the Wind Cave National Park sign and travel 0.5 mile. Turn right at the campground sign and travel 0.5 mile.

About the campground: Wind tends to miss this sheltered grassy draw. Perhaps you will find it in the cave that is directly under the campground. Ponderosa pines grow haphazardly throughout, with thicker stands on the higher places. The grass grows so fast that mowing is required. Firewood is sold on an honor system. Gathering wood for fires is not allowed here. Daily guided hikes are offered, and a talk is presented at the amphitheater in the evening.

Five comfort stations, two of them accessible to persons with disabilities, are conveniently located in the campground. These stations offer tap water, flush toilets, electricity, and slop sinks. Keep in mind that Wind Cave is underneath, so don't just dump your gray water on the ground. Not many visitors camp here, though it is hard to understand why. Perhaps it is just not known.

25 Cold Brook Reservoir (South Dakota)

Location: 3 miles north of Hot Springs, South Dakota.
Facilities: Vault toilets, fire rings, grills, tables.
Sites: 11 for tents or RVs up to 50 feet long.
Fee: $ per day, 14-day maximum stay.
Reservations: First-come, first-served.
Agency: National Park Service, 1-605-745-4600.
Activities: Fishing, swimming.
Finding the campground: Take U.S. Highway 385 north of Hot Springs for 1.25 miles. Turn left onto County Road 87A (close to the population sign) and travel 1 mile. At the sign, turn right onto the gravel access road and travel 0.5 mile.

About the campground: At the entrance a large sign warns individuals of flash-flood hazard. Should you encounter such an event in this area, follow the instructions and find higher ground. The water level fluctuates a great deal, as the warning implies, and as a result the elm trees are a considerable distance from the lakeshore. The reservoir sits in a scenic, red-colored, cliff-sided canyon.

26 Cotton Wood Springs Recreation Area (South Dakota)

Location: 6 miles west of Hot Springs, South Dakota.
Facilities: Comfort station, fire rings, grills, tables, playground, drinking water.
Sites: 18 for tents or RVs up to 60 feet long.
Fee: $ per day, 14-day maximum stay.
Reservations: First-come, first-served.
Agency: National Park Service, 1-605-745-4600.
Activities: Fishing, hiking, playground toys.
Finding the campground: Take U.S. Highway 18 west out of Hot Springs for 4 miles. Turn right at the sign onto the gravel road and travel 2 miles.

About the campground: The comfort station includes flush toilets, electricity, and sinks. The centrally located station shares a mowed grassy slope with climbing bars and other playground equipment. Shade is short and for the most part the sun is intense. Cedarlike trees stand on the rim along with ponderosa pines some distance from the lakeshore. This is a good place to gaze at distant stars while listening to the crackle of your campfire. As of our visit, a site was reserved for a campground host, though no one occupied it at the time.

Casper Area

Water and shade are worth more than gold in this hot desertlike country, and in spite of first appearances, both are plentiful here. Deep canyons and forested mountains are not that far off of the main routes. The abundance of cedar wood at the Glendo area produces campfire aromas that will never be forgotten and offer added flavoring for hot dogs and other roasted goodies. Hidden getaways, like those south of Douglas, seem to be totally forgotten.

Water sports, fishing, wildlife viewing, and rockhounding abound in the vast country surrounding Casper. Pronghorn (antelope) appear in the endless open spaces prominent between camping areas. Watch the pronghorn carefully near fences—surprisingly, an antelope prefers to go under a fence as opposed to jumping it. This can create a difficult situation for them should a vehicle chance upon them when crossing a road with limited ground space. Be mindful of their behavior and give them the space and time needed. Otherwise, the next available crossing could be too far away, causing unnecessary injury.

1 Casper Mountain

Location: 7 miles south of Casper.
Facilities: Vault toilets, fire rings, tables, drinking water, picnic area, playground.
Sites: 150 for tents or RVs up to 60 feet long.
Fee: $ per day, 14-day maximum stay.
Reservations: First-come, first-served.
Agency: Natrona Road and Bridge, 1-307-235-9311.
Activities: Hiking, picnicking.
Finding the campground: Take Wyoming Highway 258 from either the Interstate 25/exit 185 in the east or Wyoming Highway 220 from the west. Wyoming Highway 251 intersects Wyoming Highway 258 just south of the main part of Casper, roughly halfway between. Turn onto Wyoming Highway 251 and travel south for 6 miles. Bear left on County Road 505 and travel 1 mile.

About the campground: There are several loops with a lot of camping places in this tired campground; however, there does not appear to have been any planning involved in placing the units. Some are very close together, while others can't be seen through the thinned lodgepole pine. Small streams can be found with sites along them, but most of the units seem to be in the flat forest along the highway. Old but functional shelters and playground equipment are available, though firewood is not. The drinking water and toilet facilities are quite a ways apart, which could be most uncomfortable for those between. Even though the forest floor looks flat, the parking areas are not. You will have to search for the level ones. Again, there is evidence of this area being a very busy place on weekends. With a little time, lots of water, and your own firewood, a pleasant spot could be attained during the week. If you prefer not to chance a noisy night, the campgrounds on Muddy Mountain would be better.

Casper Area

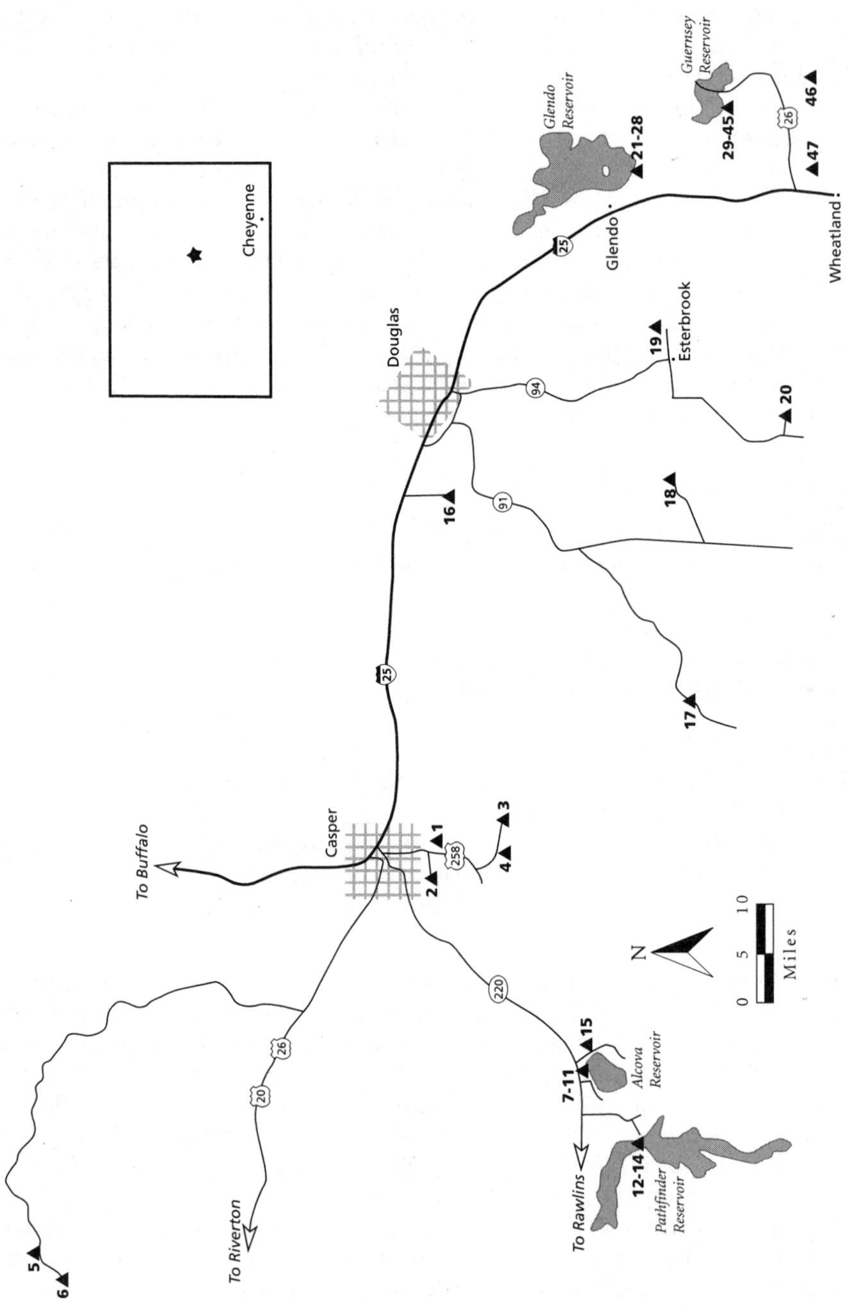

Cheyenne
Douglas
Glendo
Glendo Reservoir
Guernsey Reservoir
Esterbrook
Wheatland
Casper
To Buffalo
To Riverton
To Rawlins
Alcova Reservoir
Pathfinder Reservoir
1
2
3
4
5
6
7-11
12-14
15
16
17
18
19
20
21-28
29-45
46
47
25
26
20
91
94
220
258
N
0
5
10
Miles

	Group sites	Tents	RV sites	Total sites	Picnic area	Toilets	Hookups	Drinking water	Dump station	Phone	Disabled access	Fee ($)	Season	Can reserve	Length of stay	Recreation
1 Casper Mountain			150	150	X	V		X				$	4/1-10/15		14	H
2 Adams Archery Range			6	6		C						$	4/1-10/15		3	HR
3 Rim			10	10		V						$	6/15-10/31		14	HW
4 Lodgepole			19	19		V		?				$	6/15-10/31		14	HW
5 Grave Springs			6	6		V						N	Summer			H
6 Buffalo Creek				D		V						N	Summer			FH
Alcova Reservoir																
7 Okie Beach				D		V						$	4/1-10/15		14	FBS
8 Lakeshore Drive			50	50		V	X		X			$	4/1-10/15		14	FBS
9 Fremont Canyon			12	12		V						$	4/1-10/15		14	FBS
10 Black Beach				D		V						$	4/1-10/15		14	FHBS
11 Cottonwood Creek			15	15		V						$	4/1-10/15		14	FHBS
Pathfinder Reservoir																
12 Bishops Point				D		V						$	4/1-10/15		14	FBS
13 Diabase				D		V						$	4/1-10/15		14	FBS
14 Weiss				D		V						$	4/1-10/15		14	FBS
15 Grey Reef				D		V						$	4/1-10/15		14	FB
16 Ayres Park			6	6	X	V						D	4/1-10/15		3	PFHSW
17 Campbell Creek			9	9		V		X				$	6/1-10/31		14	FH
18 Curtis Gulch			6	6		V		X				$	5/1-10/31		14	FH
19 Esterbrook			12	12		V		X				$	5/1-10/31	X	14	H
20 Friend Park		3	6	9		V		X				$	5/1-10/31		14	H
Glendo State Park									X							
21 Whiskey Gulch	1		100	100		V		X				$	5/1-10/1		14	FHBS
22 Custer Cove			40	40		V						$	5/1-10/1		14	FHBS
23 Shelter Point			20	20		V						$	5/1-10/1		14	FHBS
24 Reno Cove			20	20		V		X				$	5/1-10/1		14	FHBS
25 Red Hills			30	30		V		X				$	5/1-10/1		14	FHBS
26 Elkhorn			20	20		V						$	5/1-10/1		14	FHBS
27 Two Moon			200	200		V		X				$	5/1-10/1		14	FHBS
28 Sandy Beach			100s	100s		V		X				$	5/1-10/1		14	FHBS
Guernsey State Park																
29 Skyline Drive			17	17		V		X				$	5/1-10/1		14	FHBS

D=dispersed, E=electricity, F=flush toilets, V=vault toilets, C=chemical toilets, N=none, F=fishing, H=hiking, B=boating, S=swimming, R=rockhounding, P=photography, W=wildlife viewing

	Group sites	Tents	RV sites	Total sites	Picnic area	Toilets	Hookups	Drinking water	Dump station	Phone	Disabled access	Fee ($)	Season	Can reserve	Length of stay	Recreation
30 Newell Bay			2	2		V						$	5/1-10/1		14	FHBS
31 Davis Bay			5	5		V						$	5/1-10/1		14	FHBS
32 Sandy Beach			32	32		V		X				$	5/1-10/1		14	FHBS
33 Cottonwood Cove			9	9		V						$	5/1-10/1		14	FHBS
34 Sandy Point			9	9								$	5/1-10/1		14	FHBS
35 Sandy Cove			20	20		V		X				$	5/1-10/1		14	FHBS
36 West Sandy			7	7								$	5/1-10/1		14	FHBS
37 Spotted Tail			18	18		V		X				$	5/1-10/1		14	FHBS
38 Sitting Bull			5	5				X				$	5/1-10/1		14	FHBS
39 Red Cloud			5	5		V		X				$	5/1-10/1		14	FHBS
40 Black Canyon Cove			3	3								$	5/1-10/1		14	FHBS
41 Black Canyon Point	1		3	4		V		X				$	5/1-10/1		14	FHBS
42 Fish Canyon			19	19		V		X				$	5/1-10/1		14	FHBS
43 Fish Canyon Cove			7	7		V		X				$	5/1-10/1		14	FHBS
44 Deadman's Gulch			2	2								$	5/1-10/1		14	FHBS
45 Long Canyon			35	35		V		X				$	5/1-10/1		14	FHBS
46 Grayrocks Reservoir			D	D		V						N	All Year			FBS
47 Wheatland City Park		8	20	28	E	F	X	X				D	All Year		3	FBS

D=dispersed, E=electricity, F=flush toilets, V=vault toilets, C=chemical toilets, N=none, F=fishing, H=hiking, B=boating, S=swimming, R=rockhounding, P=photography, W=wildlife viewing

2 Adams Memorial Archery Range

Location: 9 miles south of Casper.
Facilities: Chemical toilet, fire rings, tables.
Sites: 6 for tents or RVs up to 16 feet long.
Fee: $ per day, 3-day maximum stay.
Reservations: First-come, first-served.
Agency: Natrona Road and Bridge, 1-307-235-9311.
Activities: Hiking, rockhounding, picnicking.
Finding the campground: Take Wyoming Highway 258 from either the Interstate 25/exit 185 in the east or Wyoming Highway 220 from the west. Wyoming Highway 251 intersects Wyoming Highway 258 just south of the main part of Casper, roughly halfway between. Turn onto Wyoming Highway 251 and travel south for 6 miles. Turn right onto County Road 504 and follow the signs to the archery area, 3 miles away. The road degenerates to rough single-lane dirt toward the end.

About the campground: Sagebrush and rocky ground fill the distance between pine trees. A few aspen are scattered about, with firewood notably lacking. From appearances this would not be the best place on a weekend or holiday, but during the week this could be a very quiet place, even with resident homes very near. It seems plenty far with too much rough road. The parking areas are short and not level. Agates are found on the surface up here, but one might be better off camping elsewhere.

3 Rim

Location: 19 miles south of Casper.
Facilities: Vault toilets, fire rings, tables.
Sites: 10 for tents or RVs up to 20 feet long.
Fee: $ per day, 14-day maximum stay.
Reservations: First-come, first-served.
Agency: Bureau of Land Management, Casper District, 1-307-261-7600.
Activities: Hiking, wildlife viewing.
Finding the campground: Take Wyoming Highway 258 from either the Interstate 25/exit 185 in the east or Wyoming Highway 220 from the west. Wyoming Highway 251 intersects Wyoming Highway 258 just south of the main part of Casper, roughly halfway between. Turn onto Wyoming Highway 251 and travel south for 6 miles. Bear left on County Road 505 and travel 11 miles, following the signs to Muddy Mountain. The last 9 miles of this road are gravel. At the information area bear left and travel 0.5 mile. The campground is on the left side of the road.

About the campground: Gnarly, stubborn lodgepole pine cling tightly to the cliff's edge that houses these units. There is no drinking water here, though by the time this book is in print there could be at the nearby Lodgepole Campground. You can see a long ways perched on this mountain. A host is available at a nearby area. The parking spaces are not level, and the tables are a short hike away. Tents and pickup campers would be best suited for this campground.

4 Lodgepole

Location: 19 miles south of Casper.
Facilities: Vault toilets, fire rings, tables, water.
Sites: 19 for tents or RVs up to 30 feet long.
Fee: $ per day, 14-day maximum stay.
Reservations: First-come, first-served.
Agency: Bureau of Land Management, Casper District, 1-307-261-7600.
Activities: Hiking, wildlife viewing.
Finding the campground: Take Wyoming Highway 258 from either the Interstate 25/exit 185 in the east or Wyoming Highway 220 from the west. Wyoming Highway 251 intersects Wyoming Highway 258 just south of the main part of Casper, roughly halfway between. Turn onto Wyoming Highway 251 and travel south for 6 miles. Bear left on County Road 505 and travel 11 miles, following the signs to Muddy Mountain. At the information area turn right and travel 0.5 mile. The last 9 miles will turn to gravel. The campground is on the left side.

About the campground: Lodgepole pine are so thick that this could be considered a dog-hair forest. This newly built campground was still being worked on during our visit. All of the level units are well isolated. Two pull-thrus allow RVs of a total length of 35 feet while the other 14 are back-in only. A hand pump provided water, though as of our visit, it was untested. We learned during our stay that plans were in the works for a solar pump. Keep in mind that the water has not been tested and therefore may not be fit to drink. A host is present and firewood is plentiful. If you like a quiet secluded place, the extra miles of gravel road are well worth it.

5 Grave Springs

Location: 73 miles northwest of Casper.
Facilities: Vault toilet.
Sites: 6 dispersed.
Fee: None.
Reservations: First-come, first-served.
Agency: Bureau of Land Management, Casper District, 1-307-261-7600.
Activities: Hiking.
Finding the campground: Take U.S. Highway 26 west out of Casper. At Waltman turn right onto County Road 104 and travel about 10 miles. At Arminto turn right onto County Road 109 and travel 16 miles.

About the campground: We chose not to visit this site due to time and travel restraints. A high-profile vehicle, a good spare tire, and lots of drinking water are advised before traveling to this camping area. Badlands of dramatic colors can be expected much like those at the Outlaw Caves Campground in the Buffalo area.

6 Buffalo Creek

Location: 73 miles northwest of Casper.
Facilities: Vault toilet, table.
Sites: Dispersed.
Fee: None.
Reservations: First-come, first-served.
Agency: Bureau of Land Management, Casper District, 1-307-261-7600.
Activities: Hiking, fishing.
Finding the campground: Take U.S. Highway 26 west out of Casper. At Waltman turn right onto County Road 104 and travel about 10 miles. At Arminto turn right onto County Road 109 and travel 16 miles.

About the campground: We chose not to visit this site due to time and travel restraints. A high-profile vehicle, a good spare tire, and lots of drinking water are advised before traveling to this camping area. Badlands of dramatic colors can be expected much like those at the Outlaw Caves Campground in the Buffalo area.

Alcova Reservoir

7 Alcova Reservoir: Okie Beach

Location: 40 miles west of Casper.
Facilities: Vault toilets, fire rings, tables, boat ramp.
Sites: Dispersed, 4 tables.
Fee: $ per day, 14-day maximum stay.
Reservations: First-come, first-served.
Agency: Natrona Road and Bridge, 1-307-235-9311.
Activities: Fishing, boating, swimming.
Finding the campground: Take Wyoming Highway 220 west out of Casper for 35 miles. Turn left at the sign onto County Road 406 and travel 5 miles.

About the campground: There is more parking than tables here. The short trees basically offer no shade.

Alcova Reservoir: Lakeshore Drive

Location: 40 miles west of Casper.
Facilities: Vault toilets, fire rings, tables, RV dump, RV park.
Sites: About 50 for tents or RVs up to 40 feet long.
Fee: $ per day, 14-day maximum stay.
Reservations: First-come, first-served.
Agency: Natrona Road and Bridge, 1-307-235-9311.
Activities: Fishing, boating, swimming.
Finding the campground: Take Wyoming Highway 220 west out of Casper for 35 miles. Turn left at the sign onto County Road 406 and travel 5 miles.

About the campground: Short cedar trees offer little shade in this desert setting. Sandy beaches and cold water brings the majority of visitors. Weekends and holidays are very crowded along the shoreline. The RV park is somewhat centrally located with full hookups and a little more shade. The number of units is a function of parking. Creative forethought can fit a lot of RVs in a small area.

Alcova Reservoir: Fremont Canyon

Location: 33 to 36 miles west of Casper.
Facilities: Vault toilets, fire rings.
Sites: 12 for tents or RVs up to 40 feet long.
Fee: $ per day, 14-day maximum stay.
Reservations: First-come, first-served.
Agency: Natrona Road and Bridge, 1-307-235-9311.

Activities: Fishing, boating, swimming.
Finding the campground: Take Wyoming Highway 220 west out of Casper for 30 miles. Turn left at the Alcova Store onto County Road 407 and travel 3 to 6 miles.

About the campground: Rolling gravelly hills make leveling a chore. Shade does not exist, though there are short cedar trees present.

10 Alcova Reservoir: Black Beach

Location: 40 miles west of Casper.
Facilities: Vault toilets, fire rings, tables.
Sites: Dispersed for tents or RVs up to 40 feet long.
Fee: $ per day, 14-day maximum stay.
Reservations: First-come, first-served.
Agency: Natrona Road and Bridge, 1-307-235-9311.
Activities: Fishing, hiking, boating, swimming.
Finding the campground: Take Wyoming Highway 220 west out of Casper for 35 miles. Turn left at the sign onto County Road 406 and travel 5 miles.

About the campground: This campground settles into a much gentler hollow than Cottonwood Creek. As with the other areas, no shade offers respite from the hot sun.

11 Alcova Reservoir: Cottonwood Creek

Location: 40 miles west of Casper.
Facilities: Vault toilets, fire rings, tables.
Sites: Dispersed (15 tables) for tents or RVs up to 40 feet long.
Fee: $ per day, 14-day maximum stay.
Reservations: First-come, first-served.
Agency: Natrona Road and Bridge, 1-307-235-9311.
Activities: Fishing, hiking, boating, swimming.
Finding the campground: Take Wyoming Highway 220 west out of Casper for 35 miles. Turn left at the sign onto County Road 406 and travel 5 miles.

About the campground: Small cedar trees are scattered about on the rocky hills sloping into the reservoir. An interpretive trail adjacent to the camping area climbs to an area where dinosaur once roamed. Collecting specimens is not allowed here. The canyon housing this campground displays plenty of color for camera use. A little study will reveal the same formations on the other shore.

Pathfinder Reservoir

12 Pathfinder Reservoir: Bishops Point

Location: 50 miles west of Casper.
Facilities: Vault toilets, fire rings, tables, boat ramp.

Sites: Dispersed for tents or RVs up to 40-plus feet long.
Fee: $ per day, 14-day maximum stay.
Reservations: First-come, first-served.
Agency: Natrona Road and Bridge, 1-307-235-9311.
Activities: Fishing, boating, swimming.
Finding the campground: Take Wyoming Highway 220 west out of Casper for 40 miles. Turn left at the sign onto County Road 409 and travel about 10 miles.

About the campground: This desert-badlands setting gets hot. Most summer weekends and holidays will find the shoreline filled.

13 Pathfinder Reservoir: Diabase

Location: 50 miles west of Casper.
Facilities: Vault toilets, fire rings, tables, boat ramp.
Sites: Dispersed for tents or RVs up to 40-plus feet long.
Fee: $ per day, 14-day maximum stay.
Reservations: First-come, first-served.
Agency: Natrona Road and Bridge, 1-307-235-9311.
Activities: Fishing, boating, swimming.
Finding the campground: Take Wyoming Highway 220 west out of Casper for 40 miles. Turn left at the sign onto County Road 409 and travel about 10 miles.

About the campground: This desert-badlands setting gets hot. Most summer weekends and holidays will find the shoreline filled.

14 Pathfinder Reservoir: Weiss

Location: 50 miles west of Casper.
Facilities: Vault toilets, fire rings, tables, boat ramp.
Sites: Dispersed for tents or RVs up to 40-plus feet long.
Fee: $ per day, 14-day maximum stay.
Reservations: First-come, first-served.
Agency: Natrona Road and Bridge, 1-307-235-9311.
Activities: Fishing, boating, swimming.
Finding the campground: Take Wyoming Highway 220 west out of Casper for 40 miles. Turn left at the sign onto County Road 409 and travel about 10 miles.

About the campground: This desert-badlands setting gets hot. Most summer weekends and holidays will find the shoreline filled.

15 Grey Reef Dam

Location: 29 miles west of Casper.
Facilities: Vault toilets, fire rings, tables, boat ramp.
Sites: Dispersed for tents or RVs up to 50 feet long.

Fee: $ per day, 14-day maximum stay.
Reservations: First-come, first-served.
Agency: Natrona Road and Bridge, 1-307-235-9311.
Activities: Fishing, boating.
Finding the campground: Take Wyoming Highway 220 west out of Casper for about 29 miles. The camping area is on the left side of the road.

About the campground: Fishing seems to be the major attraction. This smaller reservoir does not compete well with the larger bodies of water upstream, at least not with those who have the toys common to water recreation.

16 Ayres Park

Location: 17 miles southwest of Douglas.
Facilities: Vault toilets, fire rings, grills, picnic area.
Sites: 6 for tents or RVs up to 40 feet long.
Fee: Donation, 3-day maximum stay.
Reservations: First-come, first-served.
Agency: Converse County Park, 1-307-358-3532.
Activities: Fishing, hiking, swimming, photography, bird watching.
Finding the campground: Take Interstate 25 west out of Douglas for 12 miles. At exit 151 take the paved Natural Bridge Road south for 5 miles.

About the campground: The stone bridge spanning these refreshing stream waters offers good photographs. The cool stream provides an oasis of refreshment for hot travelers slipping away from the sweltering desert engulfing the interstate. Paved parking allows for more units than tables when the occasion calls for it. Bring your own firewood, as all of the available firewood has long been used up. Don't forget that no drinking water exists here either. Bring your looking glasses and inner tubes. About 150 different types of birds challenge identification. Cottonwood, green ash, and other trees help shelter birds and shade onlookers.

17 Campbell Creek

Location: 31 miles south of Douglas.
Facilities: Vault toilets, fire rings, tables, grills, drinking water.
Sites: 9 for tents or RVs up to 16 feet long.
Fee: $ per day, 14-day maximum stay.
Reservations: First-come, first-served.
Agency: Medicine Bow National Forest, Laramie Ranger District, 1-307-745-2300.
Activities: Fishing, hiking.
Finding the campground: Take Wyoming Highway 91 south out of Douglas for 20 miles. Wyoming Highway 91 turns into County Road 24 and remains paved another 5 miles. Bear right to stay on County Road 24 and travel 11 miles. The campground is on the left side.

About the campground: This campground is crunched into a forested draw. A small creek crashes through the middle of the area, bouncing over large boulders. Fir trees share the available ground with compact but not crowded parking units. There is no garbage service and no host. At the time of our visit, the last 7 or 8 miles were very rough from what looked like a lot of runoff. Trailers will take an extra effort to properly level. Most of the spots are suited for tents. If you like seclusion this would be the place.

18 Curtis Gulch

Location: 49 miles south of Douglas.
Facilities: Vault toilet, fire rings, grills, tables, drinking water.
Sites: 6 for tents or RVs up to 45 feet long.
Fee: $ per day, 14-day maximum stay.
Reservations: First-come, first-served.
Agency: Medicine Bow National Forest, Laramie Ranger District, 1-307-745-2300.
Activities: Fishing, hiking.
Finding the campground: Take Wyoming Highway 91 south out of Douglas for 20 miles. Wyoming Highway 91 turns into County Road 24 and remains paved another 5 miles. Turn left onto County Road 16 and travel 14 miles. Turn left onto the degenerating Forest Road 658 and travel 4 miles. The campground is at the end of the road.

About the campground: Old cottonwood trees are grouped around these close units. Granite cliffs tower well above the tops of the trees and force Labonte Creek into a variety of pools. Douglas-fir take up residence on the shadow side of the mountains. There is no garbage service, so if you pack it in full, surely you can pack it out empty. Numerous private property signs are posted along the way. Some of these signs are placed in such a way that they look like the road is private. That may or may not be the intent; however, the road is public. Just be sure to stay on the road in areas of question.

19 Esterbrook

Location: 32 miles south of Douglas.
Facilities: Vault toilets, fire rings, tables, drinking water.
Sites: 12 for tents or RVs up to 30 feet long.
Fee: $ per day, 14-day maximum stay.
Reservations: 1-877-444-6777.
Agency: Medicine Bow National Forest, Laramie Ranger District, 1-307-745-2300.
Activities: Hiking.
Finding the campground: Take Wyoming Highway 94 south out of Douglas for 29 miles. At Esterbrook follow the signs through the old buildings of the town to Forest Road 633. Turn left onto this rough gravel road and travel about

3 miles. The campground is on the left side of the road. Be cautious—some of the washouts in the last stretch are very deep and somewhat hidden.

About the campground: The granite outcrops are not as dramatic as the ones near Friend Park. All the same there are some very colorful mineral combinations to investigate. The campground settles neatly into the lodgepole pine forest, with deadfall available for firewood. Longer trailers could be unhooked and leveled relatively easily, compared to other nearby places. The camping units spread out nicely in the shade of the pines. A host is not present; however, the Esterbrook Ranger Station is nearby.

20 Friend Park

Location: 49 miles south of Douglas.
Facilities: Vault toilets, fire rings, grills, tables, drinking water.
Sites: 3 for tents and 6 for tents or RVs up to 20 feet long.
Fee: $ per day, 14-day maximum stay.
Reservations: First-come, first-served.
Agency: Medicine Bow National Forest, Laramie Ranger District, 1-307-745-2300.
Activities: Hiking.
Finding the campground: Take Wyoming Highway 94 south out of Douglas for 45 miles. This road becomes the Esterbrook Road/Forest Road 653. Turn

Dramatic granite outcroppings and old farmsteads share Medicine Bow National Forest with Friend Park.

left onto the gravel Bear Creek Road/Forest Road 671 and travel 3 miles. Turn left onto Forest Road 661 and travel 1 mile. The highway turns to gravel about 17 miles south of Douglas.

About the campground: Perhaps friends designed this campground. Some of the available lodgepole pines in the campground shade more than one parking area. If things get cramped for you, there are numerous places to explore. The walk-in sites have more space between them and the parking. A host occupies one of the available sites. Gathering firewood does not appear to be hard, with a lot of deadfall in the forest. The granite peaks of this area have a jagged, unequal sawtooth form. At the time of our visit, during the week, only one site remained open. A larger fifth-wheel trailer filled one spot, though leveling appeared to take blocking and time. Even pickup campers will take some temporary landscaping, making tents more suitable. If you happen to be in the area when rain moves in, you would be advised to wait awhile before traveling. This could be a good place to make new friends and discover a part of Wyoming that few know exists.

Glendo State Park

21 Glendo State Park: Whiskey Gulch

Location: 26 miles southeast of Douglas.
Facilities: Vault toilets, fire rings, tables, group shelter, drinking water.
Sites: 100 for tents or RVs up to 60-plus feet long.
Fee: $ per day (including entrance fee), 14-day maximum stay.
Reservations: First-come, first-served.
Agency: Glendo State Park, 1-307-735-4433.
Activities: Water recreation, hiking.
Finding the campground: Take exit 111 off of Interstate 25 at Glendo. Drive into Glendo. After crossing the active railroad tracks, turn right at the stop sign and follow the signs. Travel about 1.5 miles to the fee booth. A map of the area is provided at the entrance.

About the campground: Water sports lure large numbers of campers over weekends and holidays. The large cottonwoods and easy access to the lake make this one of the first choices. Level spots with some places to tie up boats add to the appeal. It can get windy, though the trees provide some protection. On a busy weekend the beach looks like a crowded community; however, a good share of the residents are on the lake. Firewood is plentiful along the high water line. Cottonwood and aromatic cedar driftwood make up the majority.

22 Glendo State Park: Custer Cove

Location: 26 miles southeast of Douglas.
Facilities: Vault toilets, fire rings, tables.

Sites: 40 for tents or RVs up to 60 feet long.
Fee: $ per day (including entrance fee), 14-day maximum stay.
Reservations: First-come, first-served.
Agency: Glendo State Park, 1-307-735-4433.
Activities: Water recreation, hiking.
Finding the campground: Take exit 111 off of Interstate 25 at Glendo. Drive into Glendo. After crossing the active railroad tracks, turn right at the stop sign and follow the signs. Travel about 1.5 miles to the fee booth. A map of the area is provided at the entrance.

About the campground: This could be considered a continuation of the Whiskey Gulch area—without the water. The dispersed parking does not have as many level spots, either.

23 Glendo State Park: Shelter Point

Location: 26 miles southeast of Douglas.
Facilities: Vault toilets, fire rings, tables.
Sites: 20 for tents or RVs up to 50 feet long.
Fee: $ per day (including entrance fee), 14-day maximum stay.
Reservations: First-come, first-served.
Agency: Glendo State Park, 1-307-735-4433.
Activities: Water recreation, hiking.
Finding the campground: Take exit 111 off of Interstate 25 at Glendo. Drive into Glendo. After crossing the active railroad tracks, turn right at the stop sign and follow the signs. Travel about 1.5 miles to the fee booth. A map of the area is provided at the entrance.

About the campground: The cottonwood trees here are closer to the lakeshore than to the level parking spots. This, too, could be considered an extension of the Whiskey Gulch area.

24 Glendo State Park: Reno Cove

Location: 26 miles southeast of Douglas.
Facilities: Vault toilets, fire rings, tables, drinking water, boat ramp.
Sites: 20 for tents or RVs up to 20 feet long.
Fee: $ per day (including entrance fee), 14-day maximum stay.
Reservations: First-come, first-served.
Agency: Glendo State Park, 1-307-735-4433.
Activities: Water recreation, hiking.
Finding the campground: Take exit 111 off of Interstate 25 at Glendo. Drive into Glendo. After crossing the active railroad tracks, turn right at the stop sign and follow the signs. Travel about 1.5 miles to the fee booth. A map of the area is provided at the entrance.

About the campground: Larger units could fit here, but the amount of work required to level them discourages most. A protected bay helps keep boats out of the wind, but not the camping units.

25 Glendo State Park: Red Hills

Location: 26 miles southeast of Douglas.
Facilities: Vault toilets, fire rings, tables, drinking water.
Sites: 30 for tents or RVs up to 20 feet long.
Fee: $ per day (including entrance fee), 14-day maximum stay.
Reservations: First-come, first-served.
Agency: Glendo State Park, 1-307-735-4433.
Activities: Water recreation, hiking.
Finding the campground: Take exit 111 off of Interstate 25 at Glendo. Drive into Glendo. After crossing the active railroad tracks, turn right at the stop sign and follow the signs. Travel about 1.5 miles to the fee booth. A map of the area is provided at the entrance.

About the campground: As with other areas this could be an extension of the Reno Cove area, without the boat ramp. There are few shade trees.

26 Glendo State Park: Elkhorn

Location: 26 miles southeast of Douglas.
Facilities: Vault toilets.
Sites: 20 for tents or RVs up to 40 feet long.
Fee: $ per day (including entrance fee), 14-day maximum stay.
Reservations: First-come, first-served.
Agency: Glendo State Park, 1-307-735-4433.
Activities: Water recreation, hiking.
Finding the campground: Take exit 111 off of Interstate 25 at Glendo. Drive into Glendo. After crossing the active railroad tracks, turn right at the stop sign and follow the signs. Travel about 1.5 miles to the fee booth. A map of the area is provided at the entrance.

About the campground: Cottonwood trees provide a limited amount of shade. The boat ramp falls out of service when water levels drop, usually in early July.

27 Glendo State Park: Two Moon

Location: 26 miles southeast of Douglas.
Facilities: Vault toilets, fire rings, tables, drinking water.
Sites: 200 for tents or RVs up to 60 feet long.
Fee: $ per day (including entrance fee), 14-day maximum stay.
Reservations: First-come, first-served.
Agency: Glendo State Park, 1-307-735-4433.
Activities: Water recreation, hiking.
Finding the campground: Take exit 111 off of Interstate 25 at Glendo. Drive into Glendo. After crossing the active railroad tracks, turn right at the stop sign and follow the signs. Travel about 1.5 miles to the fee booth. A map of the area is provided at the entrance.

About the campground: The small forest of pine and cedar seems out of place in this area. The carefully placed pull-thrus create a sense of privacy. There is no foot access to the water from here, which reduces the noise level to almost nothing. Sometimes the wind rustles the needles as a powerboat motor hitchhikes along. There are two minor inconveniences. First, the abundant firewood found along the shoreline does not come as easily up here. Second, drinking water is nearly impossible to find. You may want to bring your own water and haul in some wood.

28 Glendo State Park: Sandy Beach

Location: 26 miles southeast of Douglas.
Facilities: Vault toilets, fire rings, tables, drinking water.
Sites: 100s-plus for tents or RVs up to 60-plus feet long.
Fee: $ per day (including entrance fee), 14-day maximum stay.
Reservations: First-come, first-served.
Agency: Glendo State Park, 1-307-735-4433.
Activities: Water recreation, hiking.
Finding the campground: Take exit 111 off of Interstate 25 at Glendo. Drive into Glendo. After crossing the active railroad tracks, turn right at the stop sign and follow the signs. Travel about 1.5 miles to the fee booth. A map of the area is provided at the entrance.

About the campground: Large cottonwood trees shade the high water area. Camping on the shoreline has no wind protection. Low water levels move the shade and other amenities farther away. This sandy beach is the first choice of swimmers and sunbathers. At times the beach parties tend to get a bit loud; however, stricter enforcement is improving the situation.

Guernsey State Park

29 Guernsey State Park: Skyline Drive

Location: 2 miles northwest of Guernsey.
Facilities: Vault toilets, fire rings, tables, playground, drinking water.
Sites: 17 for tents or RVs up to 50 feet long.
Fee: $ per day (including entrance fee), 14-day maximum stay.
Reservations: First-come, first-served.
Agency: Guernsey State Park, 1-307-836-2334.
Activities: Hiking, fishing (limited), all the other related water sports are regulated by water levels, picnicking.
Finding the campground: At exit 92 on Interstate 25, take U.S. Highway 26 east for 15 miles. At the sign turn left onto Wyoming Highway 317 and travel 1.5 miles.

About the campground: Trees are scarce, but the wind is not. The scrubby pine trees compete with juniper to see which can get the highest. The reservoir is a long way away from this spot, as is firewood. This would be a good place for an overnight stay, but if you are water oriented or prefer more of a mountain setting, a longer stay could become boring.

30 Guernsey State Park: Newell Bay

Location: 2 miles northwest of Guernsey.
Facilities: Vault toilets, fire rings, tables.
Sites: 2 for tents or campers.
Fee: $ per day (including entrance fee), 14-day maximum stay.
Reservations: First-come, first-served.
Agency: Guernsey State Park, 1-307-836-2334.
Activities: Hiking, fishing (limited), all the other related water sports are regulated by water levels, picnicking.
Finding the campground: At exit 92 on Interstate 25, take U.S. Highway 26 east for 15 miles. At the sign turn left onto Wyoming Highway 317 and travel 1.5 miles.

About the campground: Two points reach into the waters, with lots of room between the camping units. The narrow and steep wannabe roads have no real turnaround. Don't take your trailer into this area unless you like backing up long distances. The short pines shade very little. When the water is high, shade doesn't need to be available for comfort.

31 Guernsey State Park: Davis Bay

Location: 2 miles northwest of Guernsey.
Facilities: Vault toilets, fire rings, tables.
Sites: 5 for tents or RVs up to 50 feet long.
Fee: $ per day (including entrance fee), 14-day maximum stay.
Reservations: First-come, first-served.
Agency: Guernsey State Park, 1-307-836-2334.
Activities: Hiking, fishing (limited), all the other related water sports are regulated by water levels, picnicking.
Finding the campground: At exit 92 on Interstate 25, take U.S. Highway 26 east for 15 miles. At the sign turn left onto Wyoming Highway 317 and travel 1.5 miles.

About the campground: Cottonwoods rule, with cedar and pine trees as subjects. The camping area is actually flat, though the access road is not. The winding, steep snake of a road may not be to your liking if you have a large unit. The beach here can be a muddy mess when the water level drops. A variety of birds serenade visitor and resident alike. Bird watchers could find this a very pleasant place to investigate.

32 Guernsey State Park: Sandy Beach

Location: 2 miles northwest of Guernsey.
Facilities: Vault toilets, fire pits, tables, drinking water.
Sites: 32 for tents or RVs up to 60 feet long.
Fee: $ per day (including entrance fee), 14-day maximum stay.
Reservations: First-come, first-served.
Agency: Guernsey State Park, 1-307-836-2334.
Activities: Hiking, fishing (limited), all the other related water sports are regulated by water levels, picnicking.
Finding the campground: At exit 92 on Interstate 25, take U.S. Highway 26 east for 15 miles. At the sign turn left onto Wyoming Highway 317 and travel 1.5 miles.

About the campground: The sandy beach attracts most visitors to this spot. The parking units are well developed, making leveling less of a chore. Huge cottonwood trees line the lakeshore and shade about a third of the parking units. This is probably the best area for large RVs and trailers.

33 Guernsey State Park: Cottonwood Cove

Location: 2 miles northwest of Guernsey.
Facilities: Vault toilets, fire rings, tables.
Sites: 9 for tents or RVs up to 50 feet long.
Fee: $ per day (including entrance fee), 14-day maximum stay.
Reservations: First-come, first-served.
Agency: Guernsey State Park, 1-307-836-2334.
Activities: Hiking, fishing (limited), all the other related water sports are regulated by water levels, picnicking.
Finding the campground: At exit 92 on Interstate 25, take U.S. Highway 26 east for 15 miles. At the sign turn left onto Wyoming Highway 317 and travel 1.5 miles.

About the campground: The huge cottonwood trees continue to follow the lakeshore, granting some relief from the brutal, unmerciful sun. Leveling takes more forethought here, but it is not bad.

34 Guernsey State Park: Sandy Point

Location: 2 miles northwest of Guernsey.
Facilities: Fire rings, tables.
Sites: 9 for tents or RVs up to 60 feet long.
Fee: $ per day (including entrance fee), 14-day maximum stay.
Reservations: First-come, first-served.
Agency: Guernsey State Park, 1-307-836-2334.
Activities: Hiking, fishing (limited), all the other related water sports are regulated by water levels, picnicking.

Finding the campground: At exit 92 on Interstate 25, take U.S. Highway 26 east for 15 miles. At the sign turn left onto Wyoming Highway 317 and travel 1.5 miles.

About the campground: Level parking is plentiful. Shade is not.

35 Guernsey State Park: Sandy Cove

Location: 2 miles northwest of Guernsey.
Facilities: Vault toilets, fire rings, play area, drinking water.
Sites: 20 for tents or RVs up to 60 feet long.
Fee: $ per day (including entrance fee), 14-day maximum stay.
Reservations: First-come, first-served.
Agency: Guernsey State Park, 1-307-836-2334.
Activities: Hiking, fishing (limited), all the other related water sports are regulated by water levels, picnicking.
Finding the campground: At exit 92 on Interstate 25, take U.S. Highway 26 east for 15 miles. At the sign turn left onto Wyoming Highway 317 and travel 1.5 miles.

About the campground: A host is present at this site, which has a limited amount of shade.

36 Guernsey State Park: West Sandy

Location: 2 miles northwest of Guernsey.
Facilities: Fire rings, tables.
Sites: 7 for tents or RVs up to 30 feet long.
Fee: $ per day (including entrance fee), 14-day maximum stay.
Reservations: First-come, first-served.
Agency: Guernsey State Park, 1-307-836-2334.
Activities: Hiking, fishing (limited), all the other related water sports are regulated by water levels, picnicking.
Finding the campground: At exit 92 on Interstate 25, take U.S. Highway 26 east for 15 miles. At the sign turn left onto Wyoming Highway 317 and travel 1.5 miles.

About the campground: The few level spots here go quickly in this crowded little spot. When the water level drops, it is a long, muddy hike to get wet. There is plenty of shade here, but the active railroad next to this spot doesn't keep the peace.

37 Guernsey State Park: Spotted Tail

Location: 2 miles northwest of Guernsey.
Facilities: Vault toilets, fire rings, tables, drinking water.
Sites: 18 for tents or RVs up to 20 feet long.
Fee: $ per day (including entrance fee), 14-day maximum stay.

Reservations: First-come, first-served.
Agency: Guernsey State Park, 1-307-836-2334.
Activities: Hiking, fishing (limited), all the other related water sports are regulated by water levels, picnicking.
Finding the campground: At exit 92 on Interstate 25, take U.S. Highway 26 east for 15 miles. At the sign turn left onto Wyoming Highway 317 and travel 1.5 miles.

About the campground: Cedar and pine alike seem stunted here. This area seems like a cliff-dwelling development with no easy access to the water. There are plenty of dynamic canyon views to make up for the loss. A 16-foot-long trailer was present during our visit in the upper Spotted Tail Campground. Leveling takes careful forethought and plenty of sweat on a hot day.

8 Guernsey State Park: Sitting Bull

Location: 2 miles northwest of Guernsey.
Facilities: Fire rings, tables, drinking water.
Sites: 5 for tents or RVs up to 20 feet long.
Fee: $ per day (including entrance fee), 14-day maximum stay.
Reservations: First-come, first-served.
Agency: Guernsey State Park, 307-836-2334.
Activities: Hiking, fishing (limited), all the other related water sports are regulated by water levels, picnicking.
Finding the campground: At exit 92 on Interstate 25, take U.S. Highway 26 east for 15 miles. At the sign turn left onto Wyoming Highway 317 and travel 1.5 miles.

About the campground: This is right next door to the Spotted Tail area, with the same type of trees. When Mother Nature did the landscaping here, she left no real level spots. Tents and possibly campers would be best suited for this campground.

9 Guernsey State Park: Red Cloud

Location: 2 miles northwest of Guernsey.
Facilities: Vault toilets, fire rings, tables, drinking water.
Sites: 5 for tents or RVs up to 20 feet long.
Fee: $ per day (including entrance fee), 14-day maximum stay.
Reservations: First-come, first-served.
Agency: Guernsey State Park, 1-307-836-2334.
Activities: Hiking, fishing (limited), all the other related water sports are regulated by water levels, picnicking.
Finding the campground: At exit 92 on Interstate 25, take U.S. Highway 26 east for 15 miles. At the sign, turn left onto Wyoming Highway 317 and travel 1.5 miles.

About the campground: Sitting Bull Campground borders this area, which has the same terrain and constraints.

40 Guernsey State Park: Black Canyon Cove

Location: 2 miles northwest of Guernsey.
Facilities: Fire rings, tables.
Sites: 3 for tents or RVs up to 20 feet long.
Fee: $ per day (including entrance fee), 14-day maximum stay.
Reservations: First-come, first-served.
Agency: Guernsey State Park, 1-307-836-2334.
Activities: Hiking, fishing (limited), all the other related water sports are regulated by water levels, picnicking.
Finding the campground: At exit 92 on Interstate 25, take U.S. Highway 26 east for 15 miles. At the sign turn left onto Wyoming Highway 317 and travel 1.5 miles.

About the campground: This parking area is abruptly off the road at a sharp corner leading around the cove area. Shade is better than most, though the water level could still leave you a long distance inland in a dry year.

41 Guernsey State Park: Black Canyon Point

Location: 2 miles northwest of Guernsey.
Facilities: Vault toilets, fire rings, tables, group shelter, drinking water.
Sites: 3 for tents or RVs up to 50 feet long.
Fee: $ per day (including entrance fee), 14-day maximum stay.
Reservations: First-come, first-served.
Agency: Guernsey State Park, 1-307-836-2334.
Activities: Hiking, fishing (limited), all the other related water sports are regulated by water levels, picnicking.
Finding the campground: At exit 92 on Interstate 25, take U.S. Highway 26 east for 15 miles. At the sign turn left onto Wyoming Highway 317 and travel 1.5 miles.

About the campground: Traveling a narrow, winding, and in some places steep road is the prerequisite to parking your RV here. Adequate, fairly level space is available. There is no shade away from the group shelter. Remains of a shipping pallet seem to indicate that firewood is in short supply. This is a scenic spot to stop and take in the canyon beauty.

42 Guernsey State Park: Fish Canyon

Location: 2 miles northwest of Guernsey.
Facilities: Vault toilets, fire rings, tables, drinking water.
Sites: 19 (6 pull-thrus) for tents or RVs up to 45 feet long.
Fee: $ per day (including entrance fee), 14-day maximum stay.
Reservations: First-come, first-served.
Agency: Guernsey State Park, 1-307-836-2334.
Activities: Hiking, fishing (limited), all the other related water sports are regulated by water levels, picnicking.

Finding the campground: At exit 92 on Interstate 25, take U.S. Highway 26 east for 15 miles. At the sign turn left onto Wyoming Highway 317 and travel 1.5 miles.

About the campground: Stubby cedar and gnarly pine trees pepper this little canyon. Grass and yucca plants fill in where the trees and rocks don't. The pull-thrus provide access to two units per site. The cool water from the numerous spigots has the familiar iron taste common to hand pumps. The reservoir does not even come into view here; however, this is a quiet little hideaway well worth spending some time in.

43 Guernsey State Park: Fish Canyon Cove

Location: 2 miles northwest of Guernsey.
Facilities: Vault toilets, fire rings, tables, drinking water.
Sites: 7 for tents or RVs up to 30 feet long.
Fee: $ per day (including entrance fee), 14-day maximum stay.
Reservations: First-come, first-served.
Agency: Guernsey State Park, 1-307-836-2334.
Activities: Hiking, fishing (limited), all the other related water sports are regulated by water levels, picnicking.
Finding the campground: At exit 92 on Interstate 25, take U.S. Highway 26 east for 15 miles. At the sign turn left onto Wyoming Highway 317 and travel 1.5 miles.

About the campground: Cottonwood shade this tight little area. When the water is up, this would be a pleasant spot. It would be a little bit difficult getting larger units in, though not impossible. Low water seems to produce a fishy smell, at least it did during our visit.

44 Guernsey State Park: Deadman's Gulch

Location: 2 miles northwest of Guernsey.
Facilities: Fire rings, tables.
Sites: 2 for tents or RVs up to 16 feet long.
Fee: $ per day (including entrance fee), 14-day maximum stay.
Reservations: First-come, first-served.
Agency: Guernsey State Park, 1-307-836-2334.
Activities: Hiking, fishing (limited), all the other related water sports are regulated by water levels, picnicking.
Finding the campground: At exit 92 on Interstate 25, take U.S. Highway 26 east for 15 miles. At the sign turn left onto Wyoming Highway 317 and travel 1.5 miles.

About the campground: This area is accessed from a corner with no real room. When the water is high, it could be a good spot for water recreation. Without the high water, it is not the best place to camp.

45 Guernsey State Park: Long Canyon

Location: 2 miles northwest of Guernsey.
Facilities: Vault toilets, fire rings, tables, drinking water.
Sites: 35 for tents or RVs up to 45 feet long.
Fee: $ per day (including entrance fee), 14-day maximum stay.
Reservations: First-come, first-served.
Agency: Guernsey State Park, 1-307-836-2334.
Activities: Hiking, fishing (limited), all the other related water sports are regulated by water levels, picnicking.
Finding the campground: At exit 92 on Interstate 25, take U.S. Highway 26 east for 15 miles. At the sign turn left onto Wyoming Highway 317 and travel 1.5 miles.

About the campground: Camping units are settled all along the shore, with two and three units per point. If you choose to utilize one of the points, the toilets will be a pretty good hike. Longer trailers would find the first part easiest for access and setting up. This is near the other entrance to the park and is accessed from Wyoming State Highway 270, as well.

46 Grayrocks Reservoir

Location: 10 miles east of Wheatland.
Facilities: Vault toilets.
Sites: Dispersed.
Fee: None.
Reservations: First-come, first-served.
Agency: Wyoming Game and Fish, 1-307-777-7735.
Activities: Fishing, boating, waterskiing, all related water sports.
Finding the campground: Take exit 80 off Interstate 25 at Wheatland and travel east toward town. Turn left onto Wheatland Road and travel a short distance. Turn right at the Laramie Power Station Road and travel 9 miles.

About the campground: Water recreation brings a lot of people out into this windy prairie. The thick trees and brush lining the shores create little useable shade and even less of a windbreak. When the wind isn't blowing, fishing, boating, waterskiing, and other sports come alive. There is a small store in the area.

47 Wheatland City Park

Location: Wheatland.
Facilities: Flush toilets, electricity, picnic area.
Sites: 8 for tents and 20 for RVs up to 50 feet long.
Fee: Donation, 3-day maximum stay.

Wheatland City Park can be a welcome stopover if you have laundry or shopping to do.

Reservations: First-come, first-served.
Agency: City of Wheatland, 1-307-322-2322.
Activities: Baseball and other related park recreation.
Finding the campground: Take exit 78 to leave Interstate 25 at Wheatland. Travel east a short distance to the stop sign; you will have to go left or right here. Turn right and travel 1 block. Turn left onto Cole Street and travel about 1 mile. Turn left onto Eighth Street and travel 1 block. The camping access is on the left side of the street.

About the campground: Ancient cottonwood trees grant a lot of shade and drink deeply from the irrigation ditch bordering the parking area. The local community actively supports the baseball field behind the camping area. Horns and loud cheers fill just about any summer evening. When the sun goes down, for the most part, everything else does as well. If you have laundry to do or need repairs, this is a good spot. The Laramie Peak Museum is on the other side of this small town.

Saratoga Area

Aspen Alley resides in the little-known Sierra Madre Mountains, not far from where Thomas Edison discovered the material for light filament. As the report goes, he was on a fishing trip and a bamboo rod combined with a campfire, triggering the event that ultimately gave us the light bulb. Fishing is still popular, though access is undoubtedly improved.

Moss beards frequently adorn a countless number of older trees, indicating that this is relatively untouched land. Plentiful oak trees make for a most panoramic view when pooled with the aspen and mixed evergreens, especially in the fall.

1 Dugway

Location: 7 miles north of Sinclair.
Facilities: Vault toilets, fire rings, tables.
Sites: 4 for tents or RVs up to 50 feet long.
Fee: None, 14-day maximum stay.
Reservations: First-come, first-served.
Agency: Bureau of Land Management, Rawlins District Office, 1-307-328-4200.
Activities: Fishing.
Finding the campground: Take exit 219 off of Interstate 80 at Sinclair. Follow directions toward Seminoe State Park and travel 7 miles. The campground is on the right side of the road.

About the campground: The North Platte sleepily passes by in plain sight of this campground, but no shade could make this a very uncomfortable place on a late summer day. It could be a very pleasant place in the evening and an excellent place to star gaze. If you want a campfire, don't forget to bring the wood. Pronghorn look on, along with the available livestock nibbling on abundant sagebrush.

2 Seminoe State Park: Sunshine Beach

Location: 35 miles north of Sinclair.
Facilities: Vault toilets, fire rings, tables.
Sites: Dispersed for tents or RVs up to 16 feet long.
Fee: $ per day, 14-day maximum stay.
Reservations: First-come, first-served.
Agency: Seminoe State Park, 1-307-320-3013.
Activities: Fishing, hiking, boating, swimming.
Finding the campground: Take exit 219 off of Interstate 80 at Sinclair and follow directions to access County Road 351. Travel this paved road for 33 miles. Turn right and travel 2 miles. NOTE: Only four-wheel drives are advised. A warning sign further states that trailers and campers should not attempt the road. To do so will be at your own risk.

Saratoga Area

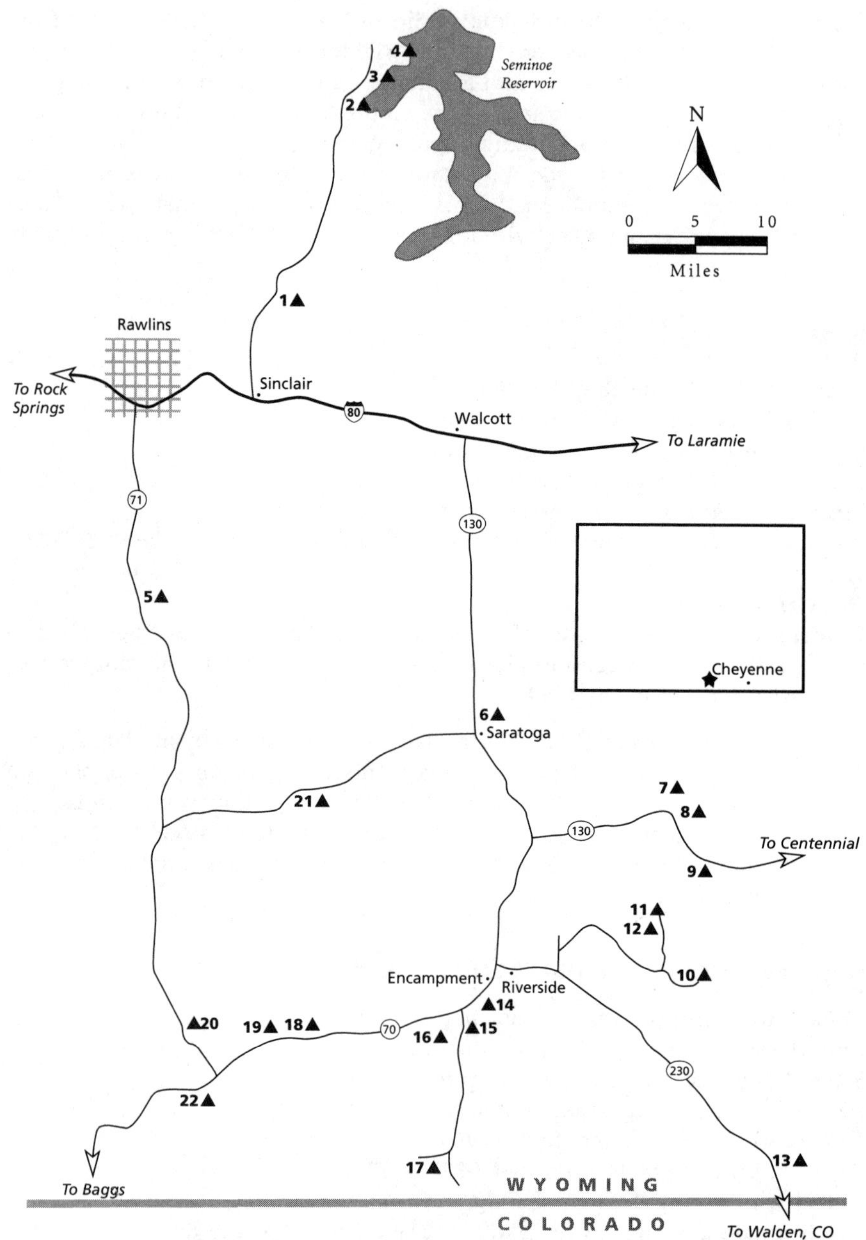

	Group sites	Tents	RV sites	Total sites	Picnic area	Toilets	Utilities	Drinking water	Dump station	Phone	Disabled access	Fee ($)	Season	Can reserve	Length of stay	Recreation
1 Dugway			4	4		V						N	6/1-10/31		14	F
2 Sunshine Beach				D		V						$	All Year		14	FHBS
3 South Red Hills			20	20		V		X				$	All Year		14	FHBS
4 Red Hills North			35	35		V		X	X	X		$	All Year		14	FHBS
5 Teton Reservoir			5	5		V						N	6/1-10/31		14	FB
6 Saratoga Lake		20	50	70		V	E	X				$	All Year		3	FB
7 Lincoln Park			12	12		V		X				$	5/15-10/1	X	14	FHW
8 South Brush Creek			21	21		V		X				$	6/1-10/1	X	14	FHW
9 Ryan Park			48	48		V		X				$	5/15-10/15	X	14	FHW
10 French Creek			11	11		V		X				$	6/1-10/1		14	FHW
11 Bennett Peak			11	11	X	V		X			X	$	6/1-10/31		14	FHTW
12 Corral Creek			7	7		V						N	6/1-10/31		14	FHTW
13 Sixmile Gap		5	4	9		V		X				$	5/15-10/31		14	FH
14 Encampment City Park			7	7		F	A	X	X			D	All Year		3	
15 Encampment River			8	8		V		X				$	6/1-10/31		14	FH
16 Bottle Creek			12	12	X	V		X				$	5/25-10/30	X	14	H
17 Lakeview			50	50	X	V		X				$	6/10-10/31	X	14	FHBS
18 Haskins Creek			10	10		V		X				$	6/15-10/31		14	FH
19 Lost Creek			13	13		V		X				$	6/15-10/31		14	FH
20 Little Sandstone			D	D		P						N	All Year			FH
21 Jack Creek			16	16		V		X				$	6/15-10/31		14	FH
22 Battle Creek			4	4		P						N	6/1-10/31		14	FH

D=dispersed, F=flush toilets, P=pit toilets, V=vault toilets, A=all services, E=electricity, D=donation, N=none, F=fishing, H=hiking, T=rafting, W=wildlife viewing, B=boating, S=swimming

About the campground: The name of this huge reservoir came from an early mountain man. This Frenchman camped here long before the dam existed, but the pronouncement of his name lives on. This particular area is restricted to four-wheel drives due to steep grades. The desert badlands get hot under this huge expanse of open sky.

3 Seminoe State Park: South Red Hills

Location: 34 miles north of Sinclair.
Facilities: Vault toilets, fire rings, tables (some sheltered), drinking water, playground, boat ramp.
Sites: 20 for tents or RVs up to 60-plus feet long.
Fee: $ per day, 14-day maximum stay.

Though South Red Hills Campground on Seminoe Reservoir is short on shade, it's rarely short of campers.

Reservations: First-come, first-served.
Agency: Seminoe State Park, 1-307-320-3013.
Activities: Fishing, hiking, boating, swimming.
Finding the campground: Take exit 219 off of Interstate 80 at Sinclair and follow directions for 34 miles. The paved access road turns to gravel in 32 miles.

About the campground: Not all units have shelters. The ones closer to the shore of Seminoe Reservoir go quickly. The stark badlands and sage hills hint of intense sun and little rain. Forget about gathering firewood. There aren't even living trees here. Hiking might be a stretch for those who like wooded trails. In spite of the barren appearance, a lot of things remain to be discovered. Exploring the geological features could prove very rewarding for rockhounds. When all else fails the cold lake water takes the sting out of the hot sun.

4 Seminoe State Park: Red Hills North

Location: 34 miles north of Sinclair.
Facilities: Vault toilets, fire rings, tables, drinking water, boat ramp, RV dump, pay phone.
Sites: About 35 sites for tents or RVs up to 60-plus feet long.
Fee: $ per day, 14-day maximum stay.

Reservations: First-come, first-served.
Agency: Seminoe State Park, 1-307-320-3013.
Activities: Fishing, hiking, swimming, boating.
Finding the campground: Take exit 219 off of Interstate 80 at Sinclair and follow signs for 34 miles. The paved access road turns to gravel in 32 miles.

About the campground: The camping area here is a bit more compact than that of the adjacent South Red Hills. Parking is somewhat organized, with lots of room for multiple vehicles, trailers, or boats. Sagebrush carpets more of the rolling terrain. A few vacant units were present on our visit toward the end of a weekend. Most, if not all, campers found water recreation to be the activity of choice.

5 Teton Reservoir

Location: 15 miles south of Rawlins.
Facilities: Vault toilets, fire rings, tables, boat ramp.
Sites: 5 for tents or RVs up to 50 feet long.
Fee: None, 14-day maximum stay.
Reservations: First-come, first-served.
Agency: Bureau of Land Management, Rawlins District Office, 1-307-328-4200.
Activities: Fishing, boating.
Finding the campground: Get off of Interstate 80 at exit 214 and travel to the north side of Rawlins road. Turn left onto Locust Road and travel past the KOA, continuing dead ahead. This will turn into Wyoming Highway 71. Continue on Wyoming Highway 71 south out of Rawlins for 15 miles. Turn left onto the gravel access road. Bear right on the access road to reach the camping area.

About the campground: No shade or firewood are to be found here. Obviously, fishing brings campers out to this panoramic setting. Endless distant cliffs stretch out overlooking the sagebrush hills. Stars and coyotes can be expected in full force on just about any night in this country. This would be an excellent place to get a feel for what the pioneers experienced on their journeys to the West.

6 Saratoga Lake

Location: 2 miles north of Saratoga.
Facilities: Vault toilets, fire rings, tables, drinking water, electricity.
Sites: 20 for tents and 50 for RVs up to 60-plus feet long.
Fee: $ per day, 3-day maximum stay.
Reservations: First-come, first-served.
Agency: City of Saratoga, 1-307-326-5629.
Activities: Fishing, boating.
Finding the campground: Take Wyoming Highway 130 north out of Saratoga for 1 mile. Turn right at the sign onto the gravel access road and travel 1 mile. Saratoga Lake is visible from the road.

About the campground: Trout are getting larger every day in this replenished reservoir. In the not-too-distant past, nongame fish had taken over the waters, resulting in draining the lake. There is no shade or firewood to gather, though wood is advertised for sale. A caretaker passes through the area to collect fees, generally in the evening. If you just came out of the backcountry, this might be a good stop to catch trout and clean up a mountain of laundry in nearby Saratoga. Hobo Hot Springs, located near the laundry facility, offers refreshment and temperatures over 104 degrees F. Native Americans shunned the hot mineral waters after attempting to treat smallpox by soaking ill members. The name was changed from Warm Springs to Saratoga after a visitor compared them to a place in New York. Hobo Hot Springs may not be the official title, but signs directing visitors to the area are labeled as such.

7 Lincoln Park

Location: 20 miles southeast of Saratoga.
Facilities: Vault toilets, fire rings, tables, drinking water.
Sites: 12 for tents or RVs up to 40 feet long.
Fee: $ per day, 14-day maximum stay.
Reservations: 1-877-444-6777.
Agency: Medicine Bow National Forest, Brush Creek Ranger District, 1-307-326-5258.
Activities: Fishing, hiking, wildlife viewing.
Finding the campground: Take Wyoming Highway 130 south and east out of Saratoga for 19 miles. Turn left onto the gravel Forest Road 100 and travel 1 mile. The campground is on the right side.

About the campground: Pine and spruce trees live in the forest holding this campground. Willow brush outlines the creek banks flowing through. Open meadows offer wildlife viewing opportunities for the observant.

8 South Brush Creek

Location: 21 miles southeast of Saratoga.
Facilities: Vault toilets, fire rings, tables, drinking water.
Sites: 21 for tents or RVs up to 40 feet long.
Fee: $ per day, 14-day maximum stay.
Reservations: 1-877-444-6777.
Agency: Medicine Bow National Forest, Brush Creek Ranger District, 1-307-326-5258.
Activities: Fishing, hiking, wildlife viewing.
Finding the campground: Take Wyoming Highway 130 south and east out of Saratoga for 19 miles. Turn left onto the gravel Forest Road 100 and travel a short distance. Turn right onto the gravel Forest Road 200 and travel 2 miles.

About the campground: As of our visit, blowdown had closed this area. Obviously, the forest was thinned, but reports of damage to some tables and other structures were not confirmed. The number of units and other services could change by the time this book is printed. This is a popular place at a lower elevation very near the beginning of the Snowy Range Scenic Byway.

9 Ryan Park

Location: 23 miles east of Saratoga.
Facilities: Vault toilets, fire rings, tables, drinking water.
Sites: 48 for tents or RVs up to 40 feet long.
Fee: $ per day, 14-day maximum stay.
Reservations: 1-877-444-6777.
Agency: Medicine Bow National Forest, Brush Creek Ranger District, 1-307-326-5258.
Activities: Fishing, hiking, wildlife viewing.
Finding the campground: Take Wyoming Highway 130 south and east out of Saratoga for 23 miles. The campground is on the right side of the road.

About the campground: As with the previous South Brush Creek, blowdown also rendered this camping area unusable. There appear to be wide-open spaces where pines filled the gap before the storm. The easy access off of the highway makes this a popular place.

Travelers on Wyoming Highway 130 are treated to fabulous views of alpine scenery.

0 French Creek

Location: 19 miles east of Riverside.
Facilities: Vault toilets, fire rings, tables, drinking water.
Sites: 11 for tents or RVs up to 30 feet long.
Fee: $ per day, 14-day maximum stay.
Reservations: First-come, first-served.
Agency: Medicine Bow National Forest, Brush Creek Ranger District, 1-307-326-5258.
Activities: Fishing, hiking, wildlife viewing.
Finding the campground: Take Wyoming Highway 230 east out of Riverside for 4 miles. Turn left onto the gravel French Creek Road and travel a short distance. Turn right at the Bennett Peak sign onto County Road 660 and travel 14 miles. Turn left at the Wyoming Highway 130 directional sign onto Forest Road 206 and travel 1 mile. The campground is on the left side of the road.

About the campground: An old but somewhat stunted aspen grove houses these spaces. Rose bushes share the space between trees with grass and an assortment of other plants. Nearby French Creek refreshes deer and plenty of other wildlife. If the trout prove too fussy, a quick wading spree could cool you off very quickly.

1 Bennett Peak

Location: 23 miles east of Riverside.
Facilities: Vault toilets, fire rings, tables, drinking water, picnic area, boat ramp.
Sites: 11 for tents or RVs up to 50 feet long.
Fee: $ per day, 14-day maximum stay.
Reservations: First-come, first-served.
Agency: Bureau of Land Management, Rawlins District, 1-307-328-4200.
Activities: Fishing, hiking, rafting, wildlife viewing.
Finding the campground: Take Wyoming Highway 230 east out of Riverside for 4 miles. Turn left onto the gravel French Creek Road and travel a short distance. Turn right at the Bennett Peak sign onto County Road 660 and travel 11 miles. Turn left onto the gravel BLM Road 3404 and travel 8 miles.

About the campground: Level, well-groomed parking spaces are well divided by an assortment of sagebrush, cedar, stunted pine, and sand. This very well-kept site has little shade but lots of river access. Surrounding cliffs and rock outcrops invite old and young alike to explore. After traveling the long and dusty badlands to get here, this oasis seems like the pot at the end of the rainbow. Pine trees and mature cedar add an enchanted sort of quality to this river canyon.

2 Corral Creek

Location: 22 miles east of Riverside.
Facilities: Vault toilets, fire rings, tables.
Sites: 7 for tents or RVs up to 50 feet long.

Fee: None, 14-day maximum stay.
Reservations: First-come, first-served.
Agency: Bureau of Land Management, Rawlins District, 1-307-328-4200.
Activities: Fishing, hiking, rafting, wildlife viewing.
Finding the campground: Take Wyoming Highway 230 east out of Riverside for 4 miles. Turn left onto the gravel French Creek Road and travel a short distance. Turn right at the Bennett Peak sign onto County Road 660 and travel 11 miles. Turn left onto the gravel BLM Road 3404 and travel 7 miles.

About the campground: This campground appears to be older than nearby Bennett Peak. Drinking water was not readily available, nor was firewood. Small cedar trees grow here and there among the unusual rock formations. The North Platte River meanders by within sight, but not real close. The many granite formations appeal to young and old alike for photos or climbing.

13 Sixmile Gap

Location: 25 miles southeast of Riverside.
Facilities: Vault toilets, fire rings, tables, drinking water.
Sites: 5 for tents and 4 for RVs up to 40 feet long.
Fee: $ per day, 14-day maximum stay.
Reservations: First-come, first-served.
Agency: Medicine Bow National Forest, Hayden Ranger District, 1-307-327-5481.
Activities: Fishing, hiking.
Finding the campground: Take Wyoming Highway 230 east and south out of Riverside for 23 miles. Turn left onto the gravel Sixmile Road and travel 2 miles. Be watching for the sign, as it tends to sneak up on you.

About the campground: Aspen trees hide the south-side units, with stair steps leading up to the tables from the parking spot. Wide-open, level spaces are on the opposite side. Sagebrush and grass inhabit the ridge on the open side. A grassy, gentle dip cuts directly through the center of the camping area. Just past the campground is a parking area for river access and the Sixmile Gap Trail. Tents could be very well placed in the aspen. If you happen to have a large RV and tired eyes, this would be an excellent stopover.

14 Encampment City Park

Location: Encampment.
Facilities: Flush toilets, water, electricity, RV dump.
Sites: 7 for RVs up to 60-plus feet.
Fee: Donation (paid at Town Hall), 3-day maximum stay.
Reservations: First-come, first-served.
Agency: City of Encampment.
Activities: Shopping (limited), museum, scenic drives.
Finding the campground: In Encampment take Fourth Street west off of Main and travel 3 blocks.

About the campground: Encampment and Riverside both consider themselves to be suburbs of each other. Stores are lacking, along with shade, but there is plenty of history. The Grand Encampment Museum should be visited, and you'll want lots of time to spare in order to get the full taste. It is almost as if the clock stopped here and never got wound up again. In the effort to survive in this remote place, the timepiece refuses to catch up.

5 Encampment River

Location: 2 miles southwest of Encampment.
Facilities: Vault toilets, fire rings, tables, drinking water.
Sites: 8 for tents or RVs up to 45 feet long.
Fee: $ per day, 14-day maximum stay.
Reservations: First-come, first-served.
Agency: Bureau of Land Management, Rawlins District, 1-307-328-4200.
Activities: Fishing, hiking.
Finding the campground: Take Wyoming Highway 70 south out of Encampment for 0.5 mile. Turn left at the Encampment River Trail sign onto the gravel road and travel 2 miles bearing left.

About the campground: Tall cottonwood trees provide shade. Willow brush and young cottonwood trees conceal the river. All of the sites appear easy to level long RVs. The last part of the "road" leading into the campground is one lane and has a prominent blind spot. Firewood does not appear to be easily obtained. Steep badlands covered with sage and melted-looking rock produce little to roast marshmallows. Numerous tailings piles entice rockhounds to have a look-see. Garnets and other related minerals are found nearby.

6 Bottle Creek

Location: 7 miles southwest of Encampment.
Facilities: Vault toilet, fire rings, tables, grills, drinking water, picnic area.
Sites: 12 for tents or RVs up to 40 feet long.
Fee: $ per day, 14-day maximum stay.
Reservations: 1-877-444-6777.
Agency: Medicine Bow National Forest, Hayden Ranger District, 1-307-327-5481.
Activities: Hiking.
Finding the campground: Take Wyoming Highway 70 south out of Encampment for 7 miles. Turn left at the sign onto the gravel Forest Road 550 and travel a short distance. The campground is on the right side of the road.

About the campground: Men of the Civilian Conservation Corps camped here during the 1930s. From the Bottle Creek Camp, men would embark on a variety of projects for $30. Of that money, $25 would be sent to each family. Large aspen and pine trees cluster together on this otherwise sagebrush mountainside. A host is present at the campground. Larger units could fit in the precious few sites that are likely to fill quickly. A large group of picnic tables allows people to meet in the center of the camp. A small bubbly stream wanders through unannounced, making a pleasant addition to a very nice camping area.

17 Lakeview

Location: 26 miles southwest of Encampment.
Facilities: Vault toilets, fire rings, tables, drinking water, boat ramp, picnic area.
Sites: 50 for tents or RVs up to 50 feet long.
Fee: $ per day, 14-day maximum stay.
Reservations: 1-877-444-6777.
Agency: Medicine Bow National Forest, Hayden Ranger District, 1-307-327-5481.
Activities: Fishing, hiking, boating, swimming.
Finding the campground: Take Wyoming Highway 70 south out of Encampment for 7 miles. At the sign turn left onto the gravel Forest Road 550 and travel 17 miles. Bear left to get onto Forest Road 496 and travel 1 mile. Turn right at the sign and travel 1 mile to the campground.

About the campground: Several loops provide plenty of secluded parking within sight of Hog Park Reservoir. When the railroad first put a line through the west, this dam stored water to flood fresh-cut ties to Fort Steel. Tie hacks cut pine trees into sections and flattened opposite sides with broadaxes. Finished ties were then stacked along the creek banks to be flooded. Water from Hog Park Reservoir would be released, adding even more to the spring runoff. The enlarged reservoir provides recreation for a different kind of camper now. Fishing and boating are among the top choices. Deadfall from the lodgepole pine forest appeared to be fairly easy to pick up for firewood as of our visit. A host occupies one of the units.

18 Haskins Creek

Location: 15 miles southwest of Encampment.
Facilities: Vault toilet, fire rings, tables, drinking water.
Sites: 10 for tents or RVs up to 30 feet long.
Fee: $ per day, 14-day maximum stay.
Reservations: First-come, first-served.
Agency: Medicine Bow National Forest, Hayden Ranger District, 1-307-327-5481.
Activities: Fishing, hiking.
Finding the campground: Take Wyoming Highway 70 west out of Encampment for 15 miles. The campground is on the right side of the road.

About the campground: Huge Engelmann spruce trees outnumber the aspen and fir in this forest. A few bushes sprout out of the needle-carpeted floor between. Now and then a jake-brake from a passing log truck joins the orchestra of whispering wind and raging rapids of the nearby stream. This whole mountain area seems to be unknown. On your way to the campground from Encampment, a historic marker overlooks a majestic mountain lake. Thomas Edison conceived the light bulb on a fishing expedition here. Reportedly a bamboo pole somehow caught fire during the fishing expedition and triggered Edison's creative mind. Settling down for the night at Haskins Creek might just open yours. It is definitely a good place to reflect.

9 Lost Creek

Location: 17 miles southwest of Encampment.
Facilities: Vault toilet, fire rings, grills, tables, drinking water.
Sites: 13 for tents or RVs up to 30 feet long.
Fee: $ per day, 14-day maximum stay.
Reservations: First-come, first-served.
Agency: Medicine Bow National Forest, Hayden Ranger District, 1-307-327-5481.
Activities: Fishing, hiking.
Finding the campground: Take Wyoming Highway 70 west out of Encampment for 17 miles. The campground is on the right side of the road.

About the campground: Spruce and some aspen shade the unique parking arrangement. Lost Creek bubbles pleasantly past on one side. Long grass flourishes where the sun sneaks through the thick needles. A host occupies one of the units. Deadfall makes firewood gathering somewhat easy, but don't forget a saw.

20 Little Sandstone

Location: 28 miles west of Encampment.
Facilities: Pit toilet.
Sites: Dispersed.
Fee: None.
Reservations: First-come, first-served.
Agency: Medicine Bow National Forest, Hayden Ranger District, 1-307-327-5481.
Activities: Fishing, hiking.
Finding the campground: Take Wyoming Highway 70 west out of Encampment for 25 miles. Turn right onto the gravel Deep Creek Road/Forest Road 801 and travel 3 miles.

About the campground: Everything but the pit toilet is gone, but as of our visit the toilet displayed fairly current use. A box of empty beer cans had taken up residence along with the toilet paper. Long grass and tall bushes semioutlined what must have been the original camping units. Little Sandstone Creek wanders by in sight, but there are special regulations posted where the road crosses. Perhaps the powers that be chose to close this level little area to avoid tempting anglers beyond their access to fishing. The gravel road does create no small amount of dust when one of the scarce vehicles passes by.

21 Jack Creek

Location: 27 miles west of Saratoga.
Facilities: Vault toilet, fire rings, tables, drinking water.
Sites: 16 for tents or RVs up to 45 feet long.
Fee: $ per day, 14-day maximum stay.
Reservations: First-come, first-served.
Agency: Medicine Bow National Forest, Hayden Ranger District, 1-307-327-5481.
Activities: Fishing, hiking.
Finding the campground: Take the gravel County Road 500 west out of Saratoga for 19 miles. Bear left onto the gravel Forest Road 452 and travel 8 miles.

About the campground: The crystal-clear waters of Jack Creek hide in the willow brush as they pass. Parking divides the pine forest adjacent to the creek with enough space to create a sense of privacy. The rolling forest surrounding the campground is splattered with grassy meadows. Aspen thickets join the lodgepole pine here and there, which adds another dimension to the meaning of beauty when they turn gold in the fall. This remote treasure fills quickly on weekends and holidays. This would be an ideal place for the days in between. The trip into the campground should by all means include the "Aspen Alley," near the south end of Forest Road 800.

22 Battle Creek

Location: 29 miles west of Encampment.
Facilities: Pit toilet, fire rings, tables.
Sites: Dispersed, about 4 units for tents or RVs up to 30 feet long.
Fee: None, 14-day maximum stay.
Reservations: First-come, first-served.
Agency: Medicine Bow National Forest, Hayden Ranger District, 1-307-327-5481.
Activities: Fishing, hiking.
Finding the campground: Take Wyoming Highway 70 west out of Encampment for 27 miles. Turn left at the sign onto the gravel road and travel 2 miles.

About the campground: The large cottonwoods look almost out of place in this lonely little spot. After winding down the steep switchbacks through oak and aspen trees, the campground pops into sight in the bottom. Services could be considered nonexistent. The valley opens up, presenting visitors with wide panoramic views. Changing colors of fall create a dynamic change in character for this backcountry. The weeds might get a little tall and the road muddy, but a visit after the leaves have changed could well make it worthwhile.

Campers at Jack Creek should consider visiting Aspen Alley, near the south end of Forest Road 800.

Laramie Area

Campers have a choice between windy, flat prairie reservoirs and high-elevation cold in the Laramie area. The more popular campgrounds reside at elevations that generate cool days and cold nights all summer. Weather plays an important role in opening and closing dates for most of the campgrounds, with some not available until late July.

The Vedauwoo Rocks between Laramie and Cheyenne offer rock climbers and adventure seekers an unforgettable experience. The unusual formations and placement of these ancient granite rocks go beyond the imagination. Golden aspen leaves make for an even greater enhancement for fall visitors.

1 Johnson Creek Reservoir

Location: 32 miles southwest of Wheatland.
Facilities: Vault toilets.
Sites: Dispersed.
Fee: $ per day, 14-day maximum stay.
Reservations: First-come, first-served.
Agency: Wyoming Game and Fish, 1-307-777-7735.
Activities: Fishing, wildlife viewing.
Finding the campground: Take exit 73 off of Interstate 25 (just south of Wheatland) to access Wyoming Highway 34. Travel west on Wyoming Highway 34 for 28 miles. Be on the alert for the Johnson Creek Reservoir sign. Turn right onto the dirt road and travel 1 mile.

About the campground: This is not a developed campground. RVs and trailers were parked along the lakeshore upon our visit, though the wisdom of that endeavor could be questioned. Thick brush and trees crowd the single-lane roadway pretty much the whole distance back here. Once you reach the bottom of this 7-acre site, a more modern vault toilet is placed in a convenient area to turn around. After crawling up and over the dam with a larger unit, things are not so simple. And, unfortunately for larger units the more attractive camping spots are farther up past the dam. The trees and brush give way to jagged rock outcrops and sage-covered hillsides. Generally later in the evening the mirrorlike water begins to boil with starving trout. If rough road and tight spots are the sorts of challenges you like, the fishing may well be the best reward.

2 Hawk Springs State Park

Location: 55 miles northeast of Cheyenne.
Facilities: Vault toilets, fire rings, tables, boat ramp.
Sites: 24 for tents or RVs up to 50 feet long.
Fee: $ per day (including entrance fee), 14-day maximum stay.
Reservations: First-come, first-served.
Agency: Hawk Springs State Recreation Area, 1-307-836-2334.

LARAMIE AREA

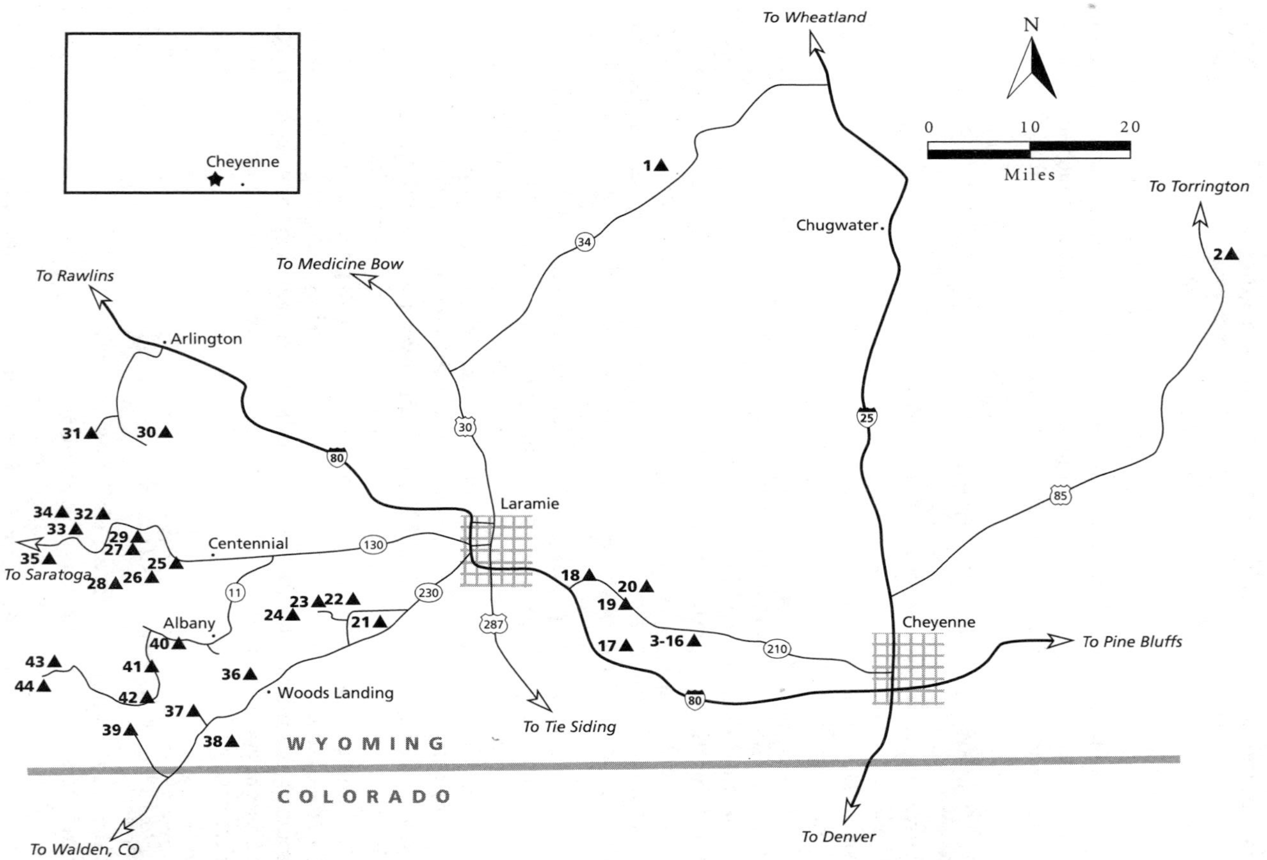

	Group sites	Tents	RV sites	Total sites	Picnic area	Toilets	Showers	Drinking water	Dump station	Phone	Disabled access	Fee ($)	Season	Can reserve	Length of stay	Recreation
1 Johnson Creek				D		V						$	Summer		14	FW
2 Hawk Springs SP			24	24		V						$	All Year		14	FBW
Curt Gowdy State Park					**X**			**X**	**X**							
3 Granite Point			6	6		V		X				$	All Year		14	FHB
4 Sherman Hills	1		6	6		V						$	All Year		14	FHB
5 Upper Sherman Hills			2	2								$	All Year		14	FHB
6 Twin Bays			3	3		V						$	All Year		14	FHB
7 Pole Mountain			2	2								$	All Year		14	FHB
8 South Causeway			15	15		V						$	All Year		14	FHB
9 Archery Range			4	4		V						$	All Year		14	FHB
10 Aspen Grove			4	4		V						$	All Year		14	FHB
11 North Causeway			8	8		V						$	All Year		14	FHB
12 Hecla Point			6	6		V						$	All Year		14	FHB
13 Federal Bay			5	5		V					X	$	All Year		14	FHB
14 Medicine Bow Point			2	2		V						$	All Year		14	FHB
15 Twin Lakes Creek	1		2	3		V						$	All Year		14	FHBS
16 Monte Cristo			4	4		V						$	All Year		14	FHBS
17 Vedauwoo			28	28		V		X				$	5/1-10/31	X	14	HCP
18 Tie City			18	18		V		X				$	5/25-10/31		14	H
19 Pole Creek			6	6		V						?	5/25-9/30	X		H
20 Yellow Pine			19	19		V		X				$	5/25-9/30		14	H
21 Meeboer Lake				D		V						N	All Year		14	F
22 Gelatt Lake				D		V						N	All Year		14	F
23 Twin Buttes Lake				D		V						N	All Year		14	FB
24 Lake Hattie				D		V						N	All Year		5	F
25 Spruce			8	8		V		X				$	5/26-9/30		14	FHW
26 Aspen			8	8		V		X				$	5/26-9/30		14	FHW
27 Pine			6	6		V		X				$	5/26-9/30		14	FH
28 Willow			16	16		V		X				$	5/26-9/30	X	14	FH
29 North Fork			60	60		V		X				$	6/15-9/30	X	14	FHW
30 Deep Creek			11	11		V		X				D	Summer		14	FH
31 Bow River			13	13		V		X				$	6/15-9/15		14	FH
32 Nash Fork			27	27		V		X				$	7/1-9/10		14	FHW

D=dispersed, V=vault toilets, N=none, D=donation, F=fishing, H=hiking, B=boating, S=swimming, W=wildlife viewing, C=rock climbing, P=photography

	Group sites	Tents	RV sites	Total sites	Picnic area	Toilets	Showers	Drinking water	Dump station	Phone	Disabled access	Fee ($)	Season	Can reserve	Length of stay	Recreation
33 Brooklyn Lake			19	19		V		X				$	7/15-9/10	X	14	FHB
34 Sugar Loaf			16	16		V		X				$	7/15-9/10	X	14	FHB
35 Silver Lake		7	11	18		V		X				$	7/1-9/15		14	FH
36 Lake Owen			35	35	X	V		X				$	6/1-10/15		14	FHBS
37 Miller Lake			7	7		V		X				$	6/1-10/15		14	FHB
38 Boswell Creek			9	9		V		X				$	6/1-10/15		14	FH
39 Pelton Creek			15	15		V		X				$	6/15-10/15		14	FH
40 Rob Roy			65	65	X	V		X				$	6/15-10/1		14	FHBS
41 Holmes			10	10		V		X				$	6/15-10/1		14	H
42 Bobbie Thompson			12	12		V		X				$	6/1-10/15		14	FH
43 Pike Pole			6	6		V						N	6/15-10/15		14	FHW
44 Pickaroon			8	8		V						N	6/15-10/15		14	FHW

D=dispersed, V=vault toilets, N=none, D=donation, F=fishing, H=hiking, B=boating, S=swimming, W=wildlife viewing, C=rock climbing, P=photography

Activities: Fishing, boating, bird watching.
Finding the campground: Take Interstate 25 north out of Cheyenne to exit 17. Take U.S. Highway 85 north for 51 miles. At the Hawk Springs sign, turn right onto the gravel County Road 225/K4 and travel 3 miles.

About the campground: Huge cottonwood trees shade the compact parking spaces. Water recreation draws the largest group of visitors. Reports of blue heron could motivate bird watchers to pack their binoculars. This popular spot is often full on weekends and holidays.

Curt Gowdy State Park

3 Curt Gowdy State Park: Granite Point

Location: 24 miles west of Cheyenne.
Facilities: Vault toilets, fire rings, tables, drinking water. An RV dump station is located just past the fee booth at Granite Springs Reservoir.
Sites: 6 for tents or RVs up to 45 feet long.
Fee: $ per day (including entrance fee), 14-day maximum stay.
Reservations: First-come, first-served.
Agency: Curt Gowdy State Park, 1-307-632-7946.
Activities: Fishing, hiking, boating.

Finding the campground: At Cheyenne take exit 10B/Happy Jack Road and follow it west out of Cheyenne for 24 miles.

About the campground: The reservoirs in this park are Cheyenne's municipal water supply. As a result no swimming, waterskiing, or jet skis are allowed. Furthermore no dogs are allowed in the water. There are several camping areas located along the two separate reservoirs. At this area, the rolling grassy hillsides collide with Granite Springs Reservoir. The only drinking water available is really not part of the camping area, but it is at the entrance. Wind and sun can both hit you hard here. Level spots take some looking, but are available. Firewood is scarce.

Curt Gowdy State Park: Sherman Hills

Location: 24 miles west of Cheyenne.
Facilities: Vault toilets, fire rings, tables, group shelter.
Sites: 6 for tents or RVs up to 50 feet long.
Fee: $ per day (including entrance fee), 14-day maximum stay.
Reservations: First-come, first-served.
Agency: Curt Gowdy State Park, 1-307-632-7946.
Activities: Fishing, hiking, boating.
Finding the campground: At Cheyenne take exit 10B/Happy Jack Road and follow it west out of Cheyenne for 24 miles.

About the campground: Rolling grassy hills dominate this spacious area. The parking places snuggle up pretty close to the lake's edge, with a lot of distance between other campers. The terrain provides little wind protection, though it could be worse.

Curt Gowdy State Park: Upper Sherman Hills

Location: 24 miles west of Cheyenne.
Facilities: Fire rings, tables.
Sites: 2 for tents or RVs up to 20 feet long.
Fee: $ per day (including entrance fee), 14-day maximum stay.
Reservations: First-come, first-served.
Agency: Curt Gowdy State Park, 1-307-632-7946.
Activities: Fishing, hiking, boating.
Finding the campground: At Cheyenne take exit 10B/Happy Jack Road and follow it west out of Cheyenne for 24 miles.

About the campground: As the name implies, this area is in the hills—complete with pine trees and steep sides. Toilet facilities are located in the adjacent camping areas.

Curt Gowdy State Park: Twin Bays

Location: 24 miles west of Cheyenne.
Facilities: Vault toilets, fire rings, tables.

Sites: 3 for tents or RVs up to 40 feet long.
Fee: $ per day (including entrance fee), 14-day maximum stay.
Reservations: First-come, first-served.
Agency: Curt Gowdy State Park, 1-307-632-7946.
Activities: Fishing, hiking, boating.
Finding the campground: At Cheyenne take exit 10B/Happy Jack Road and follow it west out of Cheyenne for 24 miles.

About the campground: Pine trees hide this hollow from the road and the lake. A small bay pokes into one of the three sites. This compact place offers the best protection from both wind and sun. In exchange for the shelter, a hike is required to access the lake, unless you happen to be next in line for the unit beside the bay.

7 Curt Gowdy State Park: Pole Mountain

Location: 24 miles west of Cheyenne.
Facilities: Fire rings, tables.
Sites: 2 for tents or RVs up to 20 feet long.
Fee: $ per day (including entrance fee), 14-day maximum stay.
Reservations: First-come, first-served.
Agency: Curt Gowdy State Park, 1-307-632-7946.
Activities: Fishing, hiking, boating.
Finding the campground: At Cheyenne take exit 10B/Happy Jack Road and follow it west out of Cheyenne for 24 miles.

About the campground: The access road slopes uphill all the way, and so do the camping units. Tents are better suited for this somewhat shaded place. Lodgepole pines line both sides of the draw, parallel with the road cutting the middle of a grassy meadow. The lake is a pretty good hike from here.

8 Curt Gowdy State Park: South Causeway

Location: 24 miles west of Cheyenne.
Facilities: Vault toilets, fire rings, tables.
Sites: 15 for tents or RVs up to 45 feet long.
Fee: $ per day (including entrance fee), 14-day maximum stay.
Reservations: First-come, first-served.
Agency: Curt Gowdy State Park, 1-307-632-7946.
Activities: Fishing, hiking, boating.
Finding the campground: At Cheyenne take exit 10B/Happy Jack Road and follow it west out of Cheyenne for 24 miles.

About the campground: These rolling sandy hills sit in the most forested part of the park. Maneuvering could be tricky but well worth the effort. Sites here are positioned to create a sense of privacy even with close neighbors. This place appears to be the first choice for most locals.

9 Curt Gowdy State Park: Archery Range

Location: 24 miles west of Cheyenne.
Facilities: Vault toilets, fire rings, tables, archery range.
Sites: 4 for tents or RVs up to 40 feet long.
Fee: $ per day (including entrance fee), 14-day maximum stay.
Reservations: First-come, first-served.
Agency: Curt Gowdy State Park, 1-307-632-7946.
Activities: Fishing, hiking, boating.
Finding the campground: At Cheyenne take exit 10B/Happy Jack Road and follow it west out of Cheyenne for 24 miles.

About the campground: Shade is short, and the parking spaces are not well designated. Leveling will take forethought. Traffic creates dust that could be very bothersome on a busy day.

0 Curt Gowdy State Park: Aspen Grove

Location: 24 miles west of Cheyenne.
Facilities: Vault toilets, fire rings, tables.
Sites: 4 for tents or RVs up to 20 feet long.
Fee: $ per day (including entrance fee), 14-day maximum stay.
Reservations: First-come, first-served.
Agency: Curt Gowdy State Park, 1-307-632-7946.
Activities: Fishing, hiking, boating.
Finding the campground: At Cheyenne take exit 10B/Happy Jack Road and follow it west out of Cheyenne for 24 miles.

About the campground: The aspen trees here are a long way from the tables. Grass is tall and the small stream crossing the access road makes thick mud from time to time, as shown by the deep ruts present during our visit. The lake is no small hike, but it could stay pretty quiet back here out of the mainstream.

1 Curt Gowdy State Park: North Causeway

Location: 24 miles west of Cheyenne.
Facilities: Vault toilets, fire rings, tables.
Sites: 8 for tents or RVs up to 40 feet long.
Fee: $ per day (including entrance fee), 14-day maximum stay.
Reservations: First-come, first-served.
Agency: Curt Gowdy State Park, 1-307-632-7946.
Activities: Fishing, hiking, boating.
Finding the campground: At Cheyenne take exit 10B/Happy Jack Road and follow it west out of Cheyenne for 24 miles.

About the campground: This is sort of a continuation of the South Causeway area on the south side—without all the trees. If you are pulling a trailer, be sure to preview your access road. Some of the points have one straight road in with no turnaround. Backing out would be a real nightmare.

12 Curt Gowdy State Park: Hecla Point

Location: 24 miles west of Cheyenne.
Facilities: Vault toilet, fire rings, tables.
Sites: 6 for tents or RVs up to 60 feet long.
Fee: $ per day (including entrance fee), 14-day maximum stay.
Reservations: First-come, first-served.
Agency: Curt Gowdy State Park, 1-307-632-7946.
Activities: Fishing, hiking, boating.
Finding the campground: At Cheyenne take exit 10B/Happy Jack Road and follow it west out of Cheyenne for 24 miles.

About the campground: There is no shade here. The level ground makes parking easy, but a windy day would not be pleasant for tenters.

13 Curt Gowdy State Park: Federal Bay

Location: 24 miles west of Cheyenne.
Facilities: Vault toilet, fire rings, tables.
Sites: 5 for tents or RVs up to 60 feet long.
Fee: $ per day (including entrance fee), 14-day maximum stay.
Reservations: First-come, first-served.
Agency: Curt Gowdy State Park, 1-307-632-7946.
Activities: Fishing, hiking, boating.
Finding the campground: At Cheyenne take exit 10B/Happy Jack Road and follow it west out of Cheyenne for 24 miles.

About the campground: There is some wind protection here, and this area is accessible to the disabled.

14 Curt Gowdy State Park: Medicine Bow Point

Location: 24 miles west of Cheyenne.
Facilities: Vault toilet, fire rings, tables.
Sites: 2 for tents or RVs up to 20 feet long.
Fee: $ per day (including entrance fee), 14-day maximum stay.
Reservations: First-come, first-served.
Agency: Curt Gowdy State Park, 1-307-632-7946.
Activities: Fishing, hiking, boating.
Finding the campground: At Cheyenne take exit 10B/Happy Jack Road and follow it west out of Cheyenne for 24 miles.

About the campground: There are trees here, but no shade to speak of. This area is more for angler convenience than camping pleasure.

15 Curt Gowdy State Park: Twin Lakes Creek

Location: 24 miles west of Cheyenne.
Facilities: Vault toilets, fire rings, tables, group shelter.
Sites: 2 for tents or RVs up to 50 feet long.
Fee: $ per day (including entrance fee), 14-day maximum stay.
Reservations: First-come, first-served.
Agency: Curt Gowdy State Park, 1-307-632-7946.
Activities: Fishing, hiking, boating, swimming.
Finding the campground: At Cheyenne take exit 10B/Happy Jack Road and follow it west out of Cheyenne for 24 miles.

About the campground: There are additional units scattered along the lakeshore, though they appear to be more for angler access than camping. Shade is scarce with the exception of the group shelter.

16 Curt Gowdy State Park: Monte Cristo

Location: 24 miles west of Cheyenne.
Facilities: Vault toilets, fire rings, tables, playground.
Sites: 4 for tents or RVs up to 50 feet long.
Fee: $ per day (including entrance fee), 14-day maximum stay.
Reservations: First-come, first-served.
Agency: Curt Gowdy State Park, 1-307-632-7946.
Activities: Fishing, hiking, boating, swimming.
Finding the campground: At Cheyenne take exit 10B/Happy Jack Road and follow it west out of Cheyenne for 24 miles.

About the campground: Cottonwood trees and willow brush crowd up to the water, granting little shade for campers. Drinking water is available at the boat ramp near Crystal Dam Overlook.

17 Vedauwoo

Location: 17 miles east of Laramie.
Facilities: Vault toilets, fire rings, tables, drinking water.
Sites: 28 for tents or RVs up to 50 feet long.
Fee: $ per day, 14-day maximum stay.
Reservations: 1-877-444-6777.
Agency: Medicine Bow National Forest, Laramie Ranger District, 1-307-745-2300.
Activities: Rock climbing, hiking, photography.
Finding the campground: Take exit 329 off of Interstate 80 southeast of Laramie. Travel east on Forest Road 700 for 1 mile. Turn left at the Vedauwoo Recreation Area sign. The campground is on the right side.

About the campground: Native Americans gave these dynamic rock formations their name, which means "earth born." Reportedly, they believed spirits piled these rocks up during a playful period. Paved roads and parking areas

The unusual rock formations in Vedauwoo Recreation Area offer both easy and technical climbing opportunities.

along with easy access to the interstate add up to a lot of use. There are both easy and technical climbing opportunities here, along with all of the related dangers, including death. Gnarly pine trees struggle for survival while stunted aspen seem to be less tormented in this environment. Level paved parking units make exploring more inviting. Our visit during the week found a few empty places. A noticeable sign at the exit explains that additional camping is available 6 miles west, and is convincing evidence that this place fills quickly. Even if you do not prefer to climb rocks, a camera is a must. Dynamic pictures can still be had without the dangers. A host occupies one of the sites. Firewood gathering requires some work.

18 Tie City

Location: 12 miles east of Laramie.
Facilities: Vault toilets, fire rings, grills, tables, drinking water.
Sites: 18 for tents or RVs up to 35 feet long.
Fee: $ per day, 14-day maximum stay.
Reservations: First-come, first-served.
Agency: Medicine Bow National Forest, Laramie Ranger District, 1-307-745-2300.
Activities: Hiking.
Finding the campground: Take exit 323 off of Interstate 80 at the Summit

Rest Area. Turn left onto Happy Jack Road and travel 1 mile. Turn right at the campground sign and travel 0.25 mile.

About the campground: Old aspen hedge in the single-lane dirt road at the entrance to the campground. Spruce trees and tall grass take over gradually, and have established complete control at the end of the campground. The pull-thrus look like the easiest to level in this rolling terrain. A host occupies one of the units. Firewood appears to be easily gathered from nearby deadfall. Getting into the campground may seem like a roller coaster, but the layout makes each site individually unique.

19 Pole Creek

Location: 13 miles east of Laramie.
Facilities: Vault toilets, fire rings, tables.
Sites: 6 for tents or RVs up to 35 feet long.
Fee: Reservation only, no other access.
Reservations: 1-877-444-6777.
Agency: Medicine Bow National Forest, Laramie Ranger District, 1-307-745-2300.
Activities: Hiking.
Finding the campground: Take exit 323 off of Interstate 80 at the Summit Rest Area. Turn left onto Happy Jack Road and travel 2 miles. Turn right at the Happy Jack Recreation Area sign and travel 1 mile. After passing the picnic area, bear right.

About the campground: This camping area is for group use only and must be reserved. As of our visit the locked gate reinforced the reservation rule. This somewhat hidden spot is rather close to Yellow Pine Campground and therefore could be very similar.

20 Yellow Pine

Location: 13 miles east of Laramie.
Facilities: Vault toilets, fire rings, tables, drinking water.
Sites: 19 (12 pull-thrus) for tents or RVs up to 50 feet long.
Fee: $ per day, 14-day maximum stay.
Reservations: First-come, first-served.
Agency: Medicine Bow National Forest, Laramie Ranger District, 1-307-745-2300.
Activities: Hiking.
Finding the campground: Take exit 323 off of Interstate 80 at the Summit Rest Area. Turn left onto Happy Jack Road and travel 2 miles. Turn right at the Happy Jack Recreation Area sign and travel 1 mile, bearing left.

About the campground: Aspen and pine trees share the campground. The units are far enough apart to help promote a feeling of privacy. A host occupies one of the sites. This would be an excellent place to set up a base camp and go exploring.

21 Meeboer Lake

Location: 14 miles southwest of Laramie.
Facilities: Vault toilet.
Sites: Dispersed.
Fee: None, 14-day maximum stay.
Reservations: First-come, first-served.
Agency: Wyoming Game and Fish, 1-307-745-4046.
Activities: Fishing.
Finding the campground: Take Wyoming Highway 230 southwest out of Laramie for 7.5 miles. Turn right onto Phalow Lane and travel 5 miles. Turn left at the sign onto the gravel County Road 422 and travel 1.5 miles.

About the campground: This is not a developed campground, but plenty of individuals use it. Large rainbow trout lure anglers who, in turn, become the campers. There are no trees or firewood. The snow you see on the distant mountains has a direct connection with this area via the wind.

22 Gelatt Lake

Location: 12 miles southwest of Laramie.
Facilities: Vault toilet.
Sites: Dispersed.
Fee: None, 14-day maximum stay.
Reservations: First-come, first-served.
Agency: Wyoming Game and Fish, 1-307-745-4046.
Activities: Fishing.
Finding the campground: Take Wyoming Highway 230 southwest out of Laramie for 7.5 miles. Turn right onto Phalow Lane and travel 5 miles. The lake is on the right side of the highway.

About the campground: Cutthroat and rainbow trout are the attraction here. May and June are typically the best times. If you are not interested in fishing, this place offers little else of interest.

23 Twin Buttes Lake

Location: 14 miles southwest of Laramie.
Facilities: Vault toilet, boat ramp.
Sites: Dispersed.
Fee: None, 14-day maximum stay.
Reservations: First-come, first-served.
Agency: Wyoming Game and Fish, 1-307-745-4046.
Activities: Fishing, boating.
Finding the campground: Take Wyoming Highway 230 southwest out of Laramie for 7.5 miles. Turn right onto Phalow Lane and travel 5 miles. Bear dead ahead onto the gravel access road and travel 1 mile.

About the campground: Like all of the Laramie Plains lakes, fishing motivates visitation. Brown trout can get large here with the added advantage of putting a boat in. Action tends to increase around late September.

24 Lake Hattie

Location: 24 miles southwest of Laramie.
Facilities: Vault toilet, boat ramp.
Sites: Dispersed.
Fee: None, 5-day maximum stay.
Reservations: First-come, first-served.
Agency: Wyoming Game and Fish, 1-307-745-4046.
Activities: Fishing.
Finding the campground: Take Wyoming Highway 230 southwest out of Laramie for 15 miles to the second access for Phalow Lane. Turn right onto Phalow Lane and travel 3.5 miles. Turn left onto the paved Hanson Lane and travel 5 miles. The Lake Hattie access road is on the right side.

About the campground: Tables are scattered about here. Camping is limited to liberal parking areas. Reports of 10-pound brown trout probably bring anglers out. Fall weather tends to be best for browns, but not for the boat ramp, as low water renders the ramp unusable.

25 Spruce

Location: 30 miles west of Laramie.
Facilities: Vault toilet, fire rings, tables, drinking water.
Sites: 8 for tents or RVs up to 45 feet long.
Fee: $ per day, 14-day maximum stay.
Reservations: First-come, first-served.
Agency: Medicine Bow National Forest, Laramie Ranger District, 1-307-745-2300.
Activities: Fishing, hiking, wildlife viewing.
Finding the campground: Take Wyoming Highway 130 west out of Laramie for 30 miles. Look for the campground sign a short distance past the Barber Lake Road. The campground is on the left side of the highway.

About the campground: Spruce trees do indeed live here, along with aspen and fir. Noisy Libby Creek rushes downstream on one side. As of our visit, a 50-foot-long motor home occupied one of the parking spaces, but it took all available space. The parking places are more suitable for smaller trailers, pickup campers, or tents. Reportedly a host should be present; however, none was to be found on our stay. The thick needles of the numerous spruce and fir help isolate the units. Firewood is not readily available, so you might want to bring some. Traffic tends to die after dark. The thick foliage helps muffle car sounds.

26 Aspen

Location: 30 miles west of Laramie.
Facilities: Vault toilet, fire rings, tables, drinking water.
Sites: 8 for tents or RVs up to 22 feet long.
Fee: $ per day, 14-day maximum stay.
Reservations: First-come, first-served.
Agency: Medicine Bow National Forest, Laramie Ranger District, 1-307-745-2300.
Activities: Fishing, hiking, wildlife viewing.
Finding the campground: Take Wyoming Highway 130 west out of Laramie for 30 miles. Turn left at the Barber Lake Road sign and travel 0.25 mile. The campground is on the right side of the highway.

About the campground: Aspen are present here, along with spruce and fir. The circular parking area designates portions for individual camping spaces, but some footwork is required to reach the tables. The traffic is not terribly heavy here, and a small knoll muffles most of the passing noise. This is a nice spot for tents.

27 Pine

Location: 31 miles west of Laramie.
Facilities: Vault toilets, fire rings, tables, drinking water.
Sites: 6 for tents or RVs up to 16 feet long.
Fee: $ per day, 14-day maximum stay.
Reservations: First-come, first-served.
Agency: Medicine Bow National Forest, Laramie Ranger District, 1-307-745-2300.
Activities: Fishing, hiking.
Finding the campground: Take Wyoming Highway 130 west out of Laramie for 30 miles. Turn left onto the paved Barber Lake Road and travel 1 mile. The campground is on the right side of the road.

About the campground: Parking spaces tend to be scrunched between pine trees in this forest. Longer trailers have been set up, but not without forethought and sweat and the telltale sign of some fender paint here and there. The units are all back-in with a one-way entrance and exit. So if you miss the main gate, don't try sneaking in the back way. If another trailer is on the way out, a real nightmare comes to life. A host is present at the campground.

28 Willow

Location: 32 miles west of Laramie.
Facilities: Vault toilets, fire rings, tables, drinking water.
Sites: 16 for tents or RVs up to 30 feet long.
Fee: $ per day, 14-day maximum stay.
Reservations: 1-877-444-6777.

Agency: Medicine Bow National Forest, Laramie Ranger District, 1-307-745-2300.
Activities: Fishing, hiking.
Finding the campground: Take Wyoming Highway 130 west out of Laramie for 30 miles. Turn left onto the paved Barber Lake Road and travel 1.5 miles. Turn right at the campground sign and travel 0.5 mile.

About the campground: Libby Creek makes a bend here that divides this campground into two areas. The willow brush hiding the ice-cold water of the creek grows high overhead. Larger RVs can fit in some of the spots, but not all. This popular campground fills quickly, perhaps because it's so far away from traffic. A host occupies a site at the campground.

29 North Fork

Location: 35 miles west of Laramie.
Facilities: Vault toilets, fire rings, tables, drinking water.
Sites: 60 for tents or RVs up to 30 feet long.
Fee: $ per day, 14-day maximum stay.
Reservations: 1-877-444-6777.
Agency: Medicine Bow National Forest, Laramie Ranger District, 1-307-745-2300.
Activities: Fishing, hiking, wildlife viewing.
Finding the campground: Take Wyoming Highway 130 west out of Laramie for 34 miles. Turn left onto the gravel Sand Lake Road/Forest Road 101 and travel 1 mile.

About the campground: The lower the elevation, the higher the spruce, fir, and pine trees. Rainbow and brook trout dwell in the nearby North Fork Little Laramie River. Weather may not allow camping in this popular area until well into July.

30 Deep Creek

Location: 55 miles west of Laramie.
Facilities: Vault toilets, fire rings, tables, drinking water.
Sites: 11 for tents or RVs up to 30 feet long.
Fee: Donation, 14-day maximum stay.
Reservations: First-come, first-served.
Agency: Medicine Bow National Forest, Brush Creek Ranger District, 1-307-326-5258.
Activities: Fishing, hiking.
Finding the campground: Take Interstate 80 west out of Laramie for 40 miles. At the Arlington exit/exit 272, go under the overpass and turn right onto the gravel Forest Road 111 and travel about 13 miles. Turn left onto the gravel Forest Road 101 and travel 1.5 miles. Forest Road 111 parallels 80 on the south side for a short distance before diving into the backcountry.

About the campground: Old fir trees stand guard over this time-worn area, with plenty of stories to tell about past visitors. Drinking water is not guaranteed, so be sure to bring plenty. A sign at the entrance explains that due to budget cuts this will no longer be a full-service campground. If donations are high enough, the water will continue to tested. There is no garbage service or host. Deadfall makes firewood gathering rather easy. If you are looking for an isolated place to hide out, this could be it.

31 Bow River

Location: 55 miles west of Laramie.
Facilities: Vault toilets, fire rings, grills, tables, drinking water.
Sites: 13 for tents or RVs up to 32 feet long.
Fee: $ per day, 14-day maximum stay.
Reservations: First-come, first-served.
Agency: Medicine Bow National Forest, Brush Creek Ranger District, 1-307-326-5258.
Activities: Fishing, hiking.
Finding the campground: Take Interstate 80 west out of Laramie for 40 miles. At the Arlington exit/exit 272, go under the overpass and turn right onto the gravel Forest Road 111 and travel about 8 miles. Turn right onto the gravel Forest Road 120 and travel 5 miles. Turn right onto the gravel Forest Road 105 and travel 2 miles.

About the campground: The forest housing this isolated camping area contains spruce, fir, and aspen. The back-in spaces are adequately placed to create a sense of privacy. A host is present. Deadfall is nearby for fairly easy firewood gathering. Medicine Bow River is close by for the anglers in your group. Do not forget bug spray. Mosquitoes have no mercy and invite all living relatives to the funeral of the one you crush. This is a perfect place to spend some quality quiet time.

32 Nash Fork

Location: 33 miles west of Laramie.
Facilities: Vault toilets, fire rings, tables, drinking water.
Sites: 27 for tents or RVs up to 22 feet long.
Fee: $ per day, 14-day maximum stay.
Reservations: First-come, first-served.
Agency: Medicine Bow National Forest, Laramie Ranger District, 1-307-745-2300.
Activities: Fishing, hiking, wildlife viewing.
Finding the campground: Take Wyoming Highway 130 west out of Laramie for 33 miles. Turn right at the sign and travel 0.5 mile.

About the campground: Spruce and scattered lodgepole pine fill the gaps between large boulders at this spot, which is at 10,000 feet. On our visit here in the middle of July, the snowdrifts still stood 4 feet high or more. The brushy alpine meadows hosted an icy breeze and wildflowers. The sun might feel warm from time to time, but there is a whole lot more cold than heat in the area. A host is present at the campground. Dry firewood could prove a little challenging to find early in the season.

Brooklyn Lake

Location: 34 miles west of Laramie.
Facilities: Vault toilets, fire rings, tables, drinking water.
Sites: 19 for tents or RVs up to 22 feet long.
Fee: $ per day, 14-day maximum stay.
Reservations: 1-877-444-6777.
Agency: Medicine Bow National Forest, Laramie Ranger District, 1-307-745-2300.
Activities: Fishing, hiking, boating (nonmotorized).
Finding the campground: Take Wyoming Highway 130 west out of Laramie for 33 miles. Turn right at the sign and travel 1 mile.

About the campground: This campground does not open until late summer, and exactly when it does is a function of weather. On our visit in the middle of July, the opening date appeared to be some time further into the future. Brooklyn Lake is nestled in alpine meadows close to the campground. Spruce trees living here show signs of a difficult life. The elevation probably makes things a bit different—since it is more than 10,000 feet above sea level. Breathing gets hard for some individuals at this height.

Sugar Loaf

Location: 37 miles west of Laramie.
Facilities: Vault toilets, fire rings, tables, drinking water.
Sites: 16 for tents or RVs up to 22 feet long.
Fee: $ per day, 14-day maximum stay.
Reservations: 1-877-444-6777.
Agency: Medicine Bow National Forest, Laramie Ranger District, 1-307-745-2300.
Activities: Fishing, hiking, boating (nonmotorized).
Finding the campground: Take Wyoming Highway 130 west out of Laramie for 36 miles. Turn right at the sign and travel 1 mile.

About the campground: This campground was full when we visited in the middle of July, but not with campers. Huge snowdrifts filled the area. At almost 11,000 feet above sea level, the air is plenty cold and thin. The same alpine terrain found in the previously mentioned campgrounds is here, too. Nearby Libby Lake offers postcard-like photographs, so don't forget your film.

35 Silver Lake

Location: 56 miles west of Laramie.
Facilities: Vault toilets, fire rings, tables, drinking water.
Sites: 7 for tents and 11 for tents or RVs up to 40 feet long.

Fee: $ per day, 14-day maximum stay.
Reservations: First-come, first-served.
Agency: Medicine Bow National Forest, Brush Creek Ranger District, 1-307-326-5258.
Activities: Fishing, hiking.
Finding the campground: Take Wyoming Highway 130 west out of Laramie for 55 miles. Turn left at the campground sign and travel about 1 mile. Just before the turnoff to the campground, a Silver Lake Scenic View sign appears—your clue to get ready for the left turn into the campground, which tends to sneak up on you.

About the campground: Large spruce shade snowdrifts well into July among these units. This campground is advertised to open on July 1, but don't count on it. The elevation is more than 10,000 feet. Between the height and lack of sun in the thick forest, opening day might well be the end of July. A foot trail leads to Silver Lake and fishing opportunities.

36 Lake Owen

Location: 36 miles west Laramie.
Facilities: Vault toilets, fire rings, tables, drinking water, boat ramp, picnic area.
Sites: 35 for tents or RVs up to 45 feet long.
Fee: $ per day, 14-day maximum stay.
Reservations: First-come, first-served.
Agency: Medicine Bow National Forest, Laramie Ranger District, 1-307-745-2300.
Activities: Fishing, hiking, boating, swimming.
Finding the campground: Take Wyoming Highway 130 west out of Laramie for 17 miles. Turn left onto the paved Wyoming Highway 11 and travel 11 miles. Continue through Albany on the gravel Forest Road 500 for 2 miles. Turn left onto the gravel Forest Road 513 and travel 2 miles. Turn left onto Forest Road 517 and travel 2 miles. At the sign turn right onto the gravel Forest Road 540 and travel 2 miles.

About the campground: An aspen thicket engulfs one side of the campground, and the remaining area finds shade under pine trees. Firewood is not too far away, though you might consider picking up some deadfall along the way. A host occupies a site in the campground. On a sunny morning the snow-capped mountains to the north stand above the green forest in stark contrast. It could prove difficult to keep your eye on a bobber if you are fishing. The railroad tracks passing by the lake appeared to be inactive when we were there. On either end, crews were busy tearing it up.

37 Miller Lake

Location: 37 miles southwest of Laramie.
Facilities: Vault toilets, fire rings, tables, drinking water.
Sites: 7 for tents or RVs up to 20 feet long.

Fee: $ per day, 14-day maximum stay.
Reservations: First-come, first-served.
Agency: Medicine Bow National Forest, Laramie Ranger District, 1-307-745-2300.
Activities: Fishing, hiking, boating (nonmotorized).
Finding the campground: Take Wyoming Highway 230 southwest out of Laramie for 37 miles. Turn right at the Foxpark sign onto the gravel Forest Road 512 and travel 0.25 mile. Turn left at the campground sign.

About the campground: This gem is not well marked along the highway, which probably accounts for some of the vacant spots. The back-in spaces circle through lodgepole pine forest. Miller Lake is not very big, but has plenty to offer. A short hike puts you along its shoreline. Fish and hot feet alike find the cold water enjoyable. Firewood can be had with a little exercise from the deadfall nearby. A host is present at the campground.

38 Boswell Creek

Location: 46 miles southwest of Laramie.
Facilities: Vault toilets, fire rings.
Sites: 9 for tents or RVs up to 20 feet long.
Fee: $ per day, 14-day maximum stay.
Reservations: First-come, first-served.
Agency: Medicine Bow National Forest, Laramie Ranger District, 1-307-745-2300.
Activities: Fishing, hiking.
Finding the campground: Take Wyoming Highway 230 southwest out of Laramie for 43 miles. Just past Mountain Home, turn left at the sign onto the gravel road and travel 3 miles.

About the campground: Firewood is plentiful here, but turnarounds are not. The main campground can accommodate longer units; however, if someone already occupies them, your nightmares may have only begun. Brook trout infest the babbling brook that cuts the campground into two units. This campground is better suited for tents or pickup campers, and has some walk-in sites. There are a lot of people living along the road accessing the area, but once you arrive the residents could just as well be hundreds of miles away. The thick lodgepole pine forest infiltrates the willow-lined Boswell Creek banks, with an aspen or two thrown in. A host is present.

39 Pelton Creek

Location: 52 miles southwest of Laramie.
Facilities: Vault toilets, fire rings, grills, tables, drinking water.
Sites: 15 for tents or RVs up to 32 feet long.
Fee: $ per day, 14-day maximum stay.
Reservations: First-come, first-served.
Agency: Medicine Bow National Forest, Laramie Ranger District, 1-307-745-2300.

Reminders of frontier life line the road to Boswell Creek Campground.

Activities: Fishing, hiking.
Finding the campground: Take Wyoming Highway 230 southwest out of Laramie for 43 miles. Just after crossing into Colorado, turn right onto Forest Road 898 and travel 9 miles. The road goes from good to bad. NOTE: There is no sign directing you to the campground. All that Colorado offers is a national forest access sign that appears abruptly after crossing from Wyoming. Be ready.

About the campground: Pelton Creek crowds up against the pine forest enclosing this campground. Willow brush lines the stream banks. Five pull-thrus offer the most level parking, and the remaining back-in units will accommodate 16-foot trailers, but not without a lot of work. A host is generally scheduled to be present, but at the time of our visit, the position had yet to be filled. The nearby trailhead makes this place popular, especially for those with horses. During the week a few places were available; however, we met campers coming in as we left. There is plenty of deadfall along the road that you should consider bringing with you for campfires.

40 Rob Roy

Location: 46 miles west of Laramie.
Facilities: Vault toilets, fire rings, tables, drinking water, boat ramp, picnic area.
Sites: 65 for tents or RVs up to 50 feet long.
Fee: $ per day, 14-day maximum stay.
Reservations: First-come, first-served.
Agency: Medicine Bow National Forest, Laramie Ranger District, 1-307-745-2300.
Activities: Fishing, hiking, boating, swimming.
Finding the campground: Take Wyoming Highway 130 west out of Laramie for 24 miles. Turn left onto the paved Wyoming Highway 11 and travel 11 miles. Continue through Albany on the gravel Forest Road 500 for 11 miles. Turn left at the campground sign.

About the campground: There are a lot of fir trees here, both standing and down on the ground. Most of the small stuff has already been picked up, and a saw or an axe is required if you plan to use any of the downed timber close by. The back-in units are not that difficult to negotiate, but finding an empty one on a weekend might be. The lure of cold water and big fish draws plenty of visitors. The picnic area is closest to the lake. Camping units are uniformly located along several loops that get progressively farther from the reservoir. The ones closest to the lake are the closest to the entrance and also the first to be occupied. Loud neighbors cannot be ignored, though the parking spaces have a pretty good distance between them. A host occupies a site at the campground.

41 Holmes

Location: 49 miles west of Laramie.
Facilities: Vault toilet, fire rings, tables, drinking water.
Sites: 10 for tents or RVs up to 22 feet long.
Fee: $ per day, 14-day maximum stay.
Reservations: First-come, first-served.
Agency: Medicine Bow National Forest, Laramie Ranger District, 1-307-745-2300.
Activities: Hiking.
Finding the campground: Take Wyoming Highway 130 west out of Laramie for 24 miles. Turn left onto the paved Wyoming Highway 11 and travel 11 miles. Continue through Albany on the gravel Forest Road 500 for 13 miles. Turn right onto the gravel Forest Road 543 and travel 1 mile. The campground is on the left side of the road. When we visited, there was no sign.

About the campground: The lodgepole pine forest is thick here, but not quite dog-hair. Drinking water pours out of a spigot near the entrance. The parking units are well separated, and firewood appeared plentiful. This campground seems almost forgotten, tucked away in this corner. On the map Rob Roy Reservoir does not look too far away. Keep in mind that inches on paper can mean miles on ground. If you don't need to be within sight of the lake, this would be an excellent place.

42 Bobbie Thompson

Location: 47 miles west of Laramie.
Facilities: Vault toilet, fire rings, tables, drinking water.
Sites: 12 for tents or RVs up to 40 feet long.
Fee: $ per day, 14-day maximum stay.
Reservations: First-come, first-served.
Agency: Medicine Bow National Forest, Laramie Ranger District, 1-307-745-2300.
Activities: Fishing, hiking.
Finding the campground: Take Wyoming Highway 130 west out of Laramie for 24 miles. Turn left onto the paved Wyoming Highway 11 and travel 11 miles. Continue through Albany on the gravel Forest Road 500 for 3 miles. Turn left onto Forest Road 542 and travel 6 miles. Turn left onto the gravel Forest Road 543 and travel 2.5 miles. At the campground sign turn right and travel 0.5 mile. This last stretch could be difficult when wet, as evidenced by the plentiful deep ruts.

About the campground: Douglas Creek hosted a mining town long before camping became a recreation. A former resident of Keystone is a permanent guest, but it is doubtful that she will be fined for staying over the maximum days. A widow, Mrs. Estus was the first death of the community in 1878. Willow brush carpets historic dredge piles from the golden days of mining. There is an active placer claim just below the campground. Lodgepole pine come in all different sizes, with firewood scattered between. Some sawing is required. For those who watch birds, the local hummingbirds show up in the warmer weather.

43 Pike Pole

Location: 57 miles west of Laramie.
Facilities: Vault toilet, fire rings, tables.
Sites: 6 for tents or RVs up to 16 feet long.
Fee: None, 14-day maximum stay.
Reservations: First-come, first-served.
Agency: Medicine Bow National Forest, Laramie Ranger District, 1-307-745-2300.
Activities: Fishing, hiking, wildlife viewing.
Finding the campground: Take Wyoming Highway 130 west out of Laramie for 24 miles. Turn left onto the paved Wyoming Highway 11 and travel 11 miles. Continue through Albany on the gravel Forest Road 500 for 3 miles. Turn left onto the gravel Forest Road 542 and travel 6 miles. Continue through Keystone to Forest Road 511. Take FR 511 for 3 miles. At the four-way intersection continue dead ahead on Forest Road 512 for 10.5 miles.

About the campground: The parking gets away from traffic dust with limited shade under large cottonwood trees. A new vault toilet sits up at the Sixmile Gap Trailhead, in stark contrast to the original. Don't be fooled by the green pump poking up out of the weeds; it has no handle. This is a remote, hard-to-get-to place, but in spite of the difficulties and sharp, steep switchbacks for the last part, there were plenty of campers. On our visit, a large fifth wheel was nestled comfortably into place. This campground would be the better choice over Pickaroon, as the parking units are off the road a short distance.

44 Pickaroon

Location: 59 miles west of Laramie.
Facilities: Vault toilet, fire rings, tables.
Sites: 8 for tents or RVs up to 16 feet long.
Fee: None, 14-day maximum stay.
Reservations: First-come, first-served.
Agency: Medicine Bow National Forest, Laramie Ranger District, 1-307-745-2300.
Activities: Fishing, hiking, wildlife viewing.
Finding the campground: Take Wyoming Highway 130 west out of Laramie for 24 miles. Turn left onto the paved Wyoming Highway 11 and travel 11 miles. Continue through Albany on the gravel Forest Road 500 for 3 miles. Turn left onto the gravel Forest Road 542 and travel 6 miles. Continue through

Keystone to Forest Road 511. Take FR 511 for 3 miles. At the four-way intersection continue dead ahead on Forest Road 512 for 12 miles.

About the campground: There seems to be more shade here—and more traffic. The units are directly next to the road. Some are along the riverbank and others hide between clumps of willow brush on the opposite side. All are in the dust zone. This is the end of the road, and everyone who makes this journey turns around here, so campers get dusted twice.

About the Author

Ken Graham, an engineer, is a recent graduate of Montana Tech in Butte, Montana. An avid rockhound, hunter, and fisherman, he is also the author of *Rockhounding Wyoming* and *Fishing Wyoming*.